国家新闻出版改革发展项目库入库项目

信息科技英语口译入门

李 平 编著

北京邮电大学出版社
www.buptpress.com

内 容 简 介

本书以信息科技类主题材料为主,主要提供英语口译入门的必要知识和初步训练。本书将理论结合实际,在介绍口译的基本技巧和训练方法的同时,结合英语听说和口译操练任务,让学生在"做中学"。本书在内容难度上循序渐进,可满足不同英语水平的学生需求。

作为国内为数不多的信息科技口译教材,本书已被选为北京邮电大学"高新课程"《初级英语口译》的教材。本书可作为高等院校非英语专业本科生、研究生的口译入门课程的教材,也可作为信息科技人才口译培训和自学的教材。

图书在版编目(CIP)数据

信息科技英语口译入门 / 李平编著. -- 北京:北京邮电大学出版社,2020.11
ISBN 978-7-5635-6260-2

Ⅰ. ①信… Ⅱ. ①李… Ⅲ. ①信息技术－英语－口译－高等学校－教材 Ⅳ. ①G202

中国版本图书馆 CIP 数据核字(2020)第 224673 号

策划编辑:姚　顺　刘纳新　　责任编辑:徐振华　王小莹　　封面设计:七星博纳

出版发行:北京邮电大学出版社
社　　址:北京市海淀区西土城路 10 号
邮政编码:100876
发 行 部:电话:010-62282185　传真:010-62283578
E-mail:publish@bupt.edu.cn
经　　销:各地新华书店
印　　刷:保定市中画美凯印刷有限公司
开　　本:720 mm×1 000 mm　1/16
印　　张:13.5
字　　数:269 千字
版　　次:2020 年 11 月第 1 版
印　　次:2020 年 11 月第 1 次印刷

ISBN 978-7-5635-6260-2　　　　　　　　　　　　　　　　　　定价:38.00 元

·如有印装质量问题,请与北京邮电大学出版社发行部联系·

前　　言

英语口译对中英文水平均有较高要求,曾经一度是英语专业的独有课程。然而近年来随着大学生英语水平的普遍提高,许多非英语专业的学生完全可以胜任一定难度的口译任务,并且开始有系统学习口译的需求。作者基于社会和学生的需求分析研究[1],发现在高校开设非英语专业口译选修课十分必要,由此设计了"以学习为中心"的"初级英语口译"课程[2],该课程于2014年起在北京邮电大学面向全校大二及以上年级非英语专业本科生开设,为全校公选课。本书是该课程的配套教材。

以下为"初级英语口译"课程的教学大纲和"以学习为中心"的课程设计方案,仅供参考。

一、"初级英语口译"课程的教学大纲

1. 课程基本信息

课程基本信息如表 0.1 所示。

表 0.1　课程基本信息

课程名称	中文:初级英语口译		课程编号	3312100550
	英文:Basics of Interpreting Skills			
学分/学时	2/32	必修(　)/选修(√)	开课学期	秋季学期
课程类别	素质教育选修课程	适用专业	除了英语专业外的其他专业	
先修课程	大学英语三四级			

2. 课程教学目标

本课程通过理论介绍和实际演练,使学生了解英语口译入门的必要知识和口译自我训练的方法,初步掌握英语口译的技巧,提升跨文化交际能力和职业素养。

3. 课程与支撑的毕业要求

本课程在课程体系(如表 0.2 所示)中,属于通识教育模块-素质教育课程(6 学分)-人文社科类中的一门选修课程(2 学分)。

前言

表0.2 各专业培养方案的课程体系

课程类别	理论教学	实践教学	学分
通识教育	思想政治理论课	思想政治理论课实践	16
	大学英语	基于计算机自主学习	8~14
		体育:4学分(128学时)	4
	军事理论、心理健康	军训	3
	计算机基础课程	计算机上机实践	
	素质教育课程: 理工类 人文社科类 艺术类	实践类课程	6
	数学与自然科学基础课程	物理实验、数学实验	
专业教育	学科基础课程 专业基础课程 专业课程	专业实验课程、课程设计 专业实习、实训 毕业设计(论文)等	
创新创业教育	创新创业课程	创新创业训练与实践	4~10
总学分	154~170		

4. 教学内容及学时安排

课程的教学内容及学时安排如表0.3所示。

表0.3 教学内容及学时安排

序号	教学内容	学时分配
1	口译概论	2
2	口译基础(听辨)	2
3	口译基础(记忆)	2
4	口译基础(笔记)	2
5	口译基础(表达)	2
6	口译操练:数字口译	2
7	口译操练:接待外宾	2
8	口译操练:宴请饮食	2
9	口译操练:礼仪致辞	2
10	口译操练:参展参会	2
11	口译操练:送客道别	2
12	口译操练:商贸洽谈	2
13	口译操练:参观访问	2
14	口译操练:教育合作	2
15	口译操练:文化交流	2
16	口译模拟实践及评析:演讲发言	2

5. 教学方法

使用网络教学平台进行混合式教学,课上进行内容精讲和学生实际技能操练、小组活动,课下学生自主学习。

6. 考核方式

采用形成性评估和终结性评估相结合的方式,期末考试采用考查的形式。

二、"初级英语口译"以学习为中心的课程设计

因篇幅较长,详细内容请见书末附录。

基于学生对课程的期望,本书的编写目标与课程目标一致:为从未接触英语口译培训的学生提供英语口译入门的必要知识。本书将理论结合实际,在介绍英语口译基本技巧和训练方法的同时,结合英语听说和口译操练任务,让学生在"做中学",培养英语口译能力和提高英语听说水平。

因为北京邮电大学学生多来自信息通信技术相关专业,如通信、计算机等,本书选材多为信息科技相关内容。鉴于公选课学生英语水平各异,为满足多样需求,本书以应用广泛、难度适中的"联络口译"为主要内容,培养学生在现实生活中常用场合的英语口译能力。本书前6章为口译入门理论和技巧;7~16章为口译情景模拟。本书的内容在难度上循序渐进,其中7~11章为初级、中级难度,12~16章的难度有所提高。

作为英语口译入门教材,本书适合所有有意了解英语口译知识、学习英语口译技巧和训练方法的人,如大学本科一至四年级学生,大专、高职院校高年级的学生,高校研究生,职场人士等。

本书的第2章参考了《英语各类口音听译突破》,第5章参考了《9小时快学国际音标》,作者在此对以上2本书的编者表示感谢! 书中的素材已尽可能给出出处,如有不慎遗漏之处,请与作者联系。本书英文录音由美国人 Larry Price、David Allen Klopfer 提供,中文录音由王赫男、严昊涵、周宇洋、赵中兴同学协助完成,同时这些同学以及夏静娴、桓欧文、向扬、曾佳豪等同学为本书的编写提供了部分素材并参与了本书的校对,在此向他们表示衷心感谢! 本书的编写和出版得到了北京市支持中央高校共建项目——"青年英才计划"(项目编号 YETP0465)和北京邮电大学研究生教育教学改革与研究项目——科技英语口译(ICT 类)——教材建设项目(项目编号 Y2016005)的资助,在此表示衷心感谢。最后,感谢北京邮电大学出版社姚顺等编辑提供的宝贵修改意见! 感谢家人的支持! 由于个人精力和水平有限,书中难免存在疏漏,敬请广大读者多提宝贵意见。

李 平
于北京邮电大学

目 录

第1篇 口译入门理论与方法

第1章 信息科技英语口译概论 ········ 3

1.1 口译的基本概念、分类 ········ 3

1.2 科技口译概述 ········ 6

1.3 口译过程揭秘 ········ 8

1.4 口译标准及质量评估 ········ 9

1.5 口译员的基本素质 ········ 12

1.6 口译员的职业素养 ········ 14

1.7 优秀口译员的人文素养 ········ 15

第2章 口译基本技能(一)听辨 ········ 17

2.1 口译中的听辨与外语教学中的听辨区别 ········ 17

2.2 口译听辨的原则"得意忘形" ········ 18

2.3 口译听辨的训练方法 ········ 19

2.4 各国口音的特点 ········ 21

第3章 口译基本技能(二)记忆 ········ 27

3.1 记忆概述 ········ 27

目录

- 3.2 口译记忆训练的方法 ········· 28
- 3.3 信息组块法 ········· 29
- 3.4 逻辑分层法 ········· 29
- 3.5 顺时记忆法 ········· 31
- 3.6 形象记忆法 ········· 31

第4章 口译基本技能（三）笔记 ········· 34

- 4.1 口译笔记概述 ········· 34
- 4.2 初学者口译笔记的记录方法 ········· 36
- 4.3 口译笔记符号举例 ········· 41

第5章 口译基本技能（四）表达 ········· 44

- 5.1 口译表达概述 ········· 44
- 5.2 英语易错语音 ········· 45
- 5.3 英语常用语调 ········· 48
- 5.4 英语地道发音窍门 ········· 50
- 5.5 英语正式语体与非正式语体 ········· 55

第6章 口译基本技能（五）数字口译 ········· 61

- 6.1 数字口译概述 ········· 61
- 6.2 数字增减及倍数的译法 ········· 62

第2篇 口译情景模拟

第7章 接待外宾 ········· 67

- 7.1 译前准备 ········· 67
- 7.2 对话全文 ········· 67
- 7.3 词汇拓展 ········· 68

第 8 章　宴请饮食 …………………………………………………… 72

8.1　译前准备 ………………………………………………………… 72
8.2　对话全文 ………………………………………………………… 72
8.3　词汇拓展 ………………………………………………………… 73

第 9 章　礼仪致辞 …………………………………………………… 79

9.1　译前准备 ………………………………………………………… 79
9.2　发言全文 ………………………………………………………… 80
9.3　词汇拓展 ………………………………………………………… 81

第 10 章　参展参会 ………………………………………………… 83

10.1　译前准备 ……………………………………………………… 83
10.2　对话全文 ……………………………………………………… 83
10.3　词汇拓展 ……………………………………………………… 85

第 11 章　送客道别 ………………………………………………… 88

11.1　译前准备 ……………………………………………………… 88
11.2　对话全文 ……………………………………………………… 88
11.3　词汇拓展 ……………………………………………………… 90

第 12 章　商贸洽谈 ………………………………………………… 91

12.1　译前准备 ……………………………………………………… 91
12.2　对话全文 ……………………………………………………… 91
12.3　词汇拓展 ……………………………………………………… 93

第 13 章　参观访问 ………………………………………………… 95

13.1　译前准备 ……………………………………………………… 95
13.2　对话全文 ……………………………………………………… 95

13.3　词汇拓展 ··· 97

第 14 章　教育合作 ··· 99

14.1　译前准备 ··· 99
14.2　对话全文 ··· 99
14.3　词汇拓展 ·· 102

第 15 章　文化交流 ·· 104

15.1　译前准备 ·· 104
15.2　对话全文 ·· 104
15.3　词汇拓展 ·· 107

第 16 章　演讲发言 ·· 110

16.1　译前准备 ·· 110
16.2　演讲全文 ·· 110
16.3　词汇拓展 ·· 115

第 3 篇　参考答案和译文

第 17 章　第 1 篇中练习的参考答案 ··· 121

17.1　第 2 章口译基本技能（一）听辨的参考答案 ································ 121
17.2　第 3 章口译基本技能（二）记忆的参考答案 ································ 127
17.3　第 4 章口译基本技能（三）笔记的参考答案 ································ 135
17.4　第 5 章口译基本技能（四）表达的参考答案 ································ 138
17.5　第 6 章口译基本技能（五）数字口译的参考答案 ························· 138

第 18 章　第 2 篇中各章的译文 ·· 140

18.1　第 7 章接待外宾的译文 ·· 140

18.2 第8章宴请饮食的译文 …………………………………………… 142
18.3 第9章礼仪致辞的译文 …………………………………………… 144
18.4 第10章参展参会的译文 ………………………………………… 148
18.5 第11章送客道别的译文 ………………………………………… 151
18.6 第12章商贸洽谈的译文 ………………………………………… 154
18.7 第13章参观访问的译文 ………………………………………… 156
18.8 第14章教育合作的译文 ………………………………………… 159
18.9 第15章文化交流的译文 ………………………………………… 163
18.10 第16章演讲发言的译文 ………………………………………… 168

参考文献 …………………………………………………………………… 176

附录 以学习为中心的《初级英语口译》课程设计 ……………………………… 182

第1篇　口译入门理论与方法

第1章 信息科技英语口译概论

1.1 口译的基本概念、分类

1. 翻译的定义

翻译的定义众说纷纭,广为接受的是尤金·奈达(Eugene A. Nida)的定义[3]: Translating consists in reproducing in the receptor language the closest natural equivalent of the source-language message, first in terms of meaning and secondly in terms of style.

译文:翻译以意义为先,风格为次,用接收语再现源语信息最相当的、自然流畅的信息[4]。

2. 翻译的分类

翻译的分类多种多样。按翻译的客体性质可分为文学翻译(如诗歌翻译)和非文学翻译(如经贸翻译和科技翻译);按翻译工具可分为口译(oral translation/interpreting)、笔译(written translation)和机辅翻译(machine translation)。按对源语语言形式的保留程度可分为直译(literal translation)和意译(liberal translation/free translation)。

直译是指在译文语言条件许可时,既保持原文内容又保持原文形式的翻译,例如,"acid rain"翻译为酸雨;"一国两制"翻译为"one country, two systems"。有时由于语言本身以及社会、文化等因素的差异,使用原文的形式无法准确、地道地表达原文的意思[5],这时就需要用到意译。意译是指舍弃原文形式,只表达原文意思的翻译。例如,"bull's eye"应翻译为"靶心"而非"牛眼睛";"Justice has long arms."翻译为"天网恢恢,疏而不漏",而非"正义有长胳膊"。

3. 口译的定义

口译是以口头表达方式将信息由一种语言形式转换成另一种语言形式的语言交际行为。口译是这样一种活动:口译员(interpreter)在听取源语(source language)后,通过口头表达的方式以目标语(target language)向听众传达讲话人的意思,使语言上无法互通的异语双方或多方之间通过口译员的传译能够进行交流沟通。

4. 口译的分类

口译的方式有交替传译（consecutive interpretation）、同声传译（simultaneous interpretation）、联络口译（liaison interpreting）和耳语传译（whispered interpreting）等，其中最基本的两种方式是交替传译和同声传译。

图 1.1 外交部张璐在进行交替传译

交替传译简称"交传"，又名连续口译、即席口译等，是在发言人讲完部分内容或全部内容后，由口译员进行翻译。这种口译方式可见于演讲、祝词、授课、谈判、会议发言、产品推介会、采访谈话、参观访问等，有时可以借助笔记进行翻译。交替传译适用的场合比较严肃，对翻译的质量和信息完整性要求最高。例如，在我国总理回答记者提问的新闻发布会上，使用的就是交替传译，如图1.1所示。

同声传译简称同传，又称同步口译，是在发言人讲话的同时进行口译，一般口译员会在同传间（booth），听众通过佩戴耳机选择口译员频道进行收听。实际上，口译员会在发言人讲话开始后略拖几秒才开始翻译，并非完全同步。因为认知难度大，听众对翻译质量有一定的容忍度。例如，在联合国会议中，常常用到同声传译的方式，如图1.2所示。

图 1.2 联合国同传间

联络口译一般用于陪同口译的场合，涉及活动安排、见面时的寒暄、用餐时的谈话、会展的解说等，如图1.3所示。联络口译适用的场合比较轻松，对口译员的语言水平和翻译质量要求相对宽松。

(a) 联络口译1　　　　　　　　　　(b) 联络口译2

图 1.3 联络口译

在实际口译市场,对联络口译的需求不低。例如,一项 2011 年发布的调查研究表明,目前中国西部的口译工作主要集中于会议口译和联络口译,从调查数据来看,联络口译占有绝对优势,超过会议口译的使用需求,达到 30%(如图 1.4 所示)[6]56。

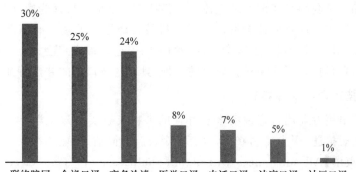

图 1.4 中国西部市场不同类型的口译需求

耳语传译俗称"咬耳朵",是指不借助设备,在听众旁边用耳语的方式进行同传的翻译方法,如图 1.5 所示。

此外,按照口译服务的场合,常见的口译类型有会议口译(conference interpreting)、陪同口译(escort interpreting)、社区口译(community interpreting)、法庭口译(legal interpreting)〔如图 1.6(a)所示〕、医疗口译(medical interpreting)、手语口译(sign language interpreting)〔如图 1.6(b)所示〕等。

图 1.5 耳语口译

(a) 法庭口译

(b) 手语口译

图 1.6 口译类型

1.2 科技口译概述

科技翻译是我国翻译事业的主体[7]。科技口译是指以口译为媒介传播科学与技术的相关知识与信息的社会交际活动。科技口译涉及的场合有国际学术会议、技术报告会、讲座、培训班、展览会、新品发布会、引进设备谈判会、施工或安装调试现场等。信息科技口译作为科技口译的一种，具有科技口译的共性特征。

1. 科技英语的文体特征

科技英语用专业语言来说明客观存在的事物或事实。与文学英语不同，科技英语没有主观描述，很少使用修辞，具有客观、准确、简洁、专业的特点。

【科技英语】All substances will permit the passage of some electric current, provided the potential difference is high enough. 只要有足够的电位差，电流便可以通过所有的物体[8]。

【文学英语】Let life be beautiful like summer flowers and death like autumn leaves. 生如夏花之绚烂，死如秋叶之静美。

在科技英语例句中，有术语 current、potential difference 等，体现了专业性；利用名词化短语 the passage of some electric current，使得语言简洁。而文学英语例句主观色彩浓，具有价值判断，使用了明喻、对比的修辞方法，重在美学享受。

因为科技英语具有自身的文体特征，所以科技口译也有其自身特征。

2. 科技口译的特征

① 客观。科技口译主要涉及客观世界的知识、事实、信息，不含有文学翻译所含的价值判断、言外之意、文化寓意，因此翻译以忠实为标准，多用客观的语言。非人称句和被动语态是科技英语的两大句式特征[9]，例如，

【原文】Face anti-spoofing is usually treated as a dichotomy between living face image and non-living face image.

【译文】人脸活体检测常被视为活体人脸图像和非活体人脸图像的二分类问题进行处理。

② 准确。不像文学文体，科技文体只有单一层次意义，即表层意义和深层意义趋向一致，因此翻译时更有可能保持源语信息的完整性，在信息传递的准确性上比一般会议口译的要求要高。为达到准确，有时采用直译，例如，

【原文】Results from aero thermodynamic calculation for the original combustor include pressure loss, combustion efficiency, flow distribution, flame tube wall temperature, exit temperature profile and exhaust emissions.

【直译】原燃烧室的气动热力计算结果包括压力损失、燃烧效率、流量分布、火

焰筒壁温、出口温度流场和排放[10]。

有时需要使用模糊限制语,如 may,could,approximately 等。例如,

【原文】This modification could presumably play a key role in substrate binding.

【译文】这种改变很可能在地层凝固中起着重要作用。

③ 简洁。科技口译的主要目的在于传递科技知识和信息,而非给予美学享受和哲学思考,因此以达意为主,尽量精简,达到简洁效果。例如,

【原文】我们在分析破损材料时,通常需要先做直观判断,再做实时检测。

【译文】When we are doing an analysis of a damaged material, usually it requires intuitive judgment followed by real-time testing.

【精简后译文】Analysis of a damaged material usually requires intuitive judgment followed by real-time testing[11]。

④ 专业。不同于一般口译,在通常情况下,科技口译涉及较专业化内容,同时服务对象双方均有一定专业背景知识,会大量使用缩略语、术语。

⑤ 灵活。科技口译尤其是现场科技口译可能涉及的范围广泛,话题多变,需要口译员知识储备深厚、灵活应变。例如,同一个词 joint 在不同语境下意思不同,需要灵活翻译,详见表 1.1[12]。

表 1.1 joint 的不同译法

专业术语	译文
expansion joint	伸缩缝
overlap joint	搭接节点
rock joint	岩石节理
supported joint	支承接头
jointing chamber	电缆交接箱

⑥ 归化。科技口译所传递的相关专业知识是普适性的、跨文化的,因此适当变换语言形式仍然可以达到翻译效果的"动态对等",应采用适合目的语听众习惯的归化的翻译方法,便于听众接受。例如,在中国石油一次技术引进谈判[13]中,外方提到了"plug flow scheme"这个名称,当时中文中并无此术语的翻译。有人建议译为"葡拉格流结构",但这一译法非常拗口,并且中国化工生产工艺中不存在这样一种流态,会引起费解。翻译专家吕世生先生采用符合中方知识体系的"断塞流"去翻译,达到了良好的效果。此后,这一概念进入该专业的术语标准。说明采用适合目的语听众的心理习惯以及构词方式的翻译策略是正确的。

1.3 口译过程揭秘

从认知心理学的角度,口译是一种复杂的认知活动。其过程可大致描述为信息输入(接受)—信息处理和存储—信息输出(运用和传递),如图1.7所示。在口译认知中,信息以一种语言(源语)的语音信号(或视觉信号)的形式,通过口译员耳朵(或眼睛)进入口译员的心理加工系统,而口译员通过知觉、注意、联想、预测、推断、表象、记忆、思维等心理认知过程,先将外部输入的信息与大脑中固有的知识存储接通,然后通过将外部输入的信息与内部固有的信息进行联系、比照、分析等操作,对输入的信息进行解码、意义建构、集成、提取、加工(分析、综合、推断等)、再加工(直至便于最优化存储),并进行记忆存储和记录存储,最后在大脑中用另一种语言对这些经过加工的意义进行表达,最终将目标语语言表达形式外化为语音信号进行发布。口译的过程就是口译员对信息进行各种心理认知加工的过程。

图1.7 口译过程简图

口译过程会对口译员的大脑产生认知负荷。口译员所能承担的认知负荷的限度,必须高于口译任务所需要的认知负荷总量,才能保障质量。口译专家Daniel Gile提出了口译的"认知负荷模型"[14],模型表明了口译过程中认知负荷的分配情况,包括"听辨和理解"(listening, L)、"语言表达"(production, P)、"记忆"(memory, M)和"协调"(coordination, C)。他将交替传译分为理解和产出两个阶段,归结为以下公式。

理解阶段:

$$\text{Interpreting} = L + N + M + C$$

其中,L(listening and analysis)代表听辨;N(note-taking)代表笔记;M(short-term memory operation)代表短时记忆;C(coordination)代表各部分的协调。

产出阶段:

$$\text{Interpreting} = \text{Rem} + NR + P + C$$

其中,Rem(remembering)代表记忆;NR(note-reading)代表解读笔记;P(speech production)代表译语产出;C(coordination)代表各部分的协调。

将上述公式译为中文,公式如下。

理解阶段：

$$口译＝听辨＋笔记＋短时记忆＋协调$$

产出阶段：

$$口译＝记忆＋解读笔记＋译语产出＋协调$$

由于大脑能承担的认知负荷总量是有限的，口译员在口译时应保证可供使用的脑力总量（total capacity available，TA）大于所需要的认知负荷总量（total requirement，TR），才能保障口译质量。基于这一认知负荷模型，口译员应该提高中英文功底和各项口译基本功，包括听辨、记忆、笔记等能力，将各项技能达到熟练的程度，才能减少认知负荷，以便完成口译任务。

1.4 口译标准及质量评估

1. 口译标准

关于口译标准，很多口译专家、学者提出了相关理论。其中，曾任新中国第一代领导人口译员的李越然认为，口译标准可以概括为"准确、通顺、及时"，简称"准、顺、快"[15]。

"准"——忠实于源语的思想内容及特定情境下的感情。

"顺"——译语形式应符合中外语言的各自规范，并同发言人的语体风格基本保持统一。

"快"——表达及时，而不是任意加快语速。

在传统口译教学中，口译测试的标准在此基础上加入"完整"，即"准确、完整、通顺、及时"，简言之就是"准、全、顺、快"。

"准确"——要求口译员把讲话人的思想和情感准确地传递给听众。译语要充分表达讲话人的意图，达到讲话人要达到的效果；要符合讲话人的身份及讲话的场合；要符合听众的认知水平和层次。口译员讲话要规范，尤其是专业术语要准确无误，不说外行话。

"完整"——要求口译员完整地传译讲话人的信息，不能遗漏内容和细节。

"通顺"——首先指译语表达要地道，符合译语的语言表达习惯，符合听众的文化习俗；其次指口译员表达要流畅。

"及时"——要求表达及时。交替传译口译员需在讲话人停止讲话后2~3 s内开始翻译，并连续译完讲话人的发言；同声传译口译员的译语发布要尽量保持与源语同步[16]。

2. 口译质量评估

国际口译评估多是通过对口译员和口译用户的调查得出的，除了类似上述

"准、全、顺、快"的语言方面的标准外,还增加了非语言层面的评估。

国际会议口译员协会(AIIC)1995年发布了一项针对会议口译用户期望的大型调查报告[17]。结果显示,从口译用户的视角来看,口译评估分为对内容和形式两方面的评估。在口译与源语的"内容匹配"方面,有三项最为重要的指标:翻译的完整度、术语的准确性、意义的忠实度;在"形式匹配"方面,有三项重要指标同步性(同声传译)、口头表达技巧、声音悦耳程度。其中,前五项基本和"准、全、顺、快"的标准一致,第六项声音悦耳程度属于非语言参数。其他对非语言参数的相关研究发现[18],有三项"重要性显著"的非语言参数,即口译员的可靠性、会前准备的充分性和团队合作能力。

3. 科技口译质量评估

针对科技口译,多年从事口译教学和研究的口译专家刘和平提出了一个科技口译标准[19],分为三大项。

(1)正确把握原讲话人意图。
(2)符合目的语表达方式。
(3)满足听众期待。

相应地,口译质量评估的方法也分为三项。

(1)讲话信息或内容转达准确(80%)。
(2)翻译表达准确和流畅(10%)。
(3)满足听众期待(10%)。

科技口译质量评估表如表1.2所示。

表1.2 科技口译质量评估表

评估标准	满分
(1) 讲话信息或内容转达准确	合计80分
① 内容量化计分	95%~100%:70分 90%~94%:65分 85%~89%:60分
② 逻辑性强,概念清楚。句间衔接自然,上下连贯,表达简明清楚。原讲话与译文中的关联词、转折词匹配	5分
③ 风格、口吻和语气恰当。口译员要根据讲话内容和讲话人的风格和口吻处理,保留必要的幽默风格	5分
(2) 翻译表达准确且流畅(=符合目的语表达方式的程度)	合计10分
① 评估衔接速度。讲话人结束后3~5 s后必须开始翻译。结束语也要同内容衔接紧密,不能丢失	3分
② 从记录的停顿、重复、卡壳数量看表达的流畅程度。口译员所用时间应小于讲话人所用时间	2分

续表

评估标准	满分
③ 记录口译员"念笔记"次数。即读笔记时翻译效果出现"蹦词"的不通畅情况。若讲话长度按 1 分钟计算,则"念笔记"次数不能超过 2 次/分钟	3 分
④ 记录口头禅数量。口头禅数量不能超过 2 次/分钟,并使用行话术语	2 分
(3) 满足听众期待	合计 10 分
① 体裁与听众期待一致	4 分
② 重点和非重点、简略程度与听众的要求相吻合	3 分
③ 译语能够产生与源语一致的内容和情感效果	3 分

4. 听众对科技口译的质量评估

如表 1.2 所示,衡量口译员口译表现的一个维度是"满足听众期待"。满足听众期待日益成为口译质量的重要标准。因此有必要了解听众期待的特点。相关实证研究发现[20]:听众整体上更重视口译的内容,而不太注重形式。但在具体情况下,听众由于自身的交际目的、知识背景、外语水平和口译使用经验的不同,会对科技口译质量因素的评价存在较大差异。

第一,听众的不同交际目的影响着对科技口译质量的评价。听众专业性目的越强,对专业术语、语法准确要求越高,对语音、翻译风格方面的要求越低。听众如果仅希望获取一般信息,则更在意口译员的表达是否流畅自如、符合逻辑,能否迅速了解具体活动的综合信息。

第二,听众的不同知识背景决定着对科技口译质量的重视程度。听众专业背景知识越丰富,对口译员专业术语的使用和表达逻辑性要求越高,但对口译员表达流畅度的要求越低,因为他们可以借助专业背景知识弥补表达中的缺陷。听众专业背景知识越少,越在意并依赖口译员的语言陈述,对口译员表达流畅度要求越高。

第三,听众的不同外语水平影响着对科技口译质量的态度。听众外语水平越高,对语言表达要求越高,对逻辑条理上的要求越低。因为外语水平较高的听众能直接从源语接收信息,以弥合译语前后衔接与译语组织上可能出现的问题。

第四,听众不同的口译使用经验影响着对科技口译质量的评价。听众的口译使用经验越丰富,越注意口译员在语音语调、声音、翻译风格等环节上的表现,越容易容忍口译员在表达逻辑上的问题。

在实际科技口译中,针对听众情况进行调整是保证口译质量的重要策略。例如,资深口译员王斌华曾为一名外国专家的讲座做了两次口译,第一次听众为科技协会成员,第二次听众为中小学学生。两次讲座内容基本一致,但口译员在口译中分别采取了不同的口译策略和方法。前者基本上按源语的专业化表达译出,后者采用了大量明晰化的策略和通俗化的用语。如果按照传统的"忠实观",给学生的译文是不够"准"的,但是,两次讲座后听众对口译员的口译评价反馈都很好[21]52。可见,科技口译中应当具体问题具体分析,分析听众情况,调整翻译策略,以满足听众期待,提高口译质量。

1.5　口译员的基本素质

关于口译员应有的基本素质,专家学者、口译从业人员、业外人士提出了许多见仁见智的观点。

国际上,国际会议口译员协会对"会议口译员"的素质提出以下要求:具有双语或多语能力;具有专题知识的充分准备能力;具有丰富的百科知识;具备职业道德。

在厦门大学陈菁教授制作的口译量化评估表中,把衡量口译员的标准划分为知识能力(包括语言知识和言外知识)、技能(包括记忆、公众演说、口译笔记、意译、概述、应对策略和职业水平等)和心理能力三个方面。

口译员王斌华提出了口译能力评估的模块如图 1.8 所示[21]51。

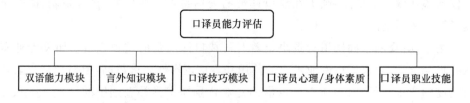

图 1.8　口译员能力评估的模块

综合以上内容可见,对于口译员必备素质达成共识的几个方面为双语能力、背景知识、口译技能、心理素质和职业道德。

(1) 双语能力

口译员对源语语言(A 语言)和目标语语言(B 语言)都应当精通。为了能够翻译准确、完整,口译员在听辨源语内容时需要高度理解,这就要求口译员对 A 语言迅速地接收和分析,尽量做到百分之百的理解。在对 A 语言和口译技巧驾轻就熟的基础上,口译员的口译产出质量就取决于 B 语言的水平层次。例如,科技口译客户衡量口译员口译质量的一个标准,就是看口译员的 B 语言是否地道、专业、流畅,翻译是否符合科技文体的简洁、专业等特征。这些对于口译员的 B 语言能力是一个巨大的挑战。

(2) 背景知识

确保口译质量的前提是对原文的理解。口译过程中的理解并非被动接收信息的过程,而是根据口译员已有的知识背景主动建构意义的过程。因此,为了准确完整地理解原文,只具备语言知识是不够的,还应该掌握大量的"言外知识"(extra-linguistic knowledge)。这一观点被口译专家Gile[22]总结为"理解等式":

$$理解＝语言知识＋言外知识$$

其中言外知识指的是语言以外各领域的百科知识,即口译员有关各主题的背景知识。Gile还指出,口译员对原文的理解水平是由语言知识和言外知识两者之间的相互作用决定的。两种知识越丰富,口译员理解能力就越强。语言知识对于理解程度的贡献率是有上限的,但言外知识对于理解程度的贡献率是没有上限的。换句话说,在语言水平一定的情况下,理解程度的高低主要取决于对背景知识的了解程度,由此可见背景知识的重要性。

(3) 口译技能

人们常常以为"中英文俱佳就可以做口译",实则不然,例如,许多美国出生的中国人精通中英双语,但是却做不好口译。这是因为口译除了需要双语能力、背景知识外,还需要具备口译技能,如记忆、听辨、表达、笔记、公众演讲等基本技能,这些技能需要通过训练去获得。

(4) 心理素质

口译是遗憾的艺术。不像笔译有充足的时间去查考资料、研究译文,在即时口译中出现错误和不完善的译文在所难免。此外,口译员往往需要在听众面前进行口译,不仅要克服在台上的压力,还要应对听众检阅的目光和随时发生的突发状况,因此需要具备极强的心理素质和良好的心理调节能力。口译员应该具备在压力下镇定、自信的素质;在出现突发状况时能够迅速调整心态,以继续工作为重,保持注意力集中,不让情绪波动影响口译工作。

(5) 职业道德

口译员在实际口译工作中,应当认真负责、守时守节、注意保密。口译员在决定是否接受口译任务之前,首先需要衡量自己的知识能力、身体情况等,然后量力而行,以保证翻译质量,对客户负责。如果超出自己能力水平和身体极限,就应果断拒绝任务。一旦接手,就需要尽最大努力做好译前准备。翻译时忠实源语,不错译、漏译,或是加添自己的观点。另外,最好提前到场,做好译前准备,不应迟到。对口译的内容应该保密,在没有取得委托人的同意之前,口译员不得将这些材料用于研究或其他用途。

1.6 口译员的职业素养

曾任国际会议口译员协会主席的 Jennifer Mackintosh 把口译职业化看作一个社会化的过程,从事同一行业的口译员将口译工作作为生活经济来源,遵循共有的职业道德公约、价值以及行为规范[23]。口译作为一种职业,对其从业人员有着特定职业素质的要求。

在针对中国西部地区规模较大的20家翻译公司网站的调查[6]56中,对应聘口译员的要求进行筛选和整理后,总结发现口译职业素养体现在以下八个方面(如表1.3所示)。

表1.3 口译职业素养

口译的职业素养	公司数	百分比(%)
中外文语言及互译能力强	19	95
团队合作能力强	17	85
人际沟通协调能力强	14	70
应变与解决问题能力强	14	70
工作压力承受能力强	13	65
为客户信息保密	12	60
能保证工作质量、吃苦耐劳	10	50
工作简历(经历)真实有效、诚实守信	8	40

厦门大学口译教研组在参照国内外众多版本的口译职业道德准则的基础上,提出以下几条口译员道德准则[24]。

① 量力而行,有所为有所不为。

② 保证质量。口译员在口译过程中,要全面、准确、清楚地表达发言人的信息、意愿和情感。如出现漏译和误译,应酌情给予纠正和补救。

③ 保持中立,不对发言人、发言内容和表达的观点进行任何评论。

④ 坚持操守,秉公办事。

⑤ 口译过程中应精神饱满,保持最佳工作状态。

⑥ 信守合约,保守秘密(替客户保守商业机密)。

⑦ 未获许可,不得私自转让口译工作任务。

可见,口译员不仅应具备口译的专业技能,更应该遵守良好的职业道德:诚实守信、敬业勤奋、严守秘密。

1.7　优秀口译员的人文素养

无论是哪个专业领域的口译员,要想达到高水平的职业水准,除了对自己专攻的领域要全面深入了解(即"Know everything about something")外,还必须"Know something about everything"。口译员对世界方方面面的知识都要保持好奇心,勤于学习。对于一个优秀口译员,一个必不可少的素养就是人文素养。

2010年3月14日,第十一届全国人民代表大会第三次会议胜利闭幕后,温家宝总理在记者会上引用了《离骚》中的经典诗句"亦余心之所善兮,虽九死其犹未悔",外交部译员张璐将其翻译为"For the ideal that I hold dear to my heart, I will not regret a thousand time to die",巧妙的翻译既表达了本意,也符合英文的表达习惯,受到了亿万观众的热捧。张璐被人赞誉的原因之一就是她拥有优秀口译员的人文素养。优秀口译员的人文素养应该包括四个方面:政治素养、文化底蕴、跨文化交际意识和职业操守。

1. 政治修养

口译工作的一大特点,就是天然地具有政治性。即便是最为平常的旅游导览或商务会谈,但凡涉及不同语言、不同国家的交际,就总会有政治因素的考量。例如,中国大陆和台湾地区在翻译时就不可以翻译为"China and Taiwan",而应翻译为"the mainland and Taiwan of China"。

2. 文化底蕴

有一年江泽民主席访问南非时,在欢迎宴会上演讲。他即兴用英语起头,"The sky is clear, the air is fresh; the breeze is gentle"。口译员心想江主席这几句非常有诗意,所以也尽量翻译得有文采,说"微风徐徐,晴空万里"。江主席后来对口译员说:"翻得还是挺好的,但我当时想的是王羲之《兰亭集序》的那句'天朗气清,惠风和畅'。"可见,如果没有深厚中文素养和文化底蕴,从这句英语联想到王羲之的名句,简直是不可能的任务。好的口译员绝不只是精通外语,更要具备非常高超的母语水平和文化底蕴。

3. 跨文化交际意识

英国民俗学家马林诺夫斯基说过:"语言深深地植根于社会生活之中,不了解语言的社会文化背景就无法理解这种语言的确切含义。"口译员需要了解双方文化背景,才能更好地理解说话人的本意,并用适合听众文化心理的方式进行翻译。例如,在某市领导与外宾会晤结束时,外宾赠送市领导自己公司生产的高级化妆品礼盒,并说"This is for your wife"。市领导没想到会收到这样的礼物,哈哈一笑,说:"我太太啊,她都是个老太婆。"考虑到双方的交际情境,口译员灵活处理,最后口译成"Thank you very much! I am sure my wife will look younger wearing your cosmetics"。可见,口译员要理解讲话人的意图,而不是简单地做字词对应的翻译。口译中的文化差异始终存在,需要真正理解双方的话语和意图,实现跨文化沟通。因此口译员需要具有跨文化交际的意识和能力。

4. 职业操守

口译员在工作中承受巨大的压力,也常常面对挑剔和指责。口译员既为发言人服务,又为听众服务,永远是两面的角色,而不是某方的代言人。为此,口译员必须进入说话人的角色,无论自己有多么独到的见解也不能够掺杂进去,要甘当辅助的角色。同时,口译员由于工作的特点,经常能够了解到外人未知的信息,但不能利用工作之便来谋取个人利益。一位曾在巴黎高等翻译学校任教、为几任法国元首担任英语口译员的老前辈,在回答为什么不写回忆录的问题时说:"如果写回忆录,将那些在世的或者已故的风云人物不为人知的事情公开出来,这对我的服务对象是不公平的。"优秀的口译员,必须在职业生涯中始终遵守职业精神:中立、守信、保守秘密。

第 2 章 口译基本技能(一)听辨

2.1 口译中的听辨与外语教学中的听辨区别

听辨源语信息是进行口译的前提。口译中的听辨和外语教学中的听辨存在差异,它们在目的、次数、理解深度、加工程度、听取材料的特点等方面都不尽相同。

在目的方面,外语教学中的听辨旨在学习、应试等。学习时以诊断自己听力盲区、学习词汇和语音语调为主要目的,考试中常常是听取大意和必要细节,以回答考试问题。而口译中的听辨不是以语言学习和应试为目的,而是要尽可能完全地输入源语信息,以达到用译语重新发布源语的目的。

在听取材料的特点方面,外语教学中的听辨常常听的是比较标准的英式或美式英语、难度经过处理了的材料,口译中的听辨则可能是夹杂各种口音的英语、难度不可控制的材料,因此挑战更大。

在次数方面,外语教学中的听辨可以反复听多次,但口译中的听辨一般只能听一次。虽然偶尔在万不得已、又有机会的情况下可以请讲话人重复一下所说的信息,但是这往往不是专业的表现,并且有时候不具备这样的条件。

在理解的深度方面,外语教学中的听辨的要求相对低一些,只需要听懂大意和必要细节,口译中的听辨要求完全地理解和记忆。

在对源语的加工程度方面,外语教学中的听辨要求较低,更多是对语音的分辨,而口译中的听辨要求较高,要做到对语义进行分辨,还要搜索相应的译语。

表 2.1 是上述几个方面的对比简表。

表 2.1 外语教学听辨与口译听辨的区别

对比点	外语教学中的听辨	口译中的听辨
目的	学习、应试	信息完全摄取以发布
听取材料的特点	标准的英式或美式英语、难度经处理	夹杂各种口音的英语、难度不可控
次数	可以多次	仅一次

续表

对比点	外语教学中的听辨	口译中的听辨
理解深度	听懂大意和必要细节	完全地理解和记忆
对源语的加工程度	加工程度浅,语音分辨	加工程度深,语义分辨

需要指出的是,科技口译员在听辨过程中,要"借助上下文,借助讲话人同听讲人的交流,不断丰富和调整认知,经历一个认知心理学中所讲的自下而上和自上而下的感知过程"[19]35。这就要求口译员在口译听辨过程中随时学习,并注重对信息的确认和定位。例如,某口译员在进行一次科技口译任务的时候,因为刚开始上下文还不明朗,她对"appreillage"(法语,本意设备、附属设施)的所指不明确,后来通过仔细听辨和学习讲话人的专业表达方式,了解到讲话人是在谈开关插座产品,由此就明白了 appreillage 的特指。

2.2 口译听辨的原则"得意忘形"

口译初学者在听辨时常出现的问题是过分受限于源语的语言形式,而不能准确、流畅、迅速地表达源语意思。因此应当特别注意摄取源语的核心意思,脱离语言外壳的束缚,这种重视内涵意义、脱离源语语言形式的思想简称"得意忘形"。

"得意忘形"的理论依据是法国塞莱斯柯维奇的释意理论。释意理论认为,翻译程序是理解原文、脱离源语言外壳、用另一语言重新表达。将这一翻译程序设定为释意理论的三角模式(见图 2.1[25])。从语言 A 到语言 B 的转换不是语言符号层次的对等,而是意义层次的对等。例如,"您辛苦了!"语言符号层次的对等是"You are tired!",但是在意义层次上,它可以翻译为"You have had a good trip?""Thank you for your contribution !"等。

图 2.1 三角模型

再例如,对于苹果手机广告"bigger than bigger"的翻译,是译文一"比更大还更大"好,还是译文二"岂止于大"更好?译文一是贴合源语形式的翻译,但是在交际目的上没有达到应有的效果。广告的真正目的在于推销,使消费者认为该产品"高大上",产生购买欲望,而"比更大还更大"只是简单的事实陈述,缺少了令人心生仰慕的效果，相比之下"岂止于大"虽然没有沿用源语的语言形式，但是在意义和功能上更能达到相应的效果。

练习

翻译以下句子，注意"得意忘形"。

（1）Less is more.

（2）He always lives ahead of his salary.

（3）The reality is far better than ten thousand words can tell.

（4）But if you're a 'glass half empty' type of person, could seeing the world through rose-tinted glasses work for you?

（5）The "Declaration" has had a transformational impact on the global oil industry. The change we have seen over the past 20 months is like night and day.

（6）Energy is a central facet that links our daily lives; it is not on call, it cannot take a holiday, it cannot call in sick. Energy is a 24-hour service.

（7）I'll love you three score and ten.

（8）He has one hundred and one things to do today.

（9）Ten to one, we shall over fulfill our production plan for this year.

（10）Putting two and two together, he came to the conclusion that mechanical energy is different from electrical energy.

2.3　口译听辨的训练方法

听辨对于口译的重要性无须赘言。而中国口译员的语言背景不同于西方国家，其"双语实际状况相对国际上普遍存在的并列性双语者口译员而言不具备可比性"[26]。因此听辨技能的培养对中国学生尤为重要。

基于认知心理学的信息加工理论，资深同传译员和口译教师卢信朝[27]提出了对口译听辨各项技能的训练方法。

（1）音流听辨技能：听辨各种口音的英语语音材料的能力。不仅需要听标准英美语音的材料，也需要听各种带口音的英语材料。训练过程应循序渐进：从单音听辨到动态音流听辨，从英美标准英语的音流听辨到各种语音变体的音流听辨。

（2）言意分离技能：透过纷繁语言形式摄取意义的能力。训练时可听辨句式或词法比较复杂的材料，做快速译出大意的练习。

（3）意群切分技能：便于意义加工和存储意义基本单位的能力。训练时循序渐进，从词句到段落进行意群切分和复述练习。

（4）关键信息识别与浓缩技能：便于意义再加工和存储意义集约化的加工能

力。训练时可学习英语话语信息的呈现规则,用各种符号、图像等在脑中或纸上对意义进行浓缩性表征或标示。

(5) 释义能力:运用分析性思维对语言或意义较为复杂的信息进行阐释的能力。训练时可选用语言或意义较为复杂的材料,用源语或目的语进行解释。

(6) 概要能力:运用归纳性思维对零碎、冗余的信息进行概要的能力。训练时可选用语言或意义较为零散、冗余较多的材料,用源语或目的语进行概述。

(7) 逻辑性重构能力:对意义进行深度逻辑加工的能力。训练时可使用逻辑较为混乱的材料,做逻辑复述或口译的练习。

(8) 联想能力:话语框架联想、话语内容联想和词汇联想能力。训练时可就某话题进行话语框架联想和话语内容联想、词汇"头脑风暴"等练习。

(9) 预测、推断能力:语言和非语言预测、推断能力。训练时可做词汇或短语的听辨预测完形练习、话题听辨接续练习等。

(10) 分心协调能力:一心多用的能力。训练时可做延迟复述、跟读+心数、跟读+写数等练习。

(11) 表征能力:对意义进行便于信息加工和存储的表征。训练时可通过数字、文字、图形、情景等途径对脑中的信息进行表征。

练习

1. 听句子,记句子关键词,然后进行复述(音频2.3-1)。

2. 听句子,根据上下文,猜测画线单词的意思(音频2.3-2)。

(1) The Internet is like alcohol in some sense. It <u>accentuates</u> what you would do anyway. If you want to be a loner, you can be more alone. If you want to connect, it makes it easier to connect.

音频2.3-1

(2) It is the mark of an educated mind to be able to <u>entertain</u> a thought without accepting it.

音频2.3-2

(3) Speak properly, and in as few words as you can, but always plainly; for the end of speech is not <u>ostentation</u>, but to be understood.

(4) There are in fact two things, science and opinion; the former <u>begets</u> knowledge, the latter ignorance.

(5) I spent five years and I don't want to tell you how much money on designing and constructing that little video camera. And now that we've lost it, well, it's <u>back to the drawing board</u>.

3. 逻辑思维训练：听下列段落，之后无笔记复述主要信息（音频 2.3-3）。

音频 2.3-3

2.4　各国口音的特点

狭义的口音是指语音和音韵的变体，即语音和音韵特征[28]。对于口译员来说，口音除语音变体之外，还包括词汇和句法的差异[29]。口译实践中，讲话人讲话往往会带有口音，这给口译员听辨带来困难。在每次翻译任务前，口译员应在熟悉讲话人的话题背景基础上，尽量与讲话人多交流，以适应其口音。平时，口译员应通过网络、电视、广播、语料库等接触不同口音的材料，掌握各种口音的特点，逐渐适应各种口音。以下为各国口音的特点。

1. 英国口音

英国各地区的口音差异很大，大致可分为标准英音（Received pronunciation）、伦敦土腔（Cockney accent）、苏格兰口音（Scottish accent）、爱尔兰口音（Irish accent）和威尔士口音（Welsh accent）等[30]。各地口音共性的特征是字正腔圆、抑扬顿挫，能够清晰区分长元音和短元音。标准英音的典型代表可参考英国女皇的讲话和 BBC 新闻英语。

2. 美国口音

美式发音比英式发音速度更快，大部分长元音被截短，常出现省音，例如，把 glass 中的长元音[ɑː]音读成短音的[æ]。美国各地的口音有差别，但大都带有卷舌音。影视作品中体现美国口音的典型代表有电视剧《老友记》《欲望都市》等。

3. 加拿大口音

加拿大口音类似于美国口音，但夹杂着英国英语和魁北克法语的特点。例如，[n]、[d]、[t]、[s]、[z]和[l]音之后，[j]音消失，所以，knew、dupe 和 Tuesday 分别发为[nuː]、[duːp]和[ˈtuːzdeɪ]。在用词方面，在大多数情况下，一个词的英式用词与美式用词并存，例如，表示裤子吊带的 braces（英式）和 suspenders（美式）常常互换使用。以"eh"代替"Pardon?"是一个典型的加拿大用法，这曾被移民官员作为辨别加拿大人的标识[31]。

4. 澳大利亚口音

澳大利亚南部口音比较接近英国口音，越往北口音越重。澳大利亚人常常省略辅音[h]，直接发后面的元音，例如，将 how 发成 ow。澳大利亚人还常将双元音[eɪ]发成类似[aɪ]的音。有一个著名的笑话，有一名澳大利亚游客问导游"Where are we going to die?",其实他说的是"Where are we going today?",由于 today 被发得和 to die 一样而成了笑话[32]。

5. 新西兰口音

传统上的新西兰英语非常接近英国英语。近年来因受美国文化的影响,年轻一代的英语杂糅了美式用法和美国俚语。新西兰口音的一个显著特点是倾向于把[e]发得与[i]相近,如 left 发成 lift;把[æ]发成[e],例如,将 back 发成类似 beck 的音。

6. 法国口音

法国人讲英语时会受到母语影响。在元音方面,许多法国人发元音时长短元音不分,如[i]和[i:]不分、[u]和[u:]不分,所以,sip 和 seep 同音,full 和 fool 同音。因为法语没有双元音,所以许多法国人发双元音会不准确,例如,把[ei]发成类似[e]的音,把[ai]发成类似[a]的音。在辅音方面,因为法语没有[h]这个辅音,因此法国人讲英语时常常省略[h]音。因为法语单词没有重音,所以法国人常常掌握不好英语单词的重音,例如,把 actually 发成"ahk chew ah lee",或者把重音放在最后一个音节[33]。

7. 意大利口音

受母语影响,意大利人讲英语时常用意大利语的语音代替英语的语音。由于意大利语中没有单元音[i]和[u],所以意大利人常会用[i:]和[u:]来替代[i]和[u],例如,sit 与 seat 同音,put 与 poot 同音。意大利语中没有舌齿摩擦音,所以意大利人常会用[t]或[f]替代[θ],用[d]替代[ð],使得 there 与 dare 听上去一样。意大利人讲英语常以强音节结尾,习惯在词尾加[ə],例如,dog 会读成[dɔgə][32]。

8. 德国口音

德国人发音时常常按照单词的拼写进行发音,语调常常显得有些生硬。很多德国人发不好[θ]和[ð],而用[s]和[z]代替,例如,把 this 发成"zis",把 things 发成 sings。有的德国人不会发[w]音,把[w]发成[v]音,例如,把 we 发成"vee""what"发成"vat"[34]。

9. 西班牙口音

西班牙口音有不区分摩擦音、省略词尾辅音等特点。由于西班牙语不区分摩擦音,所以以西班牙为母语者讲英语中往往分不清[s]和[tʃ]或[ʃ],并常用[j]替代[dʒ]和[ʒ]。在一般情况下,西班牙语中词尾辅音只有[s]、[n]、[r]、[l]和[d]五个音,因此以西班牙语为母语者常将这五个音以外的词尾辅音省略。当词首为[s]并加上另一个辅音时,西班牙人发音时常会在前加一个[e]音,例如,stamp 会发成[estæmp],而不是[stæmp][32]。

10. 东南亚口音

东南亚口音有清辅音浊化、元音长短不分、双元音及辅音(丛)简化、单词或句子重音偏移或后移等特征[35]。在辅音方面,清辅音常被浊化,例如,[p]发成[b],[t]发成[d],[k]发成[g],等等;发复辅音时常会省略其中的一个辅音。在元音方面,长短元音相混,例如,将[i]与[iː]相混,将[u]与[uː]相混,将[æ]与[ɑː]相混,等等。另外,还会出现某些音相混的情况,例如,[θ]与[t]或[s]相混,[s]与[ʃ]相混,[v]与[j]相混,等等。曾经有中国学生问新加坡人坐哪路公交车,对方回答"Dig tree tree",其实是"Take three three",即坐33路公交车,但他把take的[t]发成了[d],[k]发成了[g],three[θriː]的[θ]发成了[t],以致造成了理解的困难[36]。

11. 西亚口音

西亚国家(如伊朗、沙特阿拉伯、土耳其等)都会用母语中的近似音来替换母语体系中不存在的英语发音,例如,由于土耳其和伊朗母语中缺乏[θ]、[ð]音,常用[s]和[t]代替[θ],用[z]和[d]代替[ð],所以 three 发成[sri]或[tri],they 发成[zei]或[dei][37-39]。西亚口音还有一个特点是在辅音丛中间插音,例如,沙特阿拉伯人在辅音丛中插入元音[ə]、[i]、[u],所以[ʃn]发成了[ʃən],[dnt]发成了[dint],[fl]发成了[ful][39]。

12. 日本口音

日本口音在元音发音、重音位置和停顿等方面与标准英音差别很大。由于日语中只有五个长短一致的元音,因此日本人讲英语时通常会混淆一些元音,如[e]和[æ]、[i]和[iː]、[e]和[eə]、[ʌ]和[ɑː]等,还会将 mat [mæt] 读成[met]。在重音方面,日本人常常掌握不好英语单词的重音位置,易加重词尾音节,语句中可能会将介词、连接词等功能词发成重音,而重要信息(如否定词的重音)则发得不明显。在停顿方面,日本人讲英语时往往停顿数量更多,且停顿位置错误较多[32]。

13. 韩国口音

韩国口音有单词连读、重音后置等特点。受母语影响,很多韩国人说英语时单词连读,最后一个音节拖长。有些韩国人还分辨不出[l]和[r]音,发不出[θ]或[ð]音。在音调方面,有相当一部分人不知道除了一般疑问句外何时该读升调,往往从头到尾用降调。在节奏方面,韩国口音的英语体现出音节节拍语言的节奏特点,即元音发音普遍饱满,每个音节普遍清晰[32]。

14. 印度口音

印度人讲英语往往口音重,语速快,缺少爆破音,语调无升降,停顿难掌握,乍听起来很难懂,会给口译员造成较大的听辨困难。印度人发清辅音时常常浊化,例如,"What time"的印度发音类似"WA DIM","I'd like to change the color"的印度发音类似"I D LIG DO CHANGE DE GALA",其中清辅音[p]、[t]和[k]分别发成了[b]、[d]和[g]。在用词和句法的方面,受印地语的影响,印度英语中常常会添加一些用词,例如,问名字时说"Your good name please?",问生日的时候说"When is your happy birthday?"。印度绅士常用现在进行时代替一般现在时,例如,把"I understand it"说成"I am understanding it",把"She knows the answer"说成"She is knowing the answer"[30]。

15. 非洲口音

非洲本土语言种类繁多,达 2011 种之多,因此非洲各地英语口音也各有特点。从整体来看,非洲英语掺杂了英式英语、当地土著语借词、阿拉伯语借词、当地口音以及大舌音等诸多因素,因此,非洲英语听起来较为混沌,就像用手捂着嘴巴说话一样,而且语速很快,这给理解造成困难[40]。例如,一些非洲人把[r]发成大舌音,所以 three 听起来像 thrrrrrrrree;还有非洲人将清辅音浊化,使[p]、[t]和[k]发得像[b]、[d]和[g]。

16. 俄罗斯口音

俄罗斯人常把[r]发成大舌音,并且由于俄语中没有[w]音,所以很多俄罗斯人会用[v]音代替[w]音。大部分人在发词尾复辅音时最后一个辅音会自然脱落,有些人会刻意克服这一弱点,但有时矫枉过正,听起来像词尾多了一个音[32]。

17. 中国口音

中国口音主要是受到普通话语音系统的影响,发元音不够饱满,发辅音时常常会将清辅音浊化、在辅音后加上[ə]音等。不同地区受到地方口音的影响,会混淆某些辅音,例如,东北人多把[z]和[dʒ]互换,两湖一带的人把[h]发成[f],北京人习惯给单词加儿化音,等等。在语流方面,常有人缺少连读和爆破,发音一字一顿,听起来有一种不连贯的感觉。

练习

1. 听"英特尔手持设备业务部总监在中国移动娱乐产业发展论坛上的讲话",并进行复述,注意口音听辨(音频 2.4-1[41])。

2. 先看下列相关译前准备文件,再看视频并做交替传译。视频内容是对 2019 年诺贝尔化学奖获得者(97 岁的 John Goodenough)的采访(视频 2.4-2[42])。

音频 2.4-1

视频 2.4-2

Chemistry Nobel honours world-changing batteries[43]

The Nobel Prize in Chemistry has been awarded to John Goodenough, Stanley Whittingham and Akira Yoshino for the development of lithium-ion batteries—a technology that ushered in a revolution in energy storage.

All three contributed to the evolution of the kind of lightweight, rechargeable batteries that power today's mobile phones and other portable electronic devices—and make possible a "fossil fuel-free society", the Nobel chemistry committee said.

Goodenough, a solid-state physicist at the University of Texas at Austin who is 97, becomes the oldest ever Nobel laureate—although the committee said that it had not been able to reach him at the time of the prize announcement. The three researchers will get equal shares in the prize, worth 9 million Swedish kronor.

"I am very grateful that I had that honour, it's splendid," Goodenough, who was in London to receive a separate prize, told *Nature* later in the day. "But I am the same person I was before."

Rechargeable world

In a lithium-ion battery, lithium ions move from the negative electrode (anode) to the positive electrode (cathode) through an electrolyte while the battery discharges, then back again when it recharges.

While working for the oil company Exxon in the 1970s, Whittingham, who is now at the State University of New York at Binghamton, proposed the idea of rechargeable lithium batteries and developed a prototype that used a lithium-metal anode and a titanium disulfide cathode. The battery had a high energy density and the diffusion of lithium ions into the cathode was reversible, making the battery rechargeable. But high manufacturing costs and safety concerns meant the technology could not be commercialized.

改变世界的锂离子电池摘得诺贝尔化学奖(节选)[42]

John Goodenough、Stanley Whittingham 和吉野彰被授予2019年诺贝尔化学奖,以表彰他们在锂离子电池开发方面所做的贡献——该技术成功引领了一场储能革命。

诺贝尔化学奖委员会表示,三位科学家对这种轻便、可充电电池的开发做出了重要贡献,这些电池如今驱动着移动电话等便携式电子设备,让"零化石燃料的社会"成了可能。

现年97岁的Goodenough是美国得克萨斯大学奥斯汀分校的固体物理学家,也是迄今最高龄的诺贝尔奖得主。不过,委员会在宣布获奖名单时还无法与他本人取得联系。三位科学家将平分900万瑞典克朗。

Goodenough当时正在伦敦接受另一个奖项,他在晚些时候接受《自然》采访时说:"我非常感激能获得这个荣誉,这太美好了。但我还是之前的我。"

可充电的世界

锂离子电池在放电时,锂离子会经过电解液从负电极(负极)流向正电极(正极),充电时锂离子会从正极流回负极。

来自纽约州立大学宾汉姆顿分校的Whittingham在20世纪70年代曾就职于埃克森石油公司,他率先提出了可充电锂电池的概念,并研发了一款原型电池,使用金属锂作为负极,使用二硫化钛作为正极。这种电池的能量密度很高,锂离子向正极的传输过程也是可逆的,使得电池能够重复充电。然而,高昂的制造成本和安全隐患让这一技术的商业化困难重重。

Sustainable future The Nobel committee also highlighted the role that the battery might have in creating a more sustainable future as nations try to <u>move away from fossil fuels</u>. Batteries are increasingly being used to store energy from renewable sources, such as <u>solar and wind power</u>. Grey, who has collaborated with Whittingham, says that a number of people have made major contributions to developing the technology, but that the committee made a good choice. Goodenough, in particular, is an "<u>intellectual giant</u>" in the field of materials, with many fundamental contributions beyond batteries. "He changed the way we think about <u>magnetism</u>, and he has helped to explain <u>electronic conductivity</u>," Grey says. Asked whether lithium-ion batteries were his favourite work, Goodenough told *Nature*: "No, I think my favourite work was to investigate what's called the <u>Mott transition</u>," in which the <u>electrons</u> in a material go from being able to move freely to being linked to individual <u>atoms</u>.	**可持续的未来** 诺贝尔奖委员会还指出，随着各国努力减少<u>化石燃料的使用</u>，锂离子电池在实现可持续未来的过程中肩负着重要使命。委员会提到，电池正越来越多地被用于存储可再生能源，如<u>太阳能和风能</u>。 曾与 Whittingham 有过合作的 Grey 认为，虽然这项技术的发展离不开许多人的重要贡献，但委员会做出了正确的选择。尤其是 Goodenough，他是材料领域的一位"<u>知识巨擘</u>"，在电池以外的诸多方面都有着基础性贡献。Grey 说："他改变了我们对<u>磁性</u>的理解，还帮助阐释了<u>电子导电性</u>。" 当被问及锂离子电池是否是他最喜欢的成果时，Goodenough 告诉《自然》的记者："不是，我最喜欢的应该是对 Mott 转变的探索。" Mott 转变是指材料中的<u>电子</u>从自由移动的状态转变为和单个<u>原子</u>相连的状态。

第3章 口译基本技能(二)记忆

3.1 记忆概述

鉴于口译具有即时性、即席性的特征,口译员能否迅速完整地保存所接收到的信息至关重要,这就需要口译员具有良好的记忆能力。从脑科学的范畴来看,记忆是神经系统存储过往经验的能力。从心理学的角度来看,记忆可被理解为一种从"记"到"忆"的心理过程,它包括识记、保持和再现等过程。按照结构,记忆一般可以分为瞬时记忆(immediate memory)、短时记忆(short-term memory)和长时记忆(long-term memory)三种。

瞬时记忆是指刺激物刚停止作用时,事物映象在脑中暂时存储的现象。这种记忆在持续一瞬间后很快消失,保持时间仅为 0.25 s 至 2 s。与短时记忆比较,瞬间记忆的容量较大,但信息都处于相对未经加工的原始状态。如果人不给予注意,信息便很快流失。瞬时记忆的作用在于把环境刺激保持一定时间,以便进行更精细的加工。

短时记忆亦称操作记忆或工作记忆,指信息在一次呈现后保持的记忆,可以持续几秒钟或几分钟,其功能是对输入的信息进行加工处理。例如,在听到一个语言片段之后,要把它放在记忆里保留一段时间,以便与后续语言片段放在一起进行处理,达到准确理解。一般人短时记忆的广度平均值为 7 ± 2 个信息单位。记忆广度和记忆材料的性质有关。如果呈现的材料是无关联的数字、字母、单词或无意义音节,超过记忆广度时就会发生错误。如果呈现的材料是有意义的、有联系的并为人所熟悉的材料,则记忆广度可增加。另外,对材料进行"组块"加工,即将小单位(如字母、符号等)联合为较大单位,有利于扩大记忆容量。例如,要记住 2824714932 这样一个电话号码时,先把它分成 28(局号)、2471(总机号)和 4932(分机号)三块,就能减轻记忆的负担,扩大记忆的容量。

长时记忆又称永久记忆,保存的是人们已经贮存在大脑里的知识和经验。长时记忆所贮存的信息一旦被激活,可以用来理解新信息。长时记忆没有广度问题,其容量可以是无限的。

就口译而言,三种记忆均有作用:瞬时记忆启动信息处理的"注意"程序;短时记忆主导信息处理过程,在口译记忆中起到关键作用;长时记忆涉及已经存储的相关知识、经验,在信息处理过程中起到后台支持的作用。这三者相互作用、相辅相成。如果口译员对口译的话题具有较多背景知识储备(存储在长时记忆中),口译中就可以大量调用长时记忆,有利于将短时记忆中的信息"组块",减轻短时记忆的负担,以将更多注意力分配到信息加工、理解、输出方面,从而提高口译质量。

3.2 口译记忆训练的方法

口译记忆并不是鹦鹉学舌般地恢复源语的语音代码,而是对信息进行主动加工编码后的储存和提取。认知心理学认为,记忆痕迹是信息加工的副产品,信息加工深度越大,信息就保持得越长久[44]。因此,在进行口译记忆训练时,应特别注意对信息的加工,使源语不再是"他人的"信息,而变成自己个人化的信息。口译记忆中常用的信息加工方法有信息组块法、逻辑分层法、顺时记忆法、形象记忆法等。

在记忆不同语篇类型时,相关的信息处理建议如下[45]。

(1) 论述类:应注意观点之间的逻辑关联,保证结构清晰。

(2) 以时间为线的叙述类:应注意时间短语、日期和动词时态。

(3) 描写类:应集中精力记住最重要的信息。

(4) 极力争辩类:应保证忠实源语,并传递要旨和情感。

(5) 辞藻华丽类:源语精神比细节更重要,注意头衔、专有名词和修辞手法。

对于初学者,口译记忆常见的困难有注意力不够集中、背景知识储备不足、外语水平不够、不会做笔记或做笔记时占用注意力资源等。为此,除提高英语水平、扩大知识面之外,需要特别训练提高积极听力和做笔记的能力。要提高积极听力能力,需要培养注意力高度集中的能力,边听边主动解析源语信息点,并理解信息点之间的关系。做笔记的目标是通过学习和训练逐渐形成自己的笔记系统,使做笔记熟练到不会占用过多注意力资源的程度。

口译记忆常用的训练方法如下。

(1) 逻辑整理练习:要求在听的同时对信息进行逻辑分析。听完后概述原文中心意思,再细化为信息点,分析信息点的逻辑关系。可用不同的文体类型,也可选取逻辑性差的内容,时间长度循序渐进,由半分钟、一分钟逐渐加长。

(2) 影子跟读练习:选取中文或英文听力材料,在延迟源语半句话左右时开始用源语重复叙述。练习目的在于培养注意力高度集中和注意力分配的能力。

(3) 无笔记复述练习:在不记笔记的情况下,复述中文或英文源语信息。复述时,可以不按照源语信息的顺序,也可选择不同的语言。练习时循序渐进,可以先复述大意、关键词,然后再补充尽可能多的细节。选取材料不宜过长、过难,不含数字、专有名词等,后期逐渐加大练习长度和难度。

(4) 有笔记复述练习:在允许记笔记的情况下,复述中文或英文源语信息。要求尽量做到信息准确和完整。选取材料可以比无笔记复述选取的材料更长、更难,如含有数字、专有名词、术语等。

3.3 信息组块法

根据研究,人的记忆容量有限,为 7±2 个单位,这个记忆单位又称为块(chunk)。虽然 7±2 个单位这个数目是相对恒定的,但是每个单位的容量可以扩展。因此,为了增强记忆长度,可以尽量扩大每个记忆单位的容量,使其不仅是一个音节,还可以是一个单词、一个句子、一段话,甚至是更长的语句。这就是短时记忆的组块。

举个简单的例子来说,在记忆身份证号 370702198010152627 时,如果记忆单独的每个数字,记忆结果会非常有限,但是如果组块为以下形式就会比较容易记忆:37(代表山东省)+07(代表潍坊市)+02(代表潍城区)+19801015(出生日期1980年10月15日)+262(顺序号)+7(校验码)。再进一步整理,还可以组块成:370702(出生地)+19801015(出生日期)+262(顺序号)+5(校验码)。组块后,就更容易记忆了。

在短时记忆组块过程中,有很多因素会影响记忆组块的容量,如组块的大小、复杂性和熟悉性,以及个人的知识经验等。特别是"知识经验越多,不仅应用的组块数越多,而且每个组块所包含的相应信息量也越多"[46]。也就是说,想提高记忆组块的容量,平时应注意积累知识经验。平时的知识经验积累将形成"预制块",在记忆信息时直接嵌入使用,可以减少认知负荷,增加记忆的容量。

音频 3.3-1

练习

听段落,进行无笔记复述(音频 3.3-1)。

3.4 逻辑分层法

在记忆的时候,对信息加工程度越深,越便于记忆。逻辑分层法是记忆中运用比较广泛的一种方法。对于任何文体的语段,在听辨时都应该按照信息的重要程度进行分层,分为一级信息(主要信息)、二级信息、次级信息等,然后按照重要性的顺序去识记。此外,要特别注意语段中的逻辑关系,理顺原文脉络,以帮助记忆。

以下面这段话[47]来说明对信息的分层方法。

在人工智能(AI)的浪潮下,顶尖科学家正在发挥越来越重要的作用。那么,科学家应该如何参与AI呢?对此,李开复给出了科学家参与AI时代的四条建议路径。第一,自己撸起袖子创业,如爱迪生。科学家本质是创新,而不是创造商业价值。第二,找个商业合伙人一起干,例如,Marc Andressen和James Clark共同创办Netscape。第三,留在学校继续创新,把技术授权出去。例如,Stanford技术授权成就Google,让学生去创业。第四,提供技术开源,公开发布论文,不断利用科学加快创新发展。例如,居里夫人开创放射理论,出版《放射学》等著作,推动科技创新发展。

在这段话中,一层信息就是科学家参与AI时代的四条建议路径,二层信息是每种建议路径的名人举例。从图3.1所示的幻灯片可以直观地看出信息的层级。在实际口译中,往往没有这样明显的视觉辅助,需要在脑海中自动形成这样的逻辑分层,以帮助记忆。

图3.1 幻灯片

以记忆以下这段话为例,说明对信息的逻辑重组方法。

We have heard a lot of interesting points from the speakers who have gone before me about creating a supportive investment climate which takes into account the interests and concerns of foreign companies, while also helping Chinese companies and the various regions of China to realize their competitive advantages.

这段话的信息较为零散,在接收到这些信息时,须结合语境对其进行逻辑重组,并结合长时记忆里的相关知识(如软投资环境、论坛参与者、会议主题等),才能得到连贯的语篇信息。即在我之前的发言人已围绕"照顾外国公司的利益、创造鼓励性投资环境、同时帮助中国公司和各个地区实现其本身的竞争优势"这一话题做了很有意义的阐述。

练习

1. 听题为"张璐：如何给总理做翻译"的语段，然后做源语复述，注意记忆时按照逻辑分层的方法，优先记忆第一层的主干信息（音频3.4-1）。

音频3.4-1

2. 听香港中文大学校长沈祖尧在大学毕业典礼上发表的演讲，然后做翻译复述，注意记忆时按照逻辑分层的方法（音频3.4-2）。

音频3.4-2

3. 听题为"十大科技趋势"的文章，然后做源语复述，注意记忆时按照逻辑分层的方法，优先记忆第一层的主干信息。第一遍记录七个趋势，第二遍按照七个趋势分段进行复述（音频3.4-3）。

音频3.4-3

3.5 顺时记忆法

对于有明显时间线索的叙述性语段，可以使用顺时记忆法记忆每个时间节点和相关关键信息。例如，孔子的"吾十有五而志于学，三十而立，四十而不惑，五十而知天命，六十而耳顺，七十而从心所欲"就可以按照每个时间节点顺序去记忆。

练习

听以下语段，进行无笔记忆，然后复述（音频3.5-1至3.5-5）。

音频3.5-1　　音频3.5-2　　音频3.5-3　　音频3.5-4　　音频3.5-5

3.6 形象记忆法

形象记忆法是指口译员将讲话内容在头脑中形象化，以辅助记忆的方法。实验表明，视觉信息的记忆容量比语言信息的记忆容量大得多。由于形象记忆的方法更生动，更符合短时记忆的特点，其保持的时间相应延长，而且保持的信息更完整，所以形象记忆法十分适合用于对某种情形、故事情节、环境进行描述的情况。

例如，当要记忆马致远的《天净沙·秋思》中的"枯藤老树昏鸦，小桥流水人家，古道西风瘦马。夕阳西下，断肠人在天涯。"时，如果在脑海里立刻形象化作品所描述的场景（如图 3.2 所示），记忆就会容易很多。

图 3.2　场景图

练习

1. 用 1 分钟的时间，在无笔记的情况下记忆以下词语，看能记住多少。

第一组

(1) 草坪（lawn）　　　　　　　　(2) 戒指（ring）

(3) 池塘（pond）　　　　　　　　(4) 手枪（pistol）

(5) 秋千（swing）　　　　　　　　(6) 鹿（deer）

(7) 自行车（bike）　　　　　　　　(8) 橡树（oak）

(9) 帽子（hat）　　　　　　　　(10) 薪水（salary）

(11) 水桶（bucket）　　　　　　　(12) 香烟（cigarette）

(13) 运动服（sportswear）　　　　(14) 信（letter）

(15) 溜冰鞋（roller-skate）　　　　(16) 音箱（loudspeaker）

(17) 狗（dog）　　　　　　　　(18) 白云（cloud）

(19) 保龄球（bowling）　　　　　(20) 教师（teacher）

第二组

(1) 烟雾　　　　(2) 楼梯　　　　(3) 眼泪

(4) 电脑　　　　(5) 火花　　　　(6) 窗户

(7) 窗帘	(8) 红领巾	(9) 桌子
(10) 红色	(11) 西红柿	(12) 对讲机
(13) 直升机	(14) 记者	(15) 手机
(16) 安全帽	(17) 心形	(18) 银行卡
(19) 毛巾	(20) 灰色	

第三组

(1) 微信	(2) 收音机	(3) 酷狗音乐
(4) Wi-Max	(5) 2G	(6) 媒体平台
(7) 三星	(8) 4G	(9) 苹果
(10) 3G	(11) Wi-Fi	(12) 滑盖手机
(13) 干线中心	(14) 音乐平台	(15) 谷歌
(16) 华为	(17) 百度	(18) 智能手机
(19) 目录服务	(20) 小米	

2. 听下列片段,利用视觉化方法辅助记忆,然后进行无笔记复述(音频 3.6-1)。

音频 3.6-1

第4章 口译基本技能(三)笔记

4.1 口译笔记概述

"好记性不如烂笔头",对于较长语段的翻译,如果纯靠记忆容易遗漏,也无法持续很久的工作,因此就需要使用口译笔记法。口译笔记法是口译员在紧张的会场气氛中,在不干扰听辨源语的情况下,迅速地以简便的符号、文字等记录讲话重点内容信息的一种笔记方法[48],是口译员必备技能之一。

有人以为口译笔记就是速记,其实不然,口译笔记并不是事无巨细、不假思索地速记,而是有选择地记录经过加工处理的信息的。口译专家塞莱斯科维奇认为,口译笔记的本质是"对概念内容进行最大化提取的最小线索"[49]。从作用上说,口译笔记就像是"触发器"(trigger),口译员看到它可以引发记忆中的很多信息,是记忆的一种有力的辅助工具。

1. 口译笔记记录的内容

本着辅助记忆的作用,口译笔记主要记录要点、关键词和逻辑关系。一般来说,应该记录框架结构(第一层信息)和细节中的关键词,尤其是容易出错和难以记忆的数字、专有名词(人名、地名、机构名)等,也应该记录逻辑关系,包括转折、假设、递进等,有时候一个逻辑符号就足以提示整段内容。

口译笔记的多少并无成规,应该是在足以唤起记忆的情况下越少越好。因为口译过程中需要进行听辨、理解、产出等多线程工作,这些都需要使用认知资源,笔记作为辅助应该尽少地利用认知资源,最大限度地支持其他过程。

口译笔记的形式可以多种多样,应以"尽量精简、快速完成、能够辨识"为原则,可以尽情发挥想象力,符号、汉字偏旁、英文字母组合等都可以,只要再次阅读时自己能够辨识即可。建议在口译笔记形式自成体系后固定下来,熟悉自己的笔记符号,达到"自动化"的程度,即运用时不需要调动脑力就能条件反射般地完成辨识。口译笔记使用源语或目的语均可,用目的语记录会省去译出时语言转换的环节,但不应强求,不宜占用过多注意力资源而影响翻译。

研究表明，笔记的多少、形式（符号或缩写）、语言（源语或目的语）与口译质量没有显著相关性[50]。曾传有资深口译员在没有纸笔的情况下使用房间的四个角来代表四个方面，然后靠记忆译出。所以口译笔记可以因人而异，达到辅助记忆的功能即可。

2. 口译笔记的特点

虽然口译笔记因人而异，自成体系，但也有一些共同的特点。请观察以下两位资深口译员的笔记（如图 4.1 所示），看有什么样的特点。

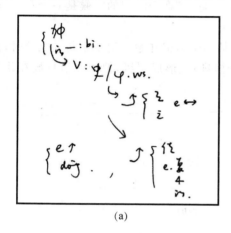
(a)

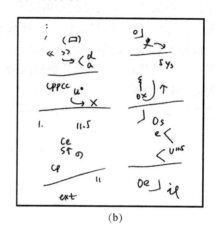
(b)

图 4.1　口译笔记

这两位口译员的笔记虽不尽相同，但也有共同之处，其特点是竖排排列、内容精简、形式简化。口译笔记不能以节省纸张为原则，如果横排排列，许多列举的内容就难以看出，各层逻辑关系也不容易显明；内容要精简，只记录主干意群和关键词（容易忘记的专有名词、数字等），一些常见词语不需要记全，如"经济发展"只用一个"e"即可；口译笔记的形式要简化、简化，再简化，遵循"最省力原则"，可以尽量用图形，例如，"因为"用数字符号的三个点表示，世界用"O"表示。另外，口译笔记往往在意群结束时有所标记，例如，图 4.1(b)所示的笔记在每个意群结束时加了一条横线。

针对口译笔记特征的表述如下[51]。

（1）纵向记录（verticalization）：也就是竖排排列，可以在版面纵向画一条中线，将版面分割成左右两半，以便竖着记录。

（2）缩格排列（indentation）：在纵向记录的同时，并不是所有信息都记录在同一列上，而是要有层层缩进，表示信息的先后顺序和逻辑位置。

（3）意群切分（division）：在每一个语意完整的意群后画一条横线，这样可以清楚地知道各个段落，从而一段一段地翻译。

（4）条列层叠（superposition）：在表达并列信息或是对立的信息等语意内涵时，竖向层叠这些信息，以便口译时更清楚地辨别。

4.2 初学者口译笔记的记录方法

对于口译初学者,其记忆容量有限,口译笔记可以由多到少,循序渐进。以下介绍初学者口译笔记的记录方法。

需要注意的是,笔记记的是意群,意群是在意义和结构上都紧密联系在一起的一组词。例如,"中华人民共和国国家主席习近平"在记笔记的时候是一个意群,可以简单记为"习",甚至只记作"P"(代表 president)。

最开始练习口译笔记的记录时,可以从句子笔记开始。记录整句的笔记时,需分析其主干结构,然后按照各语法成分竖排排列,形成层级,把相应信息放在相应位置,如图 4.2 所示。

```
            (状语,定语)
主语
        谓语(时态)
                    (定语,状语)
            宾语
```

图 4.2 排列示意图

以下介绍如何按照句子结构、重点词和逻辑关联词记口译笔记。

1. 简单句

(1) 我爱学习,也爱交友。

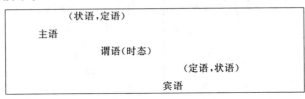

"♡"(心形):表示爱、喜欢等。
"stu":study 的缩写,代表学习。
"友":"友"的笔画少(少于或等于五笔),直接记。

(2) 俄罗斯是世界上最大的国家。

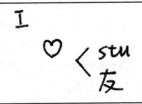

"Rus":代表 Russia 俄罗斯。
":":代表"是"、解释、说。
"O":代表国家,也可以代表全球。
"z":代表"最大的",是 zui 的拼音缩写。

2. 复杂的简单句

如今,欧洲债务危机与全球金融危机正影响着美欧国家和亚洲国家的经济。

![笔记符号]	第一行的"'"(撇):代表如今。 eu:代表欧洲。 "":专有名词用引号表示。 O:代表全球。 ♯:代表影响,"影"的简写写法的左偏旁。 ♯上面的一横:代表正在。 US:代表美国。 eu:代表欧洲。 AS:代表亚洲。 Os:代表国家的复数。 の:代表"的"(借鉴日语中"的"的写法)。 $:代表经济、金钱、美元等。

3. 汉语当中的从属关系

双方讨论了叙利亚境内流离失所人口的紧急人道要求。

![笔记符号]	2:代表双方。 ⌐:时态符号,代表已完成。 Syr:代表叙利亚。 IDP:代表流离失所人口(internally displaced people)。 nd:代表要求,是 need 的缩写。 °:代表人或者和人相关。 .:代表此处有一形容词。

4. 英语当中的介词

(1) Lawmakers in Beijing have understood the public demand for a cleaner environment.

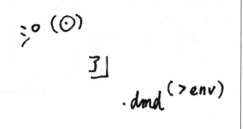

氵°:代表 lawmakers,"法"的左偏旁加"°"。
⊙:代表国家的中心,即首都。
"了":是了解(understood)的"了",因笔画少而直接记录。
dmd:demand 的缩写。
>:代表比较级,这里指代 cleaner。
env:代表 environment。

(2) The new generation does not recognize the importance of these cultural tradition.

斤G × ⊙ ＊(文 tra)	斤 G：斤是新的右偏旁，"斤 G"代表 new generation。 ×：代表没有、否定、反对等。 ⊙：眼睛的象形图，代表看见、意识到等。 ＊：代表重要。 文 tra：代表文化 tradition。

5. 汉语当中的介词

(1) 全球在预防母婴艾滋病传播方面取得了重大进步。

O ⌐ ．ᵒ̌ (×"M→子")	M→子：代表母婴。 ""：表示专有名词，这里指艾滋病。 ×：代表没有、否定、反对等，这里指预防。 ᵒ̌：这个符号像叶子托着果实，代表成果、进步。

(2) 秘书长在举行会晤时讨论了该国为实现千年发展目标所做的努力。

⌒(U) ⌐ 力 ᵒ̌ (MDG)	⌒：与刚才的果实符号"ᵒ̌"对称，像一个人戴着帽子，用来代表官员等。 (U)：U 象征 U 形会议桌，代表会议。 力：代表努力。 MDG：代表 Millennium Development Goals。

6. 被动句

2011 年，美国的实体经济遭到了次贷危机的重创。

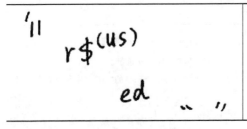

'11：代表 2011 年。
r $：代表 real 经济。
ed：代表被动语态。
""：表示专有名词，这里指次贷危机。

7. 递进关系/表目的

(1) 为了更好地保护臭氧层,国际社会开始限制含氟气体的使用。

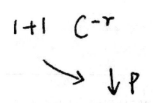	to:代表为了,表示逻辑关系的词需要记录。 >:表示比较级,这里代表更好。 ⌒:这个符号像一个章鱼横过来的形状,代表保护。 ○z:臭氧层○zone 的缩写。 ⓒ:代表国际社会,○代表全球,C 是 community。 ⌢:这个符号像一个帽子,代表镇压、限制。 F 气:代表含氟气体,f 和氟的音接近。

(2) We will work with the Chinese government to further reduce poverty.

1+1 C-r ↘ ↓P	1+1:代表合作 γ:伽马符号,"伽马"和 government 音接近。 ↘:表示目的、结果等。 ↓:代表降低、下降、减少等。 P:代表 poverty。

8. 转折关系

尽管中澳两国相距甚远,但是两国人民的友好交往不断增多。

ϟ C < A far ϟ f∽↑	ϟ:表示转折,意思是虽然、但是。 C:代表 China。 A:代表澳大利亚。 far:代表相距甚远。 f:代表 friendly。 ∽:代表交往、交流等。 ↑:代表增多、变好等。

9. 复杂句:因果关系

(1) 由于经济复苏的迹象不明朗,欧美与亚洲的各主要国家均不敢大举投资。

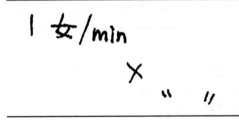

+1:代表复苏,恢复。
∵:代表因为。
×:代表不明朗、不敢。
∴:代表所以。
$ (美元符号加箭头):代表投资。

(2) One woman every minute dies as a consequence of pregnancy.

1 女:代表 one woman。
/min:代表 every minute。
×:代表 die。
"":代表专有名词,这里指 pregnancy。

以上记笔记的方法是对句子所做的口译符号,实际口译时,很少会来得及对每个句子的所有信息都做笔记,随着记忆容量的增加,笔记符号承载的信息逐渐增加,可能一个符号就代表一个句子甚至一段话。上述实例主要旨在介绍记笔记的原则,即竖排排列、内容精简、形式简化。

上述所举的口译符号只是参考,具体的口译符号因人而异,需要自成体系。初学者开始可以创制很多符号,在口译训练中进行验证和确定,逐渐巩固和强化。形成自己的口译笔记体系后,需要将笔记运用到自动化的程度,即可以自动记下笔记而非去思考要用哪个符号,关键是在记笔记的同时不影响听辨和理解。随着记忆能力的提高和对口译主题知识的熟悉,口译笔记会逐渐减少,直到最精简的形式。

此外,为了进一步拓展自己的记忆能力,建议初学者不要过早地练习记笔记,养成依赖笔记的习惯,而应以锻炼自己的记忆能力为主,当记忆能力达到一定水平之后,再加入记笔记的训练。

4.3 口译笔记符号举例

1. 韩刚口译笔记符号[52]

韩刚口译笔记符号如图 4.3 所示。

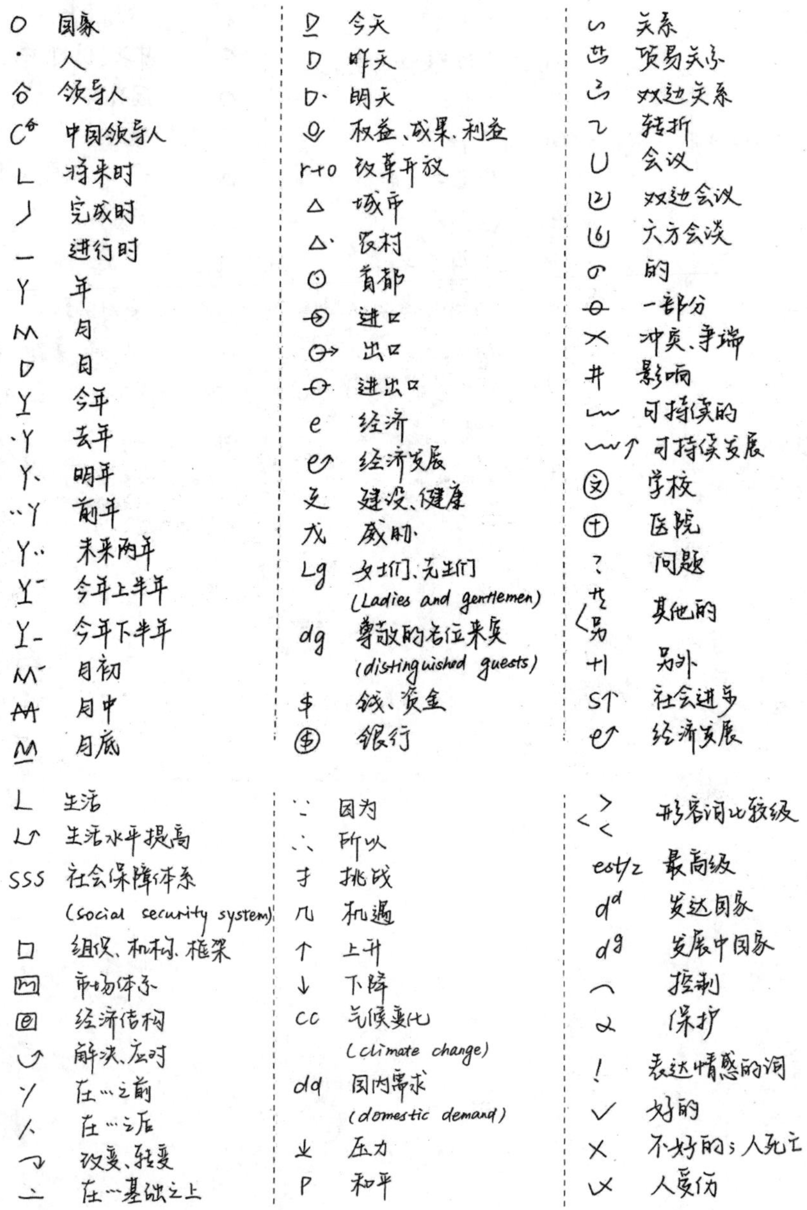

图 4.3 韩刚口译笔记符号

2. 外交部口译笔记符号[53]

外交部口译笔记符号如图 4.4 和图 4.5 所示。

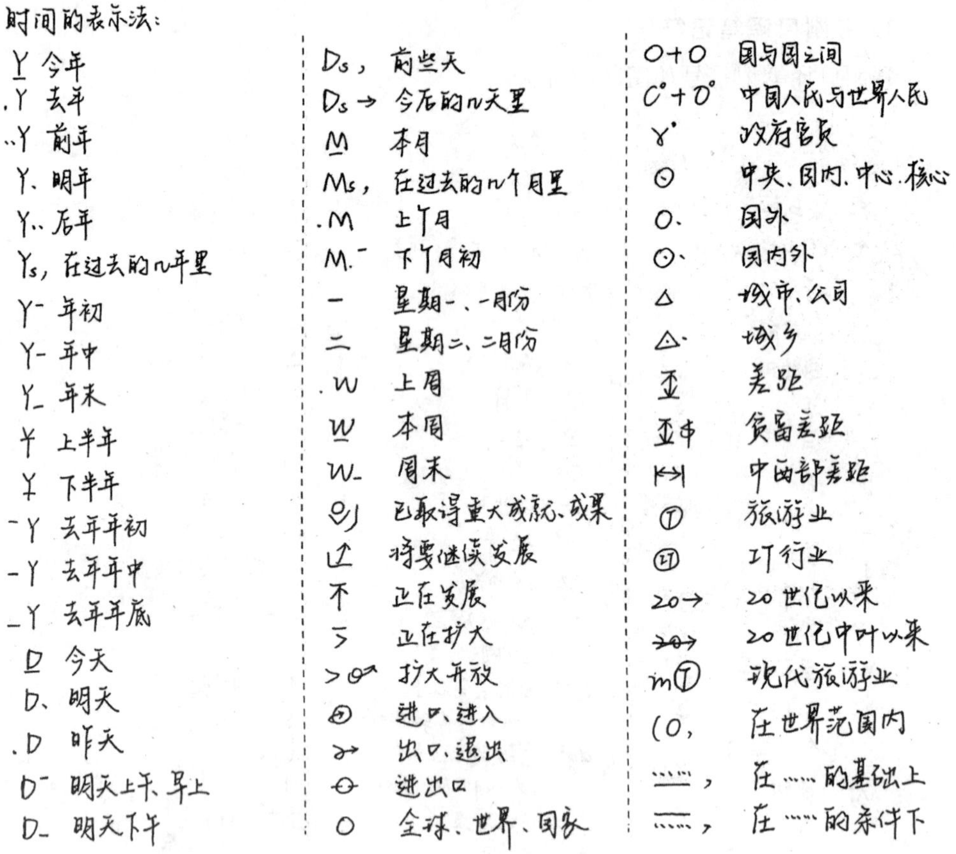

时间的表示法：

Y	今年	D̥s，	前些天	o+o	国与国之间
.Y	去年	D̥s→	今后的n天里	C°+C°	中国人民与世界人民
·Y	前年	M	本月	Y°	政府官员
Y˙	明年	M̥s，	在过去的n个月里	⊙	中央、国内、中心、核心
Y··	后年	.M	上个月	O.	国外
Ys，	在过去的n年里	M.¯	下个月初	O˙	国内外
Y⁻	年初	一	星期一、一月份	△	城市、公司
Y⁻	年中	二	星期二、二月份	⩟	城乡
Y₋	年末	.W	上周	亚	差距
Ŷ	上半年	W	本周	亚中	贫富差距
Y̌	下半年	W⌐	周末	↔	中西部差距
⁻Y	去年年初	⊕J	已取得重大成就、成果	①	旅游业
⁻Y	去年年中	⊥	将要继续发展	⊞	IT行业
₋Y	去年年底	不	正在发展	20→	20 世纪以来
D	今天	⊃	正在扩大	20⇢	20 世纪中叶以来
D˙	明天	>⊃	扩大开放	m①	现代旅游业
.D	昨天	⊙	进口、进入	(O，	在世界范围内
D¯	明天上午、早上	↷	出口、退出	——，	在……的基础上
D₋	明天下午	⇄	进出口	——，	在……的条件下
		O	全球、世界、国家		

图 4.4　外交部口译笔记符号 1

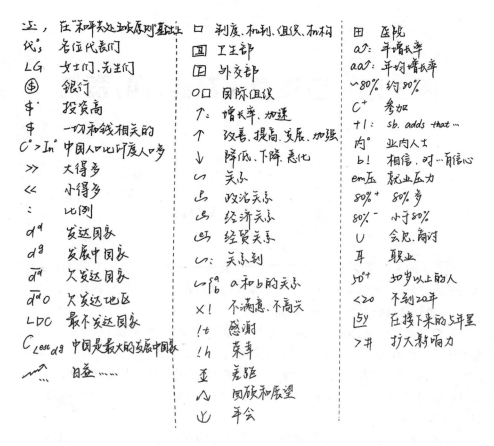

图 4.5　外交部口译笔记符号 2

练习

听题为"中印希望加强经济纽带"的英文报道,做笔记训练(音频 4.3-1 为中文版,4.3-2 为英文版)。

音频 4.3-1(中文版)　　音频 4.3-2(英文版)

第5章 口译基本技能(四)表达

5.1 口译表达概述

翻译中的表达是翻译最终产品的呈现,其质量在很大程度上决定了对翻译整体水平的评价,因此口译员应当从听众体验的角度出发,有意识地提高自己的表达能力,力争达到口译"准、顺、快"的标准。

根据口译"准、顺、快"的标准,"准"是指翻译准确、忠实原文,这是口译表达的根本要求。如前所述,这里的准确不是严格指语言形式的一一对应,而是掌握讲话人的意思,必要时打破语言外壳,以达到"动态对等"的效果。从表达呈现的形式来看,口译员的双语发音、语调都应力求规范,尽量避免错误的发音和语调(详见5.2节、5.3节、5.4节)。

口译标准中的"顺"就是要求译出语要符合语言规范和发言人的语体风格,进一步地忠实表达原意,实际上也可以视为"准"的延伸。区别于笔译,口译是为讲话人在一定的场合进行的服务。不仅发言的内容是信息的一部分,发言的语体也是信息的一部分。语体(style 或 linguistic style)即"由于使用语言的场合、场景不同而引起的语言形式和结构上的变异"[54]。例如,翻译中国领导人在正式场合的讲话和在朋友寒暄场合的讲话时所用的词汇和句式会很不一样。如果翻译时不考虑语体,就可能会出笑话。

例如,有人将"非常感谢您能邀敝人参加这次招待会,敝人的确过得愉快"翻译成"It was extremely gracious of you to have invited me to the reception, and I had bags of fun there."这句话前半部分的"extremely gracious"是正式用语,听起来很庄重严肃,但是后面的"bags of fun"非常口语化,听起来显得过于随意,前后语体很不一致,这就会令人啼笑皆非[55]。很多口译初学者语体意识不强,可能由于英语不是母语的原因。但是为了更加准确通顺地表达原意,需要学习语体知识,培养语体意识,尤其是较正式的语体(详见5.5节)。

除了英语语体知识非常重要外,中文的语言规范知识、表达能力也非常重要。

因此许多高校在培养翻译人才时也开设中文提高课程。提高中文表达水平不是一日之功，应当以提高整体语文水平为基础，进行长期积累。在此提出一个训练方法，即利用给出的中文关键词自行连接成句的方法，主要训练预测推断能力和提高语言表达流畅度。这在口译中非常重要，在只记了关键词、记忆有缺失时，还有讲话人逻辑混乱、需要梳理时，都需要把关键词连缀成句，是很实用的技巧。

　　口译标准的"快"主要是指即时性，就是在讲话人结束后应迅速给出译文，不应迟于三秒钟，这也是口译表达的基本要求。要做到"快"的标准，需要口译员在提高双语综合能力的基础上，注意力高度集中，迅速理解讲话人的意思。这就要求口译员平时锻炼口语的流畅度，可以通过朗读训练，如每天连续快速朗读半小时中英文、练习绕口令等，做到熟能生巧，以减少口译中的结巴、卡顿现象。

　　除了做到"准、顺、快"外，口译的表达还应特别考虑听众（往往也是口译的雇佣方）体验。这里作者比较倾向于翻译的"归化法"（domesticating method），即从读者角度出发，让译文尽可能符合读者文化习俗和语言习惯的译法，非常类似"意译"。根据翻译目的理论，翻译方法和翻译策略必须由译文预期的目的或功能决定，即"目的决定方式"（"ends justify means"）[56]。既然口译的目的是为了搭建两方的交际桥梁，让听众听懂对方的意思，那么口译的表达就更应倾向于听众，做到符合听众语言的规范和习惯，便于听众的理解。例如，对于同样内容的科技讲座，听众是小学生和听众是科技从业者的表达会很不一样。再例如，英译中时过于西式的句子需要进行调整，条件允许时多使用译出语所在的文化意象，多使用行内术语等。

　　以上都是从口译表达的内容和语言上进行的总结。实际上，口译表达还有一个很重要的维度，就是口译员的言外表现，如音量、姿态和手势语等。口译员需要发音清晰，音量适中，仪态大方，充满自信，才能更全面呈现讲话人信息，让听众体验到更好的口译服务。

5.2　英语易错语音

　　虽然听众对口译员的语音语调要求并不苛刻，主要关注的还是信息的传达，但毋庸置疑，较为标准的语音语调是信息传达的前提，也是口译员应具备的基本素质之一。好的语音语调更是口译员的有力工具。高水平口译员在翻译时，会巧妙利用语言本身语调的抑扬顿挫、快慢节奏来为自己赢得思考时间，使听众察觉不到翻译时的思考停顿，使翻译听起来自然流畅，就像是发言人在用另一种语言发言，这是顶级优质的听众体验。以下着重讲解中国学生容易出错的英语语音[57]和需要注意的语调。

(1) 读不好 C,G,J,L,W。

正确读音：C 为[si：]；G 为[dʒi：]；J 为[dʒei]；L 为[el]；W 为['dʌblju：]。(见音频 5.2-1。) 以上字母的正确读音与错误读音如表 5.1 所示。

音频 5.2-1

表 5.1　C,G,J,L,W 的正确读音与错误读音

英文字母	C	G	J	L	W
错误读音	西	寄、这	寄	爱喽	打不溜
正确读音	[si：] 思艺	[dʒi：] 知艺	[dʒei] zhei(拼音)	[el] ai ou(拼音)	['dʌblju：] double U(英文)

(2) 地方口音太重，辅音混淆。

陕西人前后鼻音不分，东北人多把[z]和[dʒ]互换，两湖一带的人又把[h]发成[f]，北京人和河北人习惯给单词加儿化音，南方人常把[n]和[l]、[s]和[ʃ]互换，这些都需要进行纠正。图 5.1 为 N 和 L 音的一个绕口令，读者可进行练习。

```
N 和 L 音的绕口令(音频 5.2-2)
No need to light a night-light
You've no need to light a night-light
On a light night like tonight
For a night-light's light's a slight light
And tonight's a night that's light.
When a night's light, like tonight's light
It is really not quiet right
To light night-lights with their slight-lights
On a light night like tonight
```

音频 5.2-2

图 5.1　绕口令

(3) 随意加[ə]音(音频 5.2-3)。

不少中国学生常在辅音音标[p]、[b]、[t]、[d]、[k]、[g]后面加[ə]音，这要通过练习加以改正。表 5.2 为含有上述音标的单词，读者可进行练习。

音频 5.2-3

表 5.2　辅音易发错的单词列表

[p]	[b]	[t]	[d]	[k]	[g]
top [tɔp]	job [dʒɔb]	that [ðæt]	bad [bæd]	like [laik]	dog [dɔg]
soap [səup]	cab [kæb]	sit [sit]	glad [glæd]	book [buk]	leg [leg]
stop [stɔp]	robe [rəub]	let [let]	had [hæd]	kick [kik]	beg [beg]
pop [pɔp]	pub [pʌb]	best [best]	mad [mæd]	cake [keik]	big [big]

续表

[p]	[b]	[t]	[d]	[k]	[g]
tip [tip]	Bob [bɔb]	bet [bet]	should [ʃud]	cook [kuk]	bug [bʌg]
cap [kæp]	web [web]	at [æt]	food [fuːd]	make [meik]	log [lɔg]
map [mæp]	club [klʌb]	wait [weit]	old [əuld]	mark [maːk]	egg [eg]
mop [mɔp]	bulb [bʌlb]	out [aut]	read [riːd]	dark [daːk]	vague [veig]
keep [kiːp]	bribe [braib]	meet [miːt]	card [kaːd]	lake [leik]	hug [hʌg]
up [ʌp]	lab [læb]	eat [iːt]	road [rəud]	park [paːk]	bag [bæg]

(4) [θ][s]不分,[ð][z]不分(音频 5.2-4)。

mouth——mouse　　thief——self　　thin——sin
think——sink　　south——sauce　　this——zoo
then——zest　　them——zone　　these——zip
thus——zero

音频 5.2-4

(5) 随便加儿话音[r](音频 5.2-5)。

可加儿化音和不可加儿化音示例如表 5.3 所示。

表 5.3　可加儿话音和不可加儿话音示例

可加儿话音	car, sir, far, door, hour, for, or, more, here, world
不可加儿话音	you, feel, ago, so, become, will, use, because, real, small

音频 5.2-5

(6) [l]音漏读、讹读(音频 5.2-6)。

例如,将 world[wəːld]读成[wəːd];将 all[ɔːl]读成[ɔːr]。以下单词容易出现[l]者漏读、讹读:kill, heal, field, dull, feel, cell, culture, mill, bull, steel, well, wall, ball, call, small, bulb, world, salty, casual, tall。

音频 5.2-6

(7) 不注意元音的发音长度(音频 5.2-7)。

需要发长音的长元音有两种:单元音有[iː]、[əː]、[aː]、[ɔː]、[uː];双元音有[ai]、[ei]、[ɔi]。

① No pain, no gain.
② This news has been spread all over the world.
③ You can come here and ask for help.
④ She likes kids very much.
⑤ It's cold outside.
⑥ I have a bear boy which was a gift for my birthday.
⑦ The car is out of oil.

音频 5.2-7

⑧ The girl is in a green coat.
⑨ I don't know him.
⑩ She is working in a big store.

(8) [w][v]不分(音频 5.2-8)。

we——visit　　west——very　　want——valid
wait——vivid　　word——vary　　wash——vanish
war——vote　　walk——view　　wave——victory
warm——valley

音频 5.2-8

练习

试读下列绕口令,然后通过观看视频进行跟读,尽可能把绕口令读熟练(视频 5.2-9)。

(1) Rubber baby buggy bumpers.
(2) She sells seashells by the seashore.
(3) I scream, you scream, we'll scream for ice cream.
(4) Peter Piper picked up a peck of pickled peppers.

5.3　英语常用语调

升调和降调是英语语调中常见的语调,其含义、意味和用法如表 5.4 所示[57]。

表 5.4　升调和降调

语调	升调	降调
含义	不肯定、未完结	肯定、坚定、果断、完整
意味	委婉、含蓄、礼貌、虚心、征求意见	无礼、不容置疑、唐突
用法	特殊疑问句	特殊疑问句
	祈使句	祈使句
	陈述句	陈述句
	反义疑问句	反义疑问句
	一般疑问句	感叹句

1. 升调(音频 5.3-1)

升调的基本含义是不肯定、未完结,常有委婉、含蓄、礼貌、虚心、征求意见的意味。英语的升调并不是一个词一个词地逐个上升,而是在句子着重强调的单词处上升。下面介绍升调用

音频 5.3-1

法的例子。

(1) 一般疑问句

Do you ↗understand?

(2) 祈使句(听起来会更有礼貌)

Come over ↗ here.

(3) 特殊疑问句(温和的批评或者没听清楚请求重复)

Why do you ↗ come?

What did you ↗ say?

(4) 陈述句(表示不肯定、惊讶、委婉等,也可起疑问作用)

You're a ↗ Chinese?

I beg your ↗ pardon?

(5) 反义疑问句(反义疑问句的后半部分通常用升调,表示不确定)

She is pretty, isn't ↗ she?

You will do that, won't ↗ you?

(6) 问候语

Good ↗ morning.

↗ Bye.

2. 降调(音频 5.3-2)

降调是最常用的语调,基本含义是肯定、坚定、果断、完整,有时有无礼、不容置疑、唐突的意味。下面介绍降调用法的例子。

音频 5.3-2

(1) 陈述句(一般用降调)

My name is ↘Bill.

(2) 特殊疑问句(一般在句子末尾用降调)

Where do you want to↘ go?

(3) 感叹句(表示强烈的感叹语气)

How time ↘ flies!

What a small ↘ world!

(4) 祈使句(表示表达命令,语气较强)

Be ↘ careful.

Close the ↘ door.

(5) 反义疑问句(对陈述部分把握较大时,后半部分用降调)

It's cold today, isn't ↘ it?

You don't like milk, do↘ you?

This film is boring, isn't ↘ it?

3. 混合升降调（音频 5.3-3）

除升调和降调之外，还有升降调混合用法，在选择疑问句会出现前升后降的语调。

Is she ↗Sallly or ↘Jane?

Where're you going, home, ↗gym or ↘the office?

When shall we go for a picnic, ↗Saturday or ↘Sunday?

练习

模仿视频中同一语句的五种语调，并学习其语调内涵（视频 5.3-4）。

音频 5.3-3

视频 5.3-4

5.4 英语地道发音窍门

1. 连读、缩读、弱读的基本规则[57]

（1）连读

当前一个词的词尾是辅音，后一个单词以元音开头时，应当连读。例如，

Take‿it‿easy.

慢速读法：[tei k][it][iːzi]。

连读：[ˌteikiˈtiːzi]。

更多的例子如下（音频 5.4-1）。

up‿and‿down.

连读：[ˌʌpənˈt daun]。

put‿it‿on.

连读：[ˌputitˈɔn]。

not‿at‿all.

连读：[ˌnɔtæˈtɔl]。

in‿an‿hour.

连读：[ˌinəˈnauə]。

take‿off.

连读：[teiˈkɔf]。

pick‿it‿up.

连读：[ˌpikiˈtʌp]。

good‿idea.

连读：[gʊdaiˈdiə]。

hand‿up.

音频 5.4-1

连读:[，hæn'dʌp]。
knock⌒him⌒out.
连读:[，nɔki'maut]。
stand⌒up.
连读:[stændʌp]。

(2) 缩读

为使英语发音更流利,有时会将两个相互影响的音缩读成一个音,即缩读。例如,

I am——I'm;
That is——that's;
Where is——where's;
I have ——I've;
I had——I'd;
I shall——I'll;
You will——you'll;
is not——isn't;
will not——won't;
must not——mustn't。

(3) 弱读

在英语中,名词、动词、形容词、副词(称为实词)一般会重读。冠词、物主代词、助动词、介词、连词等(虚词)一般需要弱读。

2. 发音小窍门

(1) of 的连读(音频 5.4-2)

of 后接辅音,f 不发音,念成[ə]。

- This chair is made of wood.
  ['mei-də]
- She's got a heart of stone.
  ['har-də]
- I'm out of breath.
  ['au-də]
- That's out of the question.
  ['au-də]

音频 5.4-2

(2) 清辅音变浊辅音(音频 5.4-3)

① 以[t]结尾的单词碰上以元音开头的单词,发音[t]变[d]。

音频 5.4-3

- Not at all.

  ['nɔ -də'dəl]

- What a nice surprise!

  ['wɔ-də]

- What about going to a movie?

  ['wɔ-də'bau gəuin]

② 两个元音中间的[t]要浊化成[d]，better['betə]变['bedə]。

- My mouth is watering.

  ['wɔːdəriŋ]

- Stay out of this matter, please.

  ['mædə]

- I think you'd better see a doctor.

  ['bedə]

(3) h 不发音（音频 5.4-4）

音频 5.4-4

当 he，him，his，her 与前面单词连读时，还有当 have，has 与单词连读或在句子中不重读时，h 不发音。

- I don't want to see her again.

  ['si-ə]

- Has he ever told you about that?

  ['æ-zi]

- Where have you been?

  ['we- ævjə'bin]

- Take him to the hospital.

  ['teikim]

- She has read the book.

  ['ʃiː-æz]

(4) 停顿

应当按照意群而非气群进行停顿，另外，在要发表重要信息时可以前面停顿一下，以引起听众注意。气群是指能不费力气地一口气说完的一组词，它可以是一个意群，也可以是几个意群。意群是在意义和结构上都紧密联系在一起的一组词，在意群中停顿会影响意思的表达。示例如下。

Thanks to/ space satellites/, the world itself/ is becoming/ a much smaller place/and people from different countries/ now understand/ each other better. （慢速，7 处停顿。）

Thanks to space satellites/, the world itself is becoming a much smaller place/and people from different countries/ now understand each other better. （快速，3 处停顿。）

更多例子如下（音频 5.4-5）。

- When brother stood on my shoulders he could easily reach the top of the wall.
  [wen' brʌðə stud ɔn mai 'ʃəuldəz hi kud 'iːzili riːtʃ ðə tɔp əv ðə wɔːl]

音频 5.4-5

- In the water around New York City is a very small island called Liberty Island.
  [inðə 'wɔːtə ə'raund njuː jɔk 'siti iz ə 'veri smɔːl 'ailənd kɔːld 'libəti 'ailənd]

- The little man came to me as I was about to enter the telephone box and asked me whether I had a match.
  [ðə'litl mæn keim tu mi æs ai wəs əbaut tu 'entə ðə 'telifəun bɔks ənd aːskt mi 'weðə ai hæd ə mætʃ]

（5）不发音的辅音（音频 5.4-6）

两个单词在一起时，如果前面的单词以辅音结尾，后面的单词以辅音开头，这时前面单词词尾的辅音不发音。示例如下。

音频 5.4-6

- [p] Help me.
  ['hel-mi]
- [b] I like Bob.
  ['lai bɔb]
- [t] Sit still.
  ['si-stil]
- [d] Would you mind my sitting here?
  ['main-mai]
- [k] I don't like them.
  ['lai- ðəm]
- [g] It's a big ball.
  ['bi-bɔːl]
- [f] We're out of bread.
  ['au-də-bred]
- [v] Give me a hand.
  ['gi-mi]

(6) y 的变音(音频 5.4-7)

对于以[t][d][s][z]结尾的单词接以字母 y 开头的词,连读时会发生变音。

[t]+y→[tʃ]　　　[d]+y→[dʒ]
[s]+y→[ʃ]　　　[z]+y→[ʒ]

音频 5.4-7

① [t]+y→[tʃ]

- Nice to meet you.
　　　　　['mi-tʃə]
- He's sorry he hit your car.
　　　　　　　['hitʃə]
- I got you the book you wanted.
　　　['gɔ-tʃə]

② [d]+y→[dʒ]

- Why did you quit your job?
　　　　[di-dʒə]
- Did you make this mess?
　[di-dʒə]
- He already paid you the money, didn't he?
　　　　　　['pei-dʒə]

③ [s]+y→[ʃ]

- I miss you.
　　['mi-ʃə]
- This test ranks your abilities.
　　　　　　['rænk-ʃə]
- He speaks your language.
　　　['spi:k-ʃə]

④ [z]+y→[ʒ]

- He was your friend.
　　　['wɔ-ʒə]
- Are these your CDs?
　　　['ði-ʒə]
- She made those rolls you like.
　　　　　　['rəul-ʒə]

(7) 重音变轻音(音频 5.4-8)

在美式发音中,句子中次要单词的元音需要弱读,示例如下。

① [əu]——[ə]
Mary looks so different now.
　　　　['ˈluk-sə]

② [au]——[ə]
That's our car.
[ˈðæ-tsəˈkɑːr]

③ [æ]——[ə]
I heard that you just quit.
[aiˈhəːdðət]

④ [ɔːr]——[ə]
Cash or charge?
[ˈkæ-ʃəˈtʃɑːrdʒ]

⑤ [uː]——[ə]
What do you want me to do?
　　　　[dəjə]　　　　[təˈdu]

⑥ [aːr]——[ə]
You are great!
[juəˈgreit]

音频 5.4-8

5.5　英语正式语体与非正式语体

1. 英语正式语体与非正式语体的区别

　　语体是指"由于使用语言的场合、场景不同而引起的语言形式和结构上的变异"[54]。笼统来说,语体分为口语语体和书面语语体、正式语体和非正式语体。口语语体和书面语语体不完全等同于非正式语体和正式语体。在口译中,虽然讲话人是用口语的语言媒介(medium)方式表达,但是其语言体式(mode)不一定就是非正式语体。因为有的话说出来是为了"写下来"的,如外交部的新闻发布会发言、联合国的一些正式会议发言等,相反,有的话虽然是写出来的,但是是为了"说出来"的,如大学教授的课堂讲稿等[58]126。

　　正式语体和非正式语语体并不是孤立的两极,而是一个连续体的两端,从非正式语体到正式语体是一个渐变的连续过程。很多词是否正式,在于其与其他词的比较。例如,表达聪明的用词有 astute, perceptive, intelligent, smart, on the ball 等,图 5.2 是这几个词从正式到非正式的排列,其中最正式的是 astute,最不正式的是 on the ball,位于中间的 intelligent 比 on the ball 正式,但是比 perceptive 的正式程度要低[58]163。

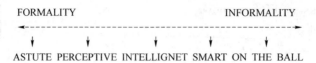

图 5.2　从正式到非正式的排列

英语语体按照正式程度从高到低分为五种变体[59]：庄严(frozen)、正式(formal)、商议(consultative)、随意(casual)和亲密(intimate)。

(1) 庄严语体

庄严语体常用于陌生听众，是为声明和出版而设的一种语体，听众不能盘问作者。

(2) 正式语体

正式语体常用于一对多人的讲话。一般听众较多，听众无法直接对讲话人做出及时反应。它主要用来提供信息。讲话人需要斟酌用词，不依赖语境，且需要保持语义的连贯性。

(3) 商洽语体

商洽语体是陌生人、不熟悉的人或者不同级别的同事之间商洽时所用的语体。说话人需要提供背景知识，听话人需要不断参与，如插话说 yes, I see 等。

(4) 随意语体

随意语体用于朋友、熟人和内行人之间的语体，常用省略和俚语。

(5) 亲密语体

亲密语体用于关系非常亲密的人之间，如夫妻之间。语言片段化，常使用彼此才懂的词。

五种语体的实例举例如下[60]。

庄严语体：Distinguished guests should make their way at once to the outside of the yard by way of corridor.

(贵宾请立即顺着走廊到花园外面去。)

正式语体：Distinguished guests should go out of the yard at once.

(贵宾请立即到花园外面。)

商洽语体：Would you mind going out of the yard right now, please?

(请你马上到花园外面好吗？)

随意语体：Time you all went out, now.

(现在你们都该下楼了)

亲密语体：Out you go, guys!

(伙计们，下去！)

在口译初学者常见的联络口译中，一般是陪同口译的场合，涉及活动安排、见面时的寒暄、用餐时的谈话、会展的解说等,比较符合商洽语体和随意语体的风格,用语可以不太正式。但是,在稍微正式的场合,如会议口译和新闻发布会的口译等,就需要用到正式语体。表 5.5 简要介绍了英语正式语体和非正式语体的区别[58]167-172。

表 5.5　正式语体和非正式语体的区别

	具体方面	非正式语体	正式语体
用词	词汇	非正式用语,如 leave, blow up, quit。再如俚语,如 mighty, lousy, talk somebody's head off	正式用语,如 depart, explode, resign 等
	缩略与否	缩略词,如 TV, it's	非缩略或非缩约形式,如 television, it is
	词源	源于古英语的英语词多用于非正式语体,如 end, look into	源于法语、拉丁语、希腊语的英语词多用于正式语体,如 conclude, investigate
	短语动词和单个动词	短语动词,如 turn in, put up with, make good use of	单个动词,如 surrender, tolerate, utilize
语法	比较句的人称代词	人称代词的宾格形式,如 Bill speaks French more fluently than me.	人称代词的主格形式,如 Bill speaks French more fluently than I.
	表达让步的连接词	but, anyway, all the same, though 等,如 He tried to prevent the marriage but it took place all the same.	Yet, however, nevertheless, in spite of, notwithstanding 等,如 He endeavored to prevent the marriage; however, they got married notwithstanding.
	方式状语	常使用副词,如 He spoke confidently.	由介词和该副词词根同根的词构成的介词短语,如 He spoke in a confident manner. He spoke with confidence.
	表达因果	常用 so, because, … 如 Since the weather had improved, we decided to go swimming. As he was a man of fixed views, he refused to listen to our arguments.	On account of, accordingly, thus, hence, consequently, owing to, … 常用分词短语、独立主格结构等,如 The weather having improved, we decided to go swimming. Being a man of fixed views, he refused to listen to our arguments.
	目的状语	so as to	in order to, in order that, …
	问句	可用省略形式,也可用陈述句形式(借助语调和标点符号),以疑问代词宾格开头,介词置于句末,如 When? Who are you talking about? What did you write it with?	完整句子,以疑问代词主格开头,介词置于句首,如 When are you going to do it? Whom are you talking about? With what did you write it?

续 表

	具体方面	非正式语体	正式语体
语法	虚拟语气	条件句中的谓语用 was，如 If he was my friend, I would ask him for help. If I had known, I would have told you earlier.	条件句中的谓语可以用 were，如 If he were my friend, I would ask him for help. Had I known before, I would have told you earlier.
	形式主语	不用形式主语 it，如 The number of books in the library has been going down.	常用 it 等，如 It has been noted with concern that the stock of books in the library has been declining alarmingly.
	祈使句	常用主动语态，如 Please gather at the gate of the school.	可用被动语态，如 The students are requested to gather at the gate of the school.
	不定代词、动名词的复合结构、主谓一致	不是很规范，如 Everybody should look after themselves. I'm surprised at John (him) making such a silly mistake.	规范，如 Everybody should look after himself. I'm surprised at John's (his) making such a silly mistake.

基于表5.5的比较，口译员可以通过语言特征，辨别源语的语体正式程度，翻译时也采取对应的语体。也可借助场合和目的来帮助判别语体。例如，正式谈判、新闻发布会和开幕式等都是严肃、庄重的活动，往往采用正式的语体，翻译时也应采用比较正式的语体。再例如，宴请场合除开头或结尾部分的祝酒外，多为随意的攀谈，语体的正式程度会降低，翻译时可多用非正式的语体，使轻松的谈话成为美食的佐餐。总之，翻译要根据情境采用相应的语体，才能更全面地表达讲话人的原意。

练习

1. 将下列画线的短语改为更正式、更精简的说法[61]。

(1) Consumer interest in electronic billing and payment is getting bigger and bigger.

(2) The competition faced by U.S. growers from imports of fresh vegetables has gotten more intense.

(3) Many urban areas do not have enough land to build new public schools.

(4) Allergic reactions to local dental anesthesia do not happen very often.

(5) The doors on these ferries were made bigger to make it easier to load and unload vehicles.

2. 正式和非正式表达的词汇

在口译中，对于同样的意思可以有更正式的表达，表5.6给出了一些正式和非正式词汇的对比[62]，其中，v 代表动词，n 代表名词，adj 代表形容词。

表 5.6　非正式和正式词汇的对比

非正式或中立	正式	非正式或中立	正式
agreement	accord	obtain, get	secure (v)
almost, more or less	virtually	obtain, get	acquire
although	albeit	only	sole(ly)
argue against, disagree with	contest (v)	even higher than	in excess of
ask	pose	pecking order	hierarchy
ask	call on	permit	sanction (v)
ask for	appeal for	point out	observe
be based on	rest on	point up	highlight
be made up of	consist of	postgrad	postgraduate
be more; greater than	exceed	promise (v)	pledge
behaviour	conduct (n)	promise (n)	undertaking (n)
carry out, do	conduct	pros and cons	advantages and disadvantages
clothes	attire	put forward	present
come back, go back, get back	return	quit	resign
deal with	treat	read, look at	consult (v)
decrease, grow smaller	diminish	recap	recapitulate
direct, order	instruct	record, write about	document (v)
dorm	dormitory	refer to	make reference to
exam	examination	rep	representative
friendly	cordial	result in	incur
get in	be accepted / be offered a place	right	correct
get rid of	dispose of	set out	describe
give	deliver	set out (to do X)	aim
give attention to	address (v)	show	demonstrate
go into	discuss	skip	omit, not attend something
go through	check	slightly, a little, a bit	somewhat
having said that	nevertheless	solve, end	resolve
house, flat, apartment	dwelling	speak/talk about	address, speak to
husband, wife	spouse	support, encourage	advocate (v)

非正式或中立	正式	非正式或中立	正式
in more detail	in greater detail	swap	exchange
in short, to sum up, summing up	in sum, in summary	take/have a look at	examine
initiate, start something	instigate	talk of, talk about	speak of
job, profession	occupation	talks	negotiations
judge	adjudicate	There's no way X…	X is not possible/not correct
keep	maintain	time	occasion
lab	laboratory	try, have a shot at	attempt
large, big	substantial	typical	characteristic (adj)
last (v)	endure	undergrad	undergraduate
last (adj)	final	unsuitable	inappropriate
lately	recently	use something effectively	utilise
list	catalogue (v)	with regard to, as far as X is concerned	in respect of, with respect to
look back over, go over	revise	write	compose
look into	investigate	write about	write of
mainly	primarily	wrong	Improper, incorrect
make up	constitute	Yours sincerely, best wishes, best	Yours faithfully

第6章 口译基本技能(五)数字口译

6.1 数字口译概述

在口译中,含有数字的信息是容易出错的地方。因为数字信息量大、相对独立且往往不能从上下文中得到任何线索和辅助,因此难以预测,并且容易忘记。除此之外,英汉数字还有"数级差异",英语是三位数字一组,而汉语是四位一组,所以在翻译时需要额外的转换,这造成更多的认知负担。因此,数字口译是口译中的一个难点和重点,需要着重进行训练。

数字口译最有效的方法是记笔记。数字口译的常用方法总结如下。

(1)表格或标尺法。提前做好表格和标尺,在口译中填入即可。此法在口译实践中并不都有条件能做到,但是非常适合初学者进行数位转换的巩固练习。表格或标尺法如表6.1所示。

表6.1 表格或标尺法

兆	千亿	百亿	十亿	亿	千万	百万	十万	万	千	百	十	个
T			B			M			T			

(2)数位转换法。牢记各个中英数字单位的对应,记笔记时采用数字+数字单位的方法,如"34 k"代表三万四千,然后迅速译出。此法的好处是笔记迅速,缺点是翻译时仍需要进行两种语言数位的转换。常用的数字单位除了千(thousand)和百万(million)外,其他容易出错的数字单位如表6.2所示。

表6.2 容易出错的数字单位

万	十万	千万	亿	十亿	百亿	千亿	万亿
ten thousand	hundred thousand	ten million	hundred million	billion	ten billion	hundred billion	trillion

(3) 点三杠四法。点三杠四法是指英文每三位数字点一个逗号,中文每四位数字划一条竖线的方法,如"322,2|23,45|6,789"(三千二百二十二万两千三百四十五万六千七百八十九)。这是普遍使用的一种方法。

(4) 小数加数位法。对于符合条件的数字,进行数位转换,然后记笔记为小数＋数位的形式。例如,把八百三十二万三千记为"8.323m",读为 eight point three two three million。这种办法的优点在于已经对数字进行数位转换,翻译时可以减少认知负荷。这种方法适合对两种语言的转换驾轻就熟的口译者。

(5) 保留大数法。在听众明确表示对精确数值兴趣不大,只要求大概数目的时候,可以只翻译出数字的大概值。例如,19 999 999 可以翻译为 around 20 million。

在各种数字口译的方法中,点三杠四法、小数加数位法是使用较多的方法。无论使用哪种方法,都要特别注意含有 0 的数字,谨防丢失数位。另外,应当熟悉各种度量、质量、长度等单位。如果可能,应了解各种单位的换算,在翻译时可以进行归化的处理,更能适合听众需要。例如,资深口译员在为中方翻译的时候,可自动把对方的美元数字换算为人民币的大致金额译出,这是数字口译可以达到的更高水平。

6.2 数字增减及倍数的译法

数字的增减和倍数是信息科技口译的常见内容。以下是数字增减和倍数的英文表达方法[63]。

1. 数字增减的表示法译法

(1) 句式特征:by＋名词＋比较级＋than。

The wire is by three inches longer than that one.

这根导线比那根长 3 英寸。

(2) 句式特征:表示增减意义的动词＋to＋n。该句式可译为增加到…或减少到…。

Metal cutting machines have been decreased to 50.

金属切割机已经减少到 50 台。

2. 百分数增减的表示法与译法

(1) 句式特征:表示增减意义的动词＋％。

The output value has increased 35％.

产值增加了 35％。

(2) 句式特征:表示增减意义的动词＋by＋％。

Retail sales should rise by 8％.

商品零售额应增加 3%。
The prime cost decreased by 60%.
主要成本减少 60%。
(3) 句式特征：表示减少意义的动词＋to＋%。该句式表示减少后剩余的数量。
By using this new-process the loss of metal was reduced to 20%.
采用这种新工艺，铁的损失量减少到 20%。
(4) 句式特征：%＋比较级＋than。该句式表示净增减的数量。
Retail sales are expected to be nine percent higher than last year.
今年零售额与去年相比，有望增加 9%。
(5) 句式特征：%＋比较级＋名词。该句式表示净减数。
The new-type machine wasted 10 percent energy supplied.
新型机械能耗量净减 10%。
(6) 句式特征：a＋%＋increase。该句式表示净增数。
There is a 20% increase of steel in comparison with last year.
与去年相比，今年钢产量净增 20%。
(7) 句式特征：%＋（of）名词（代词）。该句式表示净减数，数字照译。
The production cost is about 60 percent that of last year.
今年产值仅为去年的 60%。
(8) 句式特征：%＋up on 或 over。该句式表示净增数。
The grain output of last year in this province was 20% percent up on that of 1978.
去年粮食产量比 1978 年净增 20%。

3. 倍数增加的表示法及译法

汉语表示"增加了几倍"时，英语的倍数需减一，译成"增加了 $n-1$ 倍"，以表示净增加数。如果译成"增加到 n 倍"或"为原来的 n 倍"，则照译不误。

(1) increase＋n times 译成"增加到 n 倍"或"增加 $n-1$ 倍"。
(2) increase＋by＋n times 译成"增加到 n 倍"或"增加 $n-1$ 倍"。
(3) increase＋to＋n times 表示增加到 n 倍，译成"增加了 $n-1$ 倍"。
(4) increase＋by a factor of＋n times，译成"增加到 n 倍"。
(5) a＋n times(或 n-fold)＋increase…表示增加到 n 倍，译成"增加了 $n-1$ 倍"。
(6) double，treble，quadruple 分别表示增加到 2 倍，3 倍，4 倍。

4. 倍数减少的表达法及译法

(1) A 的大小（重量，速度，…）是 B 的 $1/n$ 或 A 比 B 小（轻，慢，…）$(n-1)/n$。
① A is n times as small (light/slow/…) as B.

② A is n times smaller (lighter/ slower/ ...) than B.

The hydrogen atom is nearly 16 times as light as the oxygen atom.

例如,氢原子的重量约为氧原子的 1/16(即比氧原子约轻 15/16)。

This sort of membrane is twice thinner than ordinary paper.

这种薄膜比普通纸张要薄一半(即是普通纸厚度的 1/2)。

注:当相比的对象 B 很明显时,than/as B 常被省去。

(2) 减少到 $1/n$ 或减少 $(n-1)/n$。

① decrease n times/n-fold

② decrease by n times

③ decrease by a factor of n

注:decrease 常被 reduce, shorten, go down, slow down 等词替代。

Switching time of the new-type transistor is shortened 3 times.

例如,新型晶体管的开关时间缩短了 1/3(即缩短到 2/3)。

When the voltage is stepped up by ten times, the strength of the current is stepped down by ten times.

电压升高 9 倍,电流强度便降低 9/10(即 90%)。

The equipment reduced the error probability by a factor of 5.

该设备误差概率降低了 4/5。

(3) 减至 $1/n$ 或减少 $(n-1)/n$。

There is a n-fold decrease/reduction…

其他形式:

A rapid decrease by a factor of 7 was observed.

发现迅速减少到 1/7。

The principal advantage of the products is a two-fold reduction in weight.

这些产品的主要优点是重量减轻了 1/2。

从上述倍数增减句型及其译法中不难看出:与汉语不同的是,英语在表述或比较倍数时,无论使用什么句型(除了不含倍数词的 again 句型外),都包括基础倍数在内,因此都不是净增或净减 n 倍,而是净增或净减 $n-1$ 倍,所以 decrease by 3 times 应译为"减少 2/3",而不是"减少 3/4"。

练习

1. 听汉语数字并做笔记,然后核对答案(音频 6.2-1)。

2. 听英语数字并做笔记,然后核对答案(音频 6.2-2)。

音频 6.2-1

音频 6.2-2

第 2 篇　口译情景模拟

第7章 接待外宾

7.1 译前准备

背景介绍:美国来宾到北京,中方接待并闲聊。

词汇准备如表 7.1 所示。

表 7.1 词汇准备

序号	词汇	翻 译
1	pen pal	笔友
2	有缘千里来相会	Though born a thousand li apart, souls which are one shall meet.
3	孝顺	filial, filial piety
4	broad and profound	博大精深
5	羔羊跪哺,乌鸦反哺	The lamb kneels down to suckle, the crown feeds its parents.

7.2 对话全文

听下列对话,进行中英、英中交替口译(音频 7.2-1)。(中方为 C;外方为 F。)

C:请问您是来自美国的普里斯先生吗?

F:Yep. That's me. Please do call me Larry.

C:好的,很荣幸见到您,Larry! 我是杨思嘉,英文名是 Scarlet。

音频 7.2-1

F:Nice to meet you, Scarlet.

C:我们的车就在外边,这边不让停车,咱们边走边谈好吗?

F:Sure. Let's go.

C:您是第一次来中国吗?

F: Actually not. My wife June is a Chinese. We had been pen pals before we first met face to face in Beijing in 2000. We married three months later.

C: 听起来很浪漫呢！真是"有缘千里来相会"呢。

F: Well said! I like Chinese sayings. They are full of wisdom and puns. Chinese culture is so broad and profound.

C: 看来您真是喜欢中国。

F: Indeed. Actually, I plan to settle down here when this business is done. June also needs to take care of her grandparents, they are in their 90s.

C: 爷爷奶奶？

F: Yes. June was raised by her grandparents. Now that they are old, June will come back to look after them.

C: 真孝顺！就像俗语说的,羔羊跪哺,乌鸦反哺。

F: What do you mean?

C: 是表示对父母的感恩：羔羊跪下表达感激和敬意,乌鸦长大后喂养年迈的父母。

F: How touching! Filial piety is truly a merit of the Chinese people. Thanks for the teaching. In return, I'd like to teach you a few Chinese characters.

C: 您教我汉字?! 我没听错吧？有意思,我洗耳恭听。

F: Yep. Now let's begin by the character "wo".

练习

1. 自编机场接外宾场景的三角对话（中方、外宾、译员）,可参考7.3节的词汇。
2. 自编协助外宾入住宾馆场景的三角对话（中方、外宾、译员）,可参考7.3节的词汇。

7.3 词汇拓展

1. 称谓的翻译

称谓中的"总""副""助理""代理""常务""执行""名誉"怎么翻译？

首席长官称谓常以"总"表示,与之相对应的英语词有 chief, general, head, managing 等,例如,总工程师为 chief engineer,总代理为 general agent,总教练为 head coach。

汉语中表示副职的头衔常以"副"字表示,英语词 vice, associate, assistant, deputy 等有相同作用。例如,副总统/大学副校长为 vice president,副教授为 associate professor,副总经理为 assistant/deputy general manager,副市长为

deputy mayor。

对于"助理"级,英语中常用 assistant 一词,例如,助理工程师为 assistant engineer,助理编辑为 assistant editor。对于"代理"一词,英语可以用 acting,例如：代理市长为 acting mayor,代理主任为 acting director。"常务"可用 managing,例如,常务理事为 managing director,常务副校长为 managing vice president。"执行"可用 executive,例如,执行主席为 executive chairman。"名誉"可用 honorary,例如,名誉主席为 honorary chairman。

2. 机场接机常见语句[64]

(1) 托运的行李 checked baggage

(2) 行李领取处 baggage claim area

(3) 随身行李 carry-on baggage

(4) 行李牌 baggage tag

(5) 行李推车 luggage cart

(6) 一路辛苦了。Did you have a good (pleasant) flight? / Is your journey enjoyable?

(7) 长途跋涉,加上时差,您一定累了。After a long flight, you must be jetlagged.

(8) 让我帮您拿行李吧。/让我来推行李车吧。Let me help you with your luggage/bags. Let me push the luggage cart for you.

(9) 您一共带了 4 件行李,是不是? So you have got altogether four pieces of baggage?

(10) 您先请。After you, please.

(11) 日程安排 schedule

(12) 预订 reserve

(13) 根据…的要求　upon…request

(14) 专程造访 come all the way

(15) 精心安排 a thoughtful arrangement

(16) 排忧解难 help out

(17) 为您设宴洗尘 host a reception banquet in your honor

(18) 有朋自远方来,不亦乐乎。How happy we are to meet friends from afar.

(19) 这是我们第一次见面。我们一直盼望着您来。This is the first time we have met. We have been expecting your arrival.

(20) 久闻大名/久仰久仰。I have heard your name before by reputation. / I have heard a lot about you.

(21) 我们的经理向您表示问候,他因不能前来迎接您而感到抱歉。Our manager sends his greetings to you. He regrets that he is not able to come to meet you personally.

(22) 我代表经理及同事们衷心欢迎您. I'd like to extend to you a warm welcome on behalf of my manager and colleagues.

(23) I'm very touched that you have come all the way to meet me in person. 您亲自来接我,我深为感动。

(24) 您一定是我们久盼的客人。You must be our long-expected guest.

(25) Excuse me, I haven't had the honor of knowing you. 不好意思,我还没能有幸认识你。

3. 宾馆入住常见语句[64]

(1) 接待处就在前面。The Reception Desk is straight ahead.

(2) 旅馆里有空余的房间吗? Have you any vacant (spare) room in the hotel?

(3) 我能为我的朋友预定一间单人房吗? Can I book a single room for my friend beforehand?

(4) double room 双人间

(5) I'd like a quiet room away from the street if it is possible. 如果可能我想要一个不临街的安静房间。

(6) (with) a front/rear view 朝阳面/背阴面

(7) 每天收费多少? How much a day do you charge?

(8) 每天1 000元,包括服务在内。1000 yuan a day, service included.

(9) What services come with that? 这个价格包括那些服务项目呢?

(10) Forty dollars, tax extra. 四十美元,外加税。

(11) It's quite reasonable. 收费十分合理。

(12) Would you mind filling in this form and pay 100 yuan in advance? 请填好这张表并预付一百元钱。

(13) May I have your check out time, please? 请问您什么时候结账退宿?

(14) We'll be leaving Sunday morning. 我们将在星期天上午离开。

(15) I'm glad that we'll be able to accept your extension request. 很高兴宾馆可以让您延长住宿。

(16) 我想设定早晨的呼叫铃。I'd like a wake-up call, please.

(17) 冷气(电视、灯)无法开启。The air-conditioner (T. V. set / light) doesn't work.

(18) I have some laundry. 我有些衣服需要送洗。

(19) I'd like these clothes cleaned (pressed). 这些衣服需要洗涤(熨平)。

(20) 请将您需要洗的衣服放在纸袋中,并将衣物内容写下来。Please put your laundry in the paper bag and write down the contents of the laundry on it.

(21) Will it be ready by tomorrow (the day after tomorrow)? 明天(后天)是否可以洗好?

(22) I'd like to check out. My bill, please. 我要退房。请给我账单。

(23) I had a coke in the mini-bar. 我拿了一瓶小吧台的可乐。

(24) How would you like to settle your bill? 您想用什么方式付账?

(25) Debit or credit? 借记卡还是信用卡?

(26) traveler's checks 旅行支票

(27) 支付宝 Alipay

(28) 微信支付 WeChat pay

第8章 宴请饮食

8.1 译前准备

背景介绍：机场接机后，王女士请从美国来的杰克逊先生吃中餐。

词汇准备如表 8.1 所示。

表 8.1 宴请饮食的词汇准备

序号	词汇	翻译
1	fried mutton slices	炸羊肉片
2	baked fish with butter	奶油烤鱼
3	roast lamb chops	烤羊排
4	steamed lamb	清蒸羊肉
5	squirrel-shaped mandarin fish	松鼠鳜鱼
6	boiled fish	水煮鱼

8.2 对话全文

听下列对话，进行中英、英中交替口译（音频 8.2-1）。（中方为 C；外方为 F。）

C：杰克逊先生，我们到了。今晚我们吃中国菜。

F：Wow, what a magnificent restaurant! It is decorated in red and gold, typical Chinese colors. I think the Chinese food here must be very delicious.

音频 8.2-1

C：这的确是一家有名的餐厅。杰克逊先生，这是菜单。今天您是客人，请随便点。

F：Thanks. But I don't know anything about Chinese food. What would you recommend?

C：请问您喜欢吃辣吗？

F：I'm afraid I can't. I love fried mutton slices and baked fish with butter in my country, does China have something similar?

C：中国也有很多关于羊肉的菜，如烤羊排和清蒸羊肉。鱼的话在中国不同的菜系中做法会各不相同，最常见的是松鼠鳜鱼和水煮鱼。

F：The Squirrel-shaped mandarin fish sounds yummy, what do you think?

C：很好的选择！中国菜十分注重"色""香""味"三方面。我想这道菜应该和您以前吃的鱼味道不一样。

F：That'll be great. Well, I can't find coffee on the menu, you guys don't drink coffee?

C：我们一般不在吃饭的时候喝咖啡。来点啤酒怎么样，北京当地产的燕京啤酒在全国都非常有名。

F：OK. Could you tell me about the custom of drinking in China?

C：我们会以"干杯"的方式向对方敬酒，需要一口喝干杯中的酒，表示敬酒人的心诚和相聚的欢乐。

F：Sounds very interesting. But for me, it might be a challenge, since I get drunk quickly. And are there any taboos about using chopsticks？

C：筷子作为用餐工具，是不能用来指向别人的，这在中国是不礼貌的行为。还有就是不能把筷子竖直插在米饭碗里，因为这象征着祭祀。实际上，在中国请人吃饭更多是一种社交，在饭桌上人们可以增进了解，成为朋友。

F：I am sure we will become good friends.

C：我同意。杰克逊先生，来，为我们的友谊和合作干杯。

F：Gan Bei！

练习

自编宴请饮食场景的三角对话（中方、外宾、译员），可参考8.3节的词汇。

8.3 词汇拓展

1. 菜谱的几种译法

中国饮食文化博大精深，不仅菜肴讲究色香味俱全，而且菜谱名称也非常讲究，常常是四字词语，音形俱佳，富有文化内涵和寓意，这对翻译提出了挑战。翻译菜谱时,首先要让听众知道菜的原料和辅料是什么,可以加上佐料名称和烹饪技术,这样菜谱的翻译公式大概为"原料＋with/in＋佐料"。如果时间允许,最好再解释一下菜肴背后的文化背景。常见的菜谱翻译的方法有音译、直译、意译、转译等。表8.2为菜谱翻译的例子。

表8.2 菜谱翻译的例子

序号	方法	中文	英文
1	原料＋with/in＋佐料	黄焖大虾 鱼香肉丝 宫保鸡丁	braised prawns in rice wine shredded pork in hot sauce diced chicken with peanuts
2	直译	过桥米线	"cross bridge" rice noodles
3	意译	发财好市(发菜、蚝豉)	black moss cooked with oysters
4	转译	凤凰玉米羹(凰;蛋黄)	corn and egg soup
5	结合烹饪方法和刀法	铁扒牛肉 叫花鸡	grilled beefsteak mud-baked chicken
6	拼音＋注释	狗不理包子	"Goubuli" steamed bun

2. 餐馆用餐常用词句[65]

常用词语如下。

(1) 主食

黑面包 brown bread

奶油土司 buttered toast

春卷 spring roll

年糕 rice cake

绿豆糕 green bean cake

通心粉 macaroni

阳春面 plain noodle

打卤面 noodles with gravy

米粉 rice noodles

肠粉 steamed vermicelli roll

元宵 rice glue ball

汤圆 glue pudding

粥 gruel/porridge

(2) 饮品

烈酒 spirits/ strong liquor

酒不加冰块 straight up

酒加冰块 on the rocks
琴酒 gin
白干 white liquor
白兰地 brandy
伏特加 vodka
兰酒 rum
黑啤 dark beer/stout beer
生啤酒 draft beer
威士忌 whiskey
香槟 champagne
佐餐酒 table wine
黄酒/花雕酒 yellow rice wine
冰咖啡 iced coffee
牛奶咖啡 white coffee
清咖啡 black coffee
全脂/脱脂奶 whole/skim milk
豆浆 soybean milk
酸梅汤 plum syrup

（3）烹饪
烹调术 cookery
爆 quick-fry
焙 roast
煸 stir-fry
熏 smoke
腌 salt
炸 deep-fry
煎 pan-fry
清炒 plain-fry
清蒸 steam
刀功 slicing technique

（4）食材
木耳 fungus
荸荠 water chestnut
山药 yam
芋头 taro

冬菇 dried mushroom
冬瓜 white gourd
苦瓜 bitter gourd
黑枣 black date
红枣 red jujube
毛豆 green soy bean
四季豆 kidney bean
黄豆芽 soybean sprout
绿豆芽 mung bean sprout
金针菇 needle mushroom
韭菜 chives
莲藕 lotus root
蒜头 garlic bulb
香菜 coriander
田螺 escargots
鱼翅 shark fin
鲍鱼 abalone
海参 sea cucumber
海带 kelp/seaweed
海蜇皮 salted jelly fish
干贝 scallops

(5) 零食

点心 dim sum
甜点 pastries
棉花糖 marshmallow
牛肉干 beef jerky
牛轧糖 nougat
葡萄干 raisin

(6) 佐料

佐料 seasoning
鸡精 essence of chicken
芥末 mustard
咖喱 curry
肉桂 cinnamon
味噌 miso

味精 gourmet powder

鱼子酱 caviar

沙茶酱 barbecue sauce

(7) 菜肴

炖牛肉 braised beef

丁骨牛排 T-bone steak

沙朗牛排 sirloin steak

菲力牛排 filet steak

腐乳 preserved bean curd

韩国泡菜 kimchi

酱瓜 pickled cucumbers

腊肉 preserved meat

萝卜干 dried turnip

皮蛋 preserved egg

臭豆腐 bean curd with odor

土豆泥 mashed potatoes

牛尾汤 ox tail soup

肉松 fried pork flakes

什锦色拉 mixed fruit salad with ham

烤乳猪 roast suckling pig

芝麻球 glutinous rice sesame balls

炒蛋 scrambled eggs

荷包蛋 poached egg

煎半熟蛋 over easy

煎两面荷包蛋 over

煎全熟蛋 over hard

煎一面荷包蛋 sunny side up

常用句子如下。

(1) 在这吃还是外带？Sit in or take away?

(2) 莲子表示的是喜生贵子。Lotus seed means having luck in having a baby boy.

(3) 肉和蔬菜一般会切成小块。Meats and vegetables are generally cut into bite-size pieces.

(4) 中国炒菜热量低、营养丰富。Chinese stir-fry is low in calorie and rich in

nutrients.

（5）竹笋意寓节节顺。Bamboo shoots means that you wish everything would be good.

（6）海带意寓财富或是发财。Black moss seaweed stands for lots of wealth.

（7）我需要预约吗？Do I need a reservation?

（8）我想要预约今晚 7 点 2 个人的位子。I'd like to reserve a table for two at seven tonight.

（9）我们大概需要等多久？How long is the wait?

（10）我们想要面对花园的位子。We'd like a table with a view of garden.

（11）晚餐前需要来点喝的吗？Would you like something to drink before dinner?

（12）餐厅有些什么餐前酒？What kind of drinks do you have for an aperitif?

（13）可否让我看看酒单？May I see the wine list?

（14）我可以点杯酒吗？May I order a glass of wine?

（15）我可以点餐了吗？May I order, please?

（16）餐厅的特色菜是什么？What is the specialty of the house?

（17）我可以点与那份相同的餐吗？Can I have the same dish as that?

（18）我想要一份开胃菜与排餐（鱼餐）。I'd like appetizers and meat（fish）dish.

（19）我必须避免含油脂（盐分/糖分）的食物。I have to avoid food containing fat（salt/ sugar）.

（20）餐厅是否有供应素食餐？Do you have vegetarian dishes?

（21）你的牛排要如何烹调？How do you like your steak?

（22）全熟（五分熟/全生）。Well done（medium/rare），please.

第 9 章 礼仪致辞

9.1 译前准备

第一段

背景介绍:万国邮政联盟大会开幕式中国领导致辞。

词汇准备如表 9.1 所示。

表 9.1 第一段词汇准备

序号	词汇	翻译
1	万国邮政联盟	Universal Postal Congress（UPC）
2	隆重开幕	grand opening
3	初秋时节的北京,万木葱茏,金风送爽	Golden autumn is embracing Beijing, bringing refreshing and pleasant breeze to the capital city
4	战略和行动纲领	strategies and programs of action
5	在国际邮政史上留下光荣的一页	be remembered as a splendid chapter in the annals of the international postal services
6	祝大会圆满成功	I wish the conference a complete success
7	宣布…开幕	I declare… open

第二段

背景介绍:国际电联秘书长赵厚麟在 2019 年世界电信和信息社会日的英文致辞,题为"缩小标准化差距"。

词汇准备如表 9.2 所示。

表 9.2 第二段词汇准备

序号	词汇	翻译
1	interoperability	互操作性
2	World Telecommunication and Information Society Day	世界电信和信息社会日
3	ITU (International Telecommunications Union)	国际电联

续表

序号	词汇	翻译
4	standardization	标准化
5	ICT	信息通信技术
6	SME（small and medium enterprises）	中小企业

9.2 发言全文

听下列演讲，进行英中口译。

第一段

下面是万国邮政联盟大会开幕词[66]20-21（音频9.2-1）。

各位嘉宾，女士们、先生们：

初秋时节的北京，万木葱茏，金风送爽。今天，第22届万国邮政联盟大会将在这里隆重开幕。这是万国邮政联盟成立125年和中国加入万国邮政联盟85年来，首次在中国举行这样的大会。我代表中国政府和中国人民，并以我个人的名义，向大会致以衷心的祝贺！向与会的各国代表和来宾表示诚挚的欢迎！

人类即将迈入新的世纪。在这样的时刻，大家共同探讨面向二十一世纪邮政发展的战略和行动纲领，其意义十分重要。我相信，这次大会将在国际邮政史上留下光荣的一页。……

最后，预祝大会取得圆满成功。祝各位在北京度过愉快的时光。

现在，我宣布：第二十二届万国邮政联盟大会开幕！谢谢！

音频 9.2-1

第二段

Bridging the Standardization Gap（视频9.2-2[67]）

ITU Secretary-General Houlin Zhao's Message
on World Telecommunication and Information Society Day

On 17 May, we will be celebrating the 50th World Telecommunication and Information Society Day.

This year, we will focus on "bridging the standardization gap".

Setting standards is a fundamental pillar of ITU's mission as the specialized agency of the United Nations for information and communication technologies.

You want to connect to the internet, enjoy a sports event on TV, listen to radio in your car or watch a video on your smartphone? ITU standards make it possible.

视频 9.2-2

The upcoming 5G standards, especially if coupled with artificial intelligence, will support a new range of applications which we will soon take for granted: from self-driving cars to safer and smart cities.

ITU standards ensure interoperability, open up global markets and spur innovation and growth. They are good for developed and developing countries.

They help accelerate ICTs for all Sustainable Development Goals.

I call upon ITU Member States, industry members, small and big companies and academia, together with UN sister agencies, our partners and all stakeholders, to support ITU's "Bridging the Standardization gap" programme and prosperity and well-being for all.

Thank you.

练习

1. 听题为"Secretary-General Message on World Telecommunication and Information Society Day"讲话[68],做笔记训练(音频 9.3-1)。

2. 自编会议致辞或祝酒词,可参考 9.3 节的词汇。

音频 9.3-1

9.3 词汇拓展

礼仪致辞常见语句如下。

(1) 海内存知己,天涯若比邻。Long distance separates no bosom friends.

(2) 不辞辛苦远道而来。Come in spite of long and tiring journey.

(3) 发表热情友好的讲话。Make a warm and friendly speech.

(4) 我们为能在我校接待如此优秀的青年团体而深感骄傲和自豪。We are very proud and honored to receive such a distinguished group of young people at our university.

(5) 请允许我向远道而来的贵宾表示热烈的欢迎和亲切的问候。Please allow me to express my warmest welcome and gracious greetings to our distinguished guests coming from afar.

(6) 我预祝大会圆满成功! I wish the conference a complete success!

(7) 今天我们很高兴在这里欢聚一堂,在金秋十月美丽的北京有幸举办这次会议,我谨代表…向…表示最热烈的祝贺。同时,我也想对…选择北京科技中心来主办这个会议表示衷心的感谢。我还想对许多尊贵的来宾和朋友不远千里参加此次会议表示感谢。

It is a good pleasure to join you all today. The beautiful city of Beijing is very lucky to be able to host the conference during this golden month of October. On behalf of ... I would firstly like to extend my warmest congratulations to .... At the same time, I would also like to express my sincere thanks to ... for choosing Beijing Science and Technology Center as the conference venue. We also thank honorable guests and friends who have traveled so far to come to this conference.

(8) 回顾过去,我们无比自豪,展望未来,我们信心百倍。让我们同心同德,再接再厉,抓住机遇,携起手来,为…做出新的贡献,并为…而奋斗,共同开创…的新局面。祝愿这次大会取得圆满成功！We feel profoundly proud of the past and immensely confident about the future. Let's work together unremittingly and capitalize on every opportunity. Let's join hands and endeavor to make new contributions to... and strive for ... and open a new chapter in .... We wish the conference much success!

第 10 章 参展参会

10.1 译前准备

背景介绍:商务洽谈的初步阶段、讨价还价阶段和签订合同阶段。

词汇准备如表 10.1 所示。

表 10.1 参展参会的词汇准备

序号	词汇	翻译
1	quote	报价单
2	brochure	宣传册
3	negotiation	谈判
4	trial order	试购
5	dispatch	派遣;分派
6	shipment	装运,装船
7	freight	运费
8	balance	余额

10.2 对话全文

听下列对话,进行中英、英中交替口译(音频 10.2-1)。(中方为 C;外方为 F。)

Dialogue 1

Scenario:initial business talk.

C:您好!我是销售代表王雷,有什么可以帮您?

F:Hi! I'm interested in your range of sweaters. Could I look at your samples?

音频 10.2-1

C：当然可以，我陪您到处看看，边走边讲解我们的产品。这些产品在国内外很受欢迎。

F：That'll be great.

C：右边是我们的最新产品，您是否愿意先看看货？

F：Quite interesting, this is the style I am looking for. How about the prices?

C：这是价格表。

F：Thank you. What about delivery time?

C：我们收到订单后几天之内即可发货。

F：Can I have the catalogue for all styles?

C：好的。给您。

F：I'll come again tomorrow.

C：好的，明天见。

Dialogue 2

Scenario: bargaining in negotiations.

C：我们开始吧？

F：Sure. I have read through the materials of your company and found the price you quote is too high.

C：俗话说一分钱一分货，如果您考虑一下质量，就会觉得我们的价格是非常合理的。我们用的原材料是最好的，而现在全国物价都在上涨，原材料成本也上涨了。

F：Why not try meeting each other half way?

C：如果你们订单下得大一些，我们价格也可以更优惠。

F：We would like to order 50 000 sweaters. As far as a trial order is concerned, the quantity is by no means small. And generally speaking, people profit from a trial order. I hope you understand.

C：好吧，因为这是我们的第一次交易，我们同意给您9折优惠价。

F：Good, I can accept that. And, I'd like to know your usual way of packing.

C：我们用纸箱，内衬防潮纸，外打铁箍两道。

F：Sounds all right.

C：贵方希望怎样发货，铁路还是海运？

F：By sea, please. And we can assume freight.

C：太好了。

F：When can you effect shipping?

C：我们最晚在今年12月或明年年初就交货。

F：That's good.

Dialogue 3

Scenario：signing the contract.

C：这是草拟的合同，请您过目。

F：OK.

（F看合同。）

C：看完了吗？

F：Yes，I have got one question about Clause 7. Are these the terms we agreed on?

C：是的，我们来看看。

F：20 percent down and the balance at the time of shipment?

C：是的。

F：I'll need a few minutes to check over my notes again.

（F查阅谈判记录。）

C：如果您有什么意见的话，请提出来。

F：OK，that's all right. I have no questions.

C：我们现在可以签合同了吗？

F：Sure. Where shall I put my signature?

C：最后一页上。我们签署两份文本，一份中文，一份英文，两份具有同等效力。

F：OK. I hope this will lead to further cooperation between us. All we have to do now is shake hands.

C：好的，谢谢您！

练习

自编参展参会场景的三角对话（中方、外宾、译员），可参考10.3节的词汇。

10.3 词汇拓展

1. 国际展会常用术语[69]

（1）convention 泛指大型会议、展览

（2）convention center 会展中心

（3）attendee brochure 分发给展会观众的宣传资料

（4）attendee 参观展会的人（不包括参展商）

(5) booth personnel 展台工作人员

(6) contractor 为展览会组织者、参展商提供服务的服务供应商

(7) demographics 参展商和观众的统计数据

(8) demonstrators （展位上的）演示和讲解员

(9) display rules & regulations 展会规则

(10) exposition 博览会

(11) distributor show 分销展（由某一个批发商举办，参展商都为该批发商的供应商，而参观展会的人一般为批发商的客户）

(12) exhibit manager 展品经理（主要负责展品，区别于负责展会全部事物的展览经理）

(13) exhibitor lounge 参展商活动室

(14) exhibitor newsletter 参展商通讯录

(15) exhibitor prospectus 展览会组织者发送给现有及潜在参展商的展览会介绍材料

(16) permanent exhibit 长期性展览

(17) press kit 袋装展览会新闻资料

(18) press room 新闻中心

(19) public show 指面向普通公众开放的展览会，观众通常需要买票进入

(20) service desk 设在展会现场、供参展商订购各种服务的服务供应处

(21) show break 展会结束和开始撤展的时间

(22) show directory 展览会会刊，包括参展商名单、摊位号、展馆位置及图示，上面还常登录广告

(23) show-within-a-show 套展（指一个有自己独立名称和主题的展览会，在另一个相关的大型展览会内举办，成为其一部分）

(24) space rate 摊位租金

(25) sponsorship 展会赞助

(26) subcontractor（展览服务）分包商

(27) hospitality area 会客区

(28) on-site registration 现场注册

(29) international traders 国际买家

(30) pre-registration 优先登记

(31) shuttle service 接送服务

(32) group visitors 团体参观者

(33) trade agreement 贸易协议

(34) business cards for registration 名片登记

（35）delegate（会议）代表,可泛指参会人

（36）off-site program 正式会议活动外的行程

2. 展会搭建常用术语[69]

（1）booth 展位

（2）booth area 展位面积

（3）backdrop 背景板

（4）sales literature 宣传材料

（5）poster 海报

（6）panel system 拉网展架

（7）X stand X 展架

（8）pamphlet 小册子

（9）brochure display 资料架

（10）slogan 标语,口号

（11）exhibit directory 参观指南

（12）reception desk 接待台

（13）move-in 展台搭建、布展期

（14）truss 桁架

（15）move-out 撤展期

（16）fireproof board 防火板

（17）multiple-story exhibit 多层展台

（18）giveaway 免费样品

（19）layout 会场布局图

（20）public address system 展厅广播设备

（21）exhibitor manual 参展商手册

（22）floor plan 展馆平面图

（23）exposition manager 展厅经理

（24）exhibit designer/producer 展台设计/搭建商

（25）floor load 展馆地面最大承重量

（26）installation & dismantlement 展台搭建和撤展

（27）installation contractor 展台搭建服务商

（28）outside exhibit 室外展台

（29）transient space 临时摊位

（30）double-decker 双层展位

（31）aisle carpet 通道地毯

（32）peninsula booth 半岛展位（展位背对通道顶端,其他三面都是过道）

第 11 章 送客道别

11.1 译前准备

背景介绍：seeing a foreign guest off after World Internet Conference at Wuzhen.

词汇准备如表 11.1 所示。

表 11.1 送客道别的词汇准备

序号	中文	英文
1	世界互联网大会	World Internet Conference
2	为某人践行	plan a farewell dinner for someone
3	相见恨晚	regret not having met earlier/sooner, regret not to have known someone before
4	互通有无	each supplies what the other needs, help supply each other's needs, exchange needed goods
5	英雄所见略同	Great minds think alike
6	枕水度假酒店	waterside resort
7	(乌镇)西栅景区	west scenic zone
8	仿古建筑	reproductions of ancient buildings
9	永久会址	permanent venue
10	虹桥机场	Shanghai Hongqiao international airport
11	送君千里,终有一别	No matter how far away you escort a guest, there will be the time to say goodbye

11.2 对话全文

听下列对话,进行中英、英中交替口译(音频 11.2-1)。(中方为 C;外方为 F。)

Dialogue 1

Scenario:at the closing ceremony of World Internet Conference.

C:时间过得真快!互联网大会这么快就结束了,今晚准备为您饯行,不知道您有时间吗?

音频 11.2-1

F:I think so. Thank you very much.

Dialogue 2

Scenario:at farewell dinner.

C:这次互联网大会举办得真不错,不但互通有无,我也结交了新朋友。史密斯先生,和您有一种相见恨晚的感觉呢!

F:Me too. It's been great pleasure knowing you. I'm deeply impressed by your vision and insights into "Internet plus". And I found myself nodding quite often during your speech.

C:哪里哪里。不过,也许是"英雄所见略同"。我提议,为我们的友谊,为我们第一次以及今后的合作,喝一杯吧,干杯!

F:Cheers!

Dialogue 3

Scenario:on the way to the airport.

F:Thank you, Mr. Wang, for coming over to pick me up.

C:我很荣幸呢。这几天会议日程比较满,也没多少机会和您交流。

F:Same here. We did have a very tight schedule during the conference.

C:您有时间逛逛乌镇景区吗?

F:Actually yes, I stayed in Waterside Resort, which is located within the West Scenic Zone. So I took a walk in the evening. It was so beautiful! By the way, the buildings on both sides of the street look great too, they have similar roofs and windows like those in the houses in the scenic zone, but they are modern.

C:对的,这些都是仿古建筑,不过您知道吗,几年前,这些房子就是白送老百姓都不愿意住呢。

F:Really? Why?

C:几年前,乌镇还没有成为互联网大会的永久会址,这里不发达,人们一般都去大城市打工去了,留下的都是老人和小孩儿。

F:Oh, I see. Wuzhen is truly becoming more developed now.

Dialogue 4

Scenario:at the airport.

C:我们到了,这就是虹桥机场了。

F:Thank you for the ride. It's been a pleasure knowing you.

C:我也很荣幸。俗话说"送君千里,终有一别",我们就此道别吧。另外,请收下这份小礼物作为中国之行的纪念吧。

F:What a nice pair of chopsticks! Thank you a lot!

C:祝您一路平安!

F:Thanks! Let's keep in touch!

C:好的,常联系,再见!

F:Bye!

练习

自编送客道别场景的三角对话(中方、外宾、译员),可参考11.3节的词汇。

11.3 词汇拓展

1. "哪里哪里"的翻译方法

由于中西文化的不同,在回应外方赞美的时候,中国人常常自谦地说"哪里哪里",而英美国家的人一般是以感谢回应。如果翻译成汉语本来的意思(如"Not really"),会让外宾觉得也许自己的称赞过分,或者对方不够自信或不够真诚。因此,为了达到跨文化交际的效果,可以顺应外宾的文化习惯,翻译为"Thanks"即可。

2. 道别常用语句

(1) 感谢热情招待! Thank you for your kind hospitality.

(2) 我想借此机会对东道主表达我最崇高的敬意。I'd like to take this opportunity to express my highest salute to the host.

(3) 在向克林顿总统告别时,我们借此机会请求他转达我们对美国人民的深厚友谊,请他转达我们对他们的亲切问候和敬意。In bidding farewell to President Clinton, we take this opportunity to request him to convey our profound friendship to the American people, and also our best regards and respect to them.

第 12 章 商贸洽谈

12.1 译前准备

背景介绍:海尔公司和开利公司有关空调产品的商务洽谈。
词汇准备如表 12.1 所示。

表 12.1 商贸洽谈的词汇准备

序号	词汇	翻译
1	满汉全席	the Man-Han banquet, the most typical local cuisine combining Manchurian and Chinese delicacies
2	Letter of credit(L/C)	信用证
3	R & D	Research and Development,研发
4	吉祥数字	auspicious number
5	terms of payment	付款方式
6	irrevocable letter of credit payable against shipping documents	不可撤销的、凭装运单据付款的信用证
7	各让一步	meet half way
8	付款交单	documents against payment

12.2 对话全文

听下列对话,进行中英、英中交替口译(音频 12.2-1)。(中方为 C;外方为 F。)

Dialogue 1

Scenario:initial talk.

C:欢迎来到海尔!我是海尔公司的 CEO 严昊涵。

F: Thanks! I'm Larry, the general manager of Carrier Corporation.

C: 您现在来北京正是时候,十月的北京气候适宜。不知您是否适应这边的饮食?

F: Indeed, we are also impressed with the fascinating scenery and exquisite dishes.

C: 今晚,我们为您安排了本地最具代表性的晚宴——满汉全席,期待您能赴宴。

F: Thank you very much! I'm pleased to receive your invitation. Your company has received a favorable reputation. We hope we can settle the deal through this negotiation.

Dialogue 2

Scenario: bargaining.

C: 好的,那我们开始吧?

F: Sure.

C: 看来贵公司提供的新型空调很符合我方的采购要求,请问贵方报价如何?

F: 600 U.S. dollars per set.

C: 贵方的报价实在是太高了,这远远超出我们的财政预算。

F: Mr. Yan, you'll find our price very reasonable if you consider the high-tech quality of our product.

C: 非常合理?贵方的报价如此离谱,我实在怀疑贵方的诚意。我们所能接受的价格为400美元一台。

F: We really cannot take your offer. We've invested huge amounts of labor, resources and funds in R&D in this product. However, to show our sincerity, we could lower our price to 500.

C: 我们已经感受到了您的诚意。我们有意订购2 000台,不知贵方可否将价格降到450美元?

F: Considering the costs we've paid, 480 is really our bottom line.

C: 虽然贵方已经做出一定的让步,但是此价格我方仍然难以接受。如果我们把订单提高到3 000台,您看460美元能接受吗?六在中国也是个吉祥数字。

F: Alright. We can take that. Hopefully this deal will bring us good fortune. Well, we've settled the price. Let's talk about the terms of payment?

C: 好的!

F: We only accept payment by irrevocable letter of credit payable against shipping documents.

C: 我明白了。您能不能破例接受承兑交单或付款交单?

F：I'm afraid not. We always require a letter of credit for our exports.

C：老实说，信用证会增加我方进口货的成本。要在银行开立信用证，我得付一笔押金。这样会占压我的资金，因而会增加成本。

F：You could consult your bank and see if they will reduce the required deposit to a minimum.

C：我们都各让一步，货价的百分之五十用信用证，其余的采用付款交单，您看怎么样？

F：Alright, we can do that.

C：这很合理。我们已谈妥大部分的合同条款，贵方是否有疑问？

F：We've reached agreement and expect further cooperation.

练习

自编商贸洽谈场景的三角对话（中方、外宾、译员）可参考12.3节的词汇。

12.3 词汇拓展

1. 商务洽谈简介[70]

商务洽谈活动是在经济活动中，洽谈双方通过协商来确定交换各种条件的一项必不可少的活动，它可以促进双方达成协议，是双方洽谈的一项重要环节。商务洽谈是双方相互调整利益，减少分歧，并最终确立共同利益的行为过程，主要包括准备、价值传递、讨价还价、促单、定案五个阶段。

2. 签约常见语句[71]

(1) Our foreign trade policy has always been based on equality and mutual benefit and exchange of needed goods.

我们的对外贸易政策一向是以平等互利、互通有无为基础的。

(2) We have adopted much more flexible methods in our dealings.

我们在具体操作方法上灵活多了。

(3) We have mainly adopted some usual international practices.

我们主要采取了一些国际上的惯例做法。

(4) How would you like to proceed with the negotiations?

您认为该怎样进行这次谈判呢？

(5) Let's move on to what makes our product sell so well.

我来说一下我们产品销量好的原因。

(6) Our service, so far, has been very well-received by our customers．

到目前为止，顾客对我们的服务质量评价很高。

(7) How about feedback from your retailers and consumers?

你们的零售商和消费者的反映怎样？

(8) Could you tell me some more about your market analysis?

请多介绍一下你们的市场分析好吗？

(9) Yes, our market analysis tells us our prime users will be between 5 and 50.

好的，市场分析表明，我们的产品主要使用者年龄将在 5 至 50 岁。

(10) How soon can you have your product ready?

你们多久才可以出货呢？

(11) We are always willing to cooperate with you and if necessary make some concessions.

我们总是愿意和您合作的，如果需要还可以做些让步。

(12) We'd like you to consider our request once again.

希望贵方再次考虑我们的要求。

(13) We'd like to clear up some points connected with the technical part of the contract.

我们希望搞清楚合同中技术方面的几个问题。

(14) The negotiations on the rights and obligations of the parties under contract turned out to be very successful.

有关合同各方的权利和义务方面的谈判非常成功。

(15) We can't agree with the alterations and amendments to the contract.

我们无法同意对合同的变动和修改。

(16) We hope that the next negotiation will be the last one before signing the contract.

希望下一轮谈判后就可以签订合同了。

(17) We don't have any different opinions about the contractual obligations of both parties.

就合同双方要承担的义务方面，我们没有意见。

第 13 章 参观访问

13.1 译前准备

背景介绍:中国外文局煦方国际 China Matters 记者来华为新研发中心参观[72]。词汇准备如表 13.1 所示。

表 13.1 参观访问的词汇准备

序号	词汇	翻译
1	telecom gear	通信设备
2	功率	power
3	爱立信	Ericsson
4	基站	base station
5	专利	patent
6	手机卡	sim card

13.2 对话全文

听下列对话,进行中英、英中交替口译(音频 13.2-1)。(中方为 C;记者为 F。)

F: Hi, I'm Sam from China Matters. I'm very honored to visit the new research center of Huawei.

C:您好,我是华为新研发中心的工程师邹博士。接下来将由我带领您参观中心。

F: Huawei is now 12 months ahead of its rivals like Nokia and Ericsson because of its superior technology especially in 5G. I'm very curious about the 5G technique and what is powering Huawei.

音频 13.2-1

C：好的，希望今天的参观过程将会满足你的好奇心。请这边走。

C：这里是5G无线基站，那是4G无线基站。在4G时代，无线基站的平均功率约为300瓦。在5G时代，平均功率高达1 000瓦。这意味着功率是原来的三倍多。

F：Awesome! I have just heard that Huawei has been developing telecoms gear to handle higher 5G performance. But how does this 5G wireless base station work?

C：5G基站是必不可少的通信设备，它以超高的速度向我们的移动设备传输信号。由于5G基站的数据传输速度更快，其消耗的能量更多，温度也会越来越高，因此需要研发新的冷却技术。你可以看到里面有一种特殊液体，不是水，这个液体很特别，它的沸点是18℃。华为有很多像我一样的工程师，正在研究如何通过巧妙的设计和材料的使用来改变部件内热气流的流速和方向，从而达到散热的目的。

F：I think these designs by your team have been funded by Huawei's massive investment in research. I have heard that the investment spent on research is more than the total of its rivals combined.

C：是的。截止到2017年，华为的研发经费已经高达130亿美元，到2019年为止，华为几乎包揽了5G中最重要的专利科技，高达2 570个，全球占比20%。这些专利技术成为推动5G在国内外发展的最坚实的保障。

F：Excellent! But please allow me to interrupt, what you said before is too technical. Could you please introduce me to some applications about 5G techniques in our daily life?

C：当然。请跟我来这边。大量的研发投入使得一项项新的技术应运而生，室内数字系统就是其中之一。有了它，就算你用的不是5G手机，也可以在室内接收5G信号。

F：So does that mean we can enjoy 5G at home even without a 5G mobile phone?

C：是的。

F：With the 4G network, I especially struggle to make video calls. That's probably because the speed is slow, and somehow the screen freezes from time to time, which I find to be annoying. This DIS is such an amazing product!

C：是的，当然你也可以用4G的手机卡，或者在4G和5G卡之间自由切换，都没有问题。华为的手机基站可以同时支持这两种选择。

F：At a time when many of the world's 5G players have been held back by the high cost of setting up more 5G base stations. Huawei is offering a solution. I do admire your company.

C：谢谢您的赞美，接下来请让我带您参观推动基站实现"极简"模式的研发核心——"天罡"芯片。请这边走。

练习

假设有外国代表团来参观北京邮电大学,自编校方与代表团代表的三角对话(中方、外宾、译员),可参考 13.3 节的词汇。

13.3　词汇拓展

1. 参观访问常见词汇

(1) 安排访问 schedule a visit

(2) 参访团 visiting group / party

(3) 出国考察 go abroad on a tour of investigation; go abroad on a study tour

(4) 代表团 delegation; deputation; mission

(5) 代表团的正式成员 the full member of the delegation

(6) 代表团长 head / leader of a delegation

(7) 中国代表 Chinese delegation; delegation from China

(8) 短期访问 brief / short visit

(9) 访问学者 visiting scholar

(10) 进行国事访问 make / pay a state visit

(11) 考察 inspect, observe and study

(12) 实地考察 make an on-the-scene investigation

(13) 礼节访问 courtesy visit

(14) 谢绝参观 Not open to visitors

(15) 致以诚挚的问候 extend one's cordial greetings

2. 解说词——以北京邮电大学为例

北京邮电大学是中华人民共和国教育部直属、首批进入"211 工程"建设的全国重点大学,是一所以信息科技为特色,工学门类为主体,工管文理相结合的多科性大学,是信息科技人才的重要培养基地。

Directly under the administration of the Ministry of Education, Beijing University of Posts and Telecommunications (BUPT) is a national key university built preferentially in the national Project 211. BUPT is a comprehensive university with information and telecommunication technology as its main feature, engineering and science as its main focus and a combination of engineering, management, humanities and sciences as its main pursuit, which has become an important base for fostering IT talents.

学校现设有信息与通信工程学院、电子工程学院、计算机学院、软件学院、经济管理学院、人文学院、理学院、国际学院、网络教育学院等14个学院。学校拥有国家重点实验室、教育部重点实验室和北京市重点实验室,以及国家一级重点学科和北京市重点学科。

BUPT has 14 schools: School of Information and Telecommunications Engineering, School of Electronic Engineering, School of Computer Science, School of Software Engineering, School of Economics and Management, School of Humanities, School of Sciences, International School, and School of Network Education etc. The university has ministerial, municipal and national key laboratories and municipal and national key disciplines.

学校现开设43个本科专业、45个硕士专业、两类专业学位硕士、14个博士专业教育教学课程,并建立了5个一级学科博士后流动站。学校现有全日制本硕博及留学生约27 000余名,正式注册的非全日制学生约55 000名。学校注重开展对外合作交流,已同美国、英国、德国、瑞典、法国等40个国家以及港澳台地区的66所大学建立了学术方面的校际合作交流关系,并与世界著名通信公司开展了富有成就的合作,为培养学生具有现代意识和国际意识创造了良好的氛围。

Currently, over 27 000 full-time undergraduates, graduates, PhDs and international students, and about 55 000 registered part-time students are studying under 43 undergraduate programs, 45 graduate programs, two types of professional master degree programs, 14 doctoral programs and 5 postdoctoral programs. BUPT attaches great importance to the exchange and cooperation with other higher learning institutions both at home and abroad and has established inter-university academic exchange programs with over 66 universities from 40 countries, including the United States, the United Kingdom, Germany, Sweden and France and with those from the regions of Hong Kong, Macao, and Chinese Taipei. BUPT has also cooperated successfully with many world-renowned enterprises in telecommunications to create a better environment for students to develop their modern and international consciousness.

北京邮电大学在"团结、勤奋、严谨、创新"的校风、"厚德、博学、敬业、乐群"的校训和"崇尚奉献、追求卓越"的北邮精神的引领下,聚精会神打造学校的核心竞争力,以建成信息科技特色突出、工管文理协调发展的世界高水平大学而努力奋斗。

Guided by its morals of being United, Diligent, Rigorous and Innovative, following its motto of striving for Great Virtue, Profound Knowledge, Total Commitment and Harmonious Cooperation and the spirit of Valuing Dedication and Pursuing Excellence, BUPT is growing in its main strength and striving to become a world-class university specializing in information and telecommunications technology with a balanced development of all disciplines.

第14章 教育合作

14.1 译前准备

背景介绍：外媒记者采访伦敦玛丽女王学院-北京邮电大学合作交流项目负责人陈月[73]。

词汇准备如表14.1所示。

表14.1 教育合作的词汇准备

序号	词汇	翻译
1	BUPT (Beijing University of Posts and Telecommunications)	北京邮电大学
2	Information and Communication Engineering	信息通信工程
3	Queen Mary University of London	伦敦大学玛丽女王学院
4	Telecommunications Engineering with Management	电信工程与管理
5	E-Commerce Engineering with Law	电子商务与法律
6	Internet of Things Engineering	物联网工程
7	accredited	（官方）认可的
8	awareness of engineering ethics	工程伦理意识
9	EECS(Electronic Engineering and Computer Science)	电子工程与计算机

14.2 对话全文

听下列对话，进行中英、英中交替口译（音频14.2-1）。（陈月为C;记者为J。）

J:Hi Ms. Chen! Could you introduce yourself to our online audience?

C:好的，我是陈月，2003年开始在玛丽女王学院工作。现在是伦敦玛丽女王学院-北京邮电大学合作项目主任。

J: Could you tell me a bit about the BUPT Program?

C: 好的。这个合作项目是由伦敦玛丽女王学院和北京邮电大学联合举办的双学位本科项目,始于2004年。北京邮电大学是中国一流大学之一,在信息和通信工程领域排名第一。合作项目的理念是将两国教育体系的优势结合起来。

音频 14.2-1

J: How is the teaching program organized?

C: 目前我们有三个学位课程,三个专业是:电信工程及管理、电子商务与法律和物联网工程。在教学方面,整个课程由两所大学共同设计,大约一半课程由北京邮电大学教授,另一半由玛丽女王学院教授。

J: Who are the students on the program?

C: 我们通过高考选拔招生,今年招生680人,他们来自中国各地,遍布30多个省份。

J: What have been some challenges of managing the Joint Program?

C: 合作项目是一种特殊的跨国项目,作为东道主大学玛丽女王学院,我们为中国学生提供学位。因此,我们面临着其他跨国教育项目面临的一样的挑战:一方面保证项目质量符合英国标准;另一方面要调整教学风格,使之适应中国背景下的学生。这是我们在执行这个项目时面临的挑战之一。

J: What have been some of the benefits?

C: 优势嘛,从学生的角度来说,这些有天分的学生可以得到更多的学习机会。如果没有这个合作项目,就没有这样的机会。此外,学生可以不用出国就能接触中英两国的教育系统。从学校的角度看,这个合作项目通过提升教育合作,提升了玛丽女王学院和北京邮电大学的国际知名度。

J: Why is the program important for Queen Mary? What do you think its wider impact will be?

C: 正如西蒙指出,国际化是一个现代化大学发展的战略计划。玛丽女王学院坐落于伦敦,教职员工和学生都来自世界各地,已经具备很高的国际化程度。这个国际合作项目提升了我校跨国教育的可信度。我们学生的毕业去向显示,迄今为止,已经有三千余名毕业生,其中大约80%选择在中国或海外继续修读研究生学位,其余20%选择直接进入职场。我们为毕业生的成就深感自豪。大学追求的目标之一,就是培养学生,让他们有更好的未来,这对学生和学校而言都是非常有益的事情。

J: What do the students get out of the program, aside from the qualification?

C: 我认为学生还可以获得丰富的学习经验,接触不同国家的教师和课程。举个例子,我们引入个人发展计划,这是一个特别设计的模块,旨在培养学生的通用技能、工程伦理意识、研究评估能力等。与传统学位课程的学生相比,这个模块丰富了他们的学习体验。我们还努力为中英两国的学生组织交流活动。由于时空的差距,组织这样的活动不太容易。不过我很高兴地看到,从这个学年开始,我们举办了"设计与建造"夏令营。其实本周就在进行,有10个中国学生去了伦敦,和玛丽女王学院电子工程与计算机专业的学生一起,做设计和建造项目,准备最后的比赛。这是个好活动,希望在未来持续下去。

J:Finally, do you have any advice for colleagues who might be embarking on similar transnational educational projects?

C:在我看来,良好的质量是任何跨国项目可持续运作的关键,对不同教育体系的深入了解至关重要。要建立双学位项目,必须确保课程满足双方的要求,学生应具备成为未来工程师所需的技能,以满足市场的需要。除了质量把控和良好计划外,积极进取、高效工作的团队也是必不可少的。我们的工作人员对这个项目非常投入,工作一直非常努力。虽然这项工作是一个挑战,但也很有益处。

练习

1. 图 14.1 是北京邮电大学马老师就学生交流项目学习的会议海报[74]。根据海报信息自编采访马老师的三角对话(马老师、外媒记者、译员),可以自由发挥。

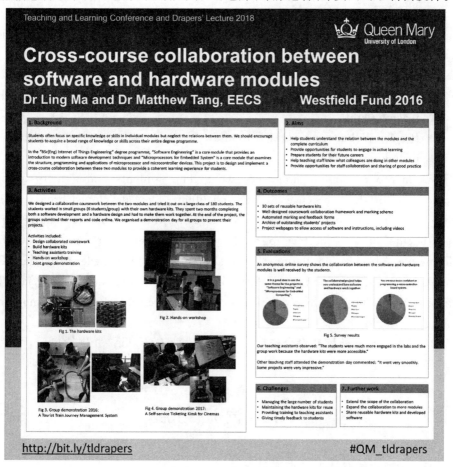

图 14.1　会议海报

信息简介:

Cross-course collaboration between software and hardware modules

Dr. Ling Ma, School of Electronic Engineering and Computer Science, BUPT

This project was to implement a cross-course collaboration between software and hardware modules to improve the students' learning experience in the Joint Programme between Queen Mary University of London and Beijing University of Posts and Telecommunications. The aims of the project were to improve the teaching quality, improve the students' appreciation for the coherence of the curriculum, help the students make connections between modules and give them a new and a more comprehensive perspective of the curriculum. It would help to improve the students' satisfaction with the teaching and assessment areas in the NSS.

The project outcomes are:

- Well-designed collaborated coursework and marking scheme.
- Joint demonstration of both software and hardware in the same scenario.
- 30 sets of reusable hardware kits.
- Hands-on technical workshops.
- Analysis of feedback from students, teaching assistants and other teaching staff.
- Project Webpages on QM+ to allow access to software and instructions, including videos.

We met our original aims very well. The students had a more general appreciation for the coherence of the curriculum. They developed broader skills and received more hands-on support. After doing this collaborated coursework, the students have a better approach to development with hardware when informative software simulations (virtual hardware) are made available. The cross-course collaboration improved the overall learning experience, especially for top students. Our teaching staff are more aware of what other modules/colleagues are doing.

2. 自编本校和外校教育合作项目筹备阶段两方的对话,并进行口译,可参考14.3节的词汇。

14.3　词汇拓展

下面是学校教育科研词汇[75]。

(1) 博士后科研流动站 center for post-doctoral studies
(2) 短训班 short-term training course
(3) 岗位培训 undergo job-specific training
(4) 国家发明奖 National Invention Prize
(5) 国家教育经费 national expenditure on education
(6) 国家科技进步奖 National Prize for Progress in Science and Technology
(7) 国家自然科学奖 National Prize for Natural Sciences
(8) 副教授 associate professor
(9) 客座教授 visiting professor
(10) 名誉教授 honorary professor
(11) 公费生 government-supported student
(12) 旁听生 auditor(美)/guest student(英)
(13) 实验员 laboratory technician
(14) 特级教师 Teacher of Special Grade
(15) 学院院长 Dean of College
(16) 学术报告会/专题讨论会 symposium
(17) 学术活动 academic activities
(18) 研究所所长 director of research institute
(19) 院士 academician
(20) 助理研究员 research associate
(21) 助理实验师 assistant experimentalist
(22) 助理讲师 assistant lecturer
(23) 综合性大学 comprehensive universities
(24) 理工院校 colleges of science and engineering
(25) 农林院校 agricultural colleges
(26) 师范院校 normal universities and colleges
(27) 医药院校 medical colleges
(28) 财经院校 colleges of finance and economics
(29) 政法院校 colleges of political science and law
(30) 德才兼备 to combine ability with character, equal stress on integrity and ability
(31) 启发式 elicitation method (of teaching), heuristic method
(32) 产学研"三结合" "3-in-1 combination" involving teaching, research, and production
(33) 学校配有现代化的教学设备并运用现代化的教学手段,以保证教学目标的实现。The university is equipped with advanced teaching facilities and modernized teaching methods so as to guarantee the realization of education targets.

第 15 章 文化交流

15.1 译前准备

背景介绍:下面是对莎士比亚研究所所长 Michael Dobson 有关莎士比亚话题的采访[76]。

词汇准备如表 15.1 所示。

表 15.1 文化交流的词汇准备

序号	词汇	翻译
1	*Midsummer Night's Dream*	《仲夏夜之梦》
2	styles and registers	语体和语域,语言风格
3	supernatural	超自然
4	Beijing People's Art Theatre	北京人民艺术剧院
5	Coriolanus	科利奥兰纳斯
6	Falstaff	福斯塔夫
7	*Henry* Ⅳ	《亨利四世》
8	*Merry Wives of Windsor*	《温莎的风流娘们儿》

15.2 对话全文

听下列对话,进行交替传译(音频 15.2-1)。(主持人为 H;外方为 F。)

H:今天我们很荣幸请到了伯明翰大学莎士比亚研究所所长 Michael Dobson 教授。让我们一起对 Dobson 教授的到来表示最热烈的欢迎。我想先从您的专业领域——莎士比亚——开始。想请问您,您对于莎士比亚的兴趣和热情来自哪里呢?

音频 15.2-1

F: Well, it comes from Shakespeare's works themselves and the influence of my family. Almost everyone has to study Shakespeare in schools around the world and many of them fall in love with his works. To be honest, I am one of the group. But what really excited me about Shakespeare was seeing it performed. I have some sort of formative memories of this. One is to see students from a local school performing "Midsummer Night's Dream" when I was quite young, which I thought was absolutely weird and incredibly funny. All of the girls dressed up as fairies and acting this play out which was extremely powerful and interesting. It was just a brilliant production and was beautifully designed. So that was a revelation. But actually, there'd been an enthusiasm for Shakespeare in a previous generation of my family. My grandfather was passionately keen on Shakespeare and even founded an amateur theatre group when he was in college. So you can see that Shakespeare is a popular writer in Britain and around the world among not only the professionals but also the amateurs. And I started to know that this was something absolutely extraordinary for me long before I left school.

H: 您提到英国的专业人士和业余爱好者都喜欢莎士比亚,在全球也是这样。那么您认为莎士比亚为什么能享誉全球呢?

F: To some extent it's historical luck. Some British people who liked Shakespeare spread out across the world, so the English language carries Shakespeare with it simultaneously. He has such an influence on the development of the English language and English culture. But also, he's the medium through which lots of stories get into wide circulation. He tells stories about families. There is a tremendous sort of core appeal of Shakespeare in that he keeps dramatizing what happens between fathers and children, what happens between lovers, what happens between siblings, as well as how does history change, how do people arguing together produce a new society. And because his works have different styles and registers between the intellectual and the popular, there will be something in the Shakespeare canon that resonates with their particular interests and their particular styles. He does some rational political plays about how people pragmatically get on with things in a secular world. But he also writes plays about ghosts, magic and the supernatural. His works are so broad that each can take what he needs from them.

H: 其他国家的观众要欣赏戏剧的话,翻译就十分重要,尤其是对于莎士比亚的作品。您认为翻译会让他的作品的精髓丢失吗?或者翻译反而能丰富他的作品?

F: Well, one thing that gets found in translation is Shakespeare's newness. Performing Shakespeare, especially translating Shakespeare keeps these texts and plays new. And you will discover things about your own language through working out how you're going to render Shakespeare's effects and how you're going to recreate them in your own context. The problem of translating Shakespeare's blank verse, the kind of rhythm in which he habitually writes in English, into Mandarin, is a great example. Because there are so many different rhythm and verse patterns in Mandarin and you get to choose which one, for particular bits of blank verse. Therefore Shakespeare's blank verse metamorphoses into different versification patterns in Mandarin, which is fascinating.

H: 近年来,更多的莎士比亚剧目在中国的各大剧场上演。您对于这些文化交流是怎么看的? 文化交流有什么重要意义?

F: They are terribly important, because they renew both parties involved. Shakespeare is all about dialogue and his plays foment dialogue. It enables culture to understand one another or for both as audiences or both as practitioners, that's tremendously enlightening. For instance, when a performer goes on a global tour, he or she may be very curious about what Chinese audience are going to make of it, where the laughs are going to be, where the attentions are going to be, which bits of the play are going to really excite a Chinese audience, compared to a British audience or a New York audience. Shakespeare's plays themselves are interested in relations between countries, they are a great means of producing discussion about that in the afterlives they have. I've seen some great Chinese Shakespeare with subtitles. And I thought that Beijing People's Art Theatre's "Coriolanus" that came to Edinburgh a couple of years ago was a terrific show.

H:对,我也知道那场演出。那么既然您已经欣赏了许多表演和作品,您也在世界各地讲授莎士比亚的课程,请问您是否发现在与不同国家的学生和人们聊天时,由于成长在不同的文化氛围中,他们对莎剧会有不同的看法?

F:Absolutely, and it's really fascinating. Quite different priorities and different responses to the stories, different things that they want to explore and want to go with. The question of political legitimacy in history plays has been very important for different countries at different times and lots of students have wanted to argue about that. In different places I've taught, for example in America, where there are some aspects of Shakespeare in comedy that don't really work for Americans. And some of them work extremely well. I remember being quite taken aback when I was first teaching at Harvard where I was teaching a class on "Henry IV" Part I, Shakespeare's great play about a prince who is waiting to inherit the crown. While he's waiting to inherit the crown, he's hanging about down at the pub with this complete fat dropout reprobate called Sir John Falstaff. And these Harvard students, they can see the point of this prince waiting to inherit the crown, but they just couldn't see the point of Falstaff at all. You know, why doesn't he just get on with inheriting the corporation? Why are they wasting our time with this fat guy. You know the sort of pub element of "Henry IV", and it just didn't translate for them at all, which I thought was very intriguing. Whereas when I met students in Central Europe, they wanted Shakespeare to be very noble and elevated, and they've been slightly embarrassed by the jokes sometimes. They prefer that kind of Julius Caesar-ish side of Shakespeare rather than the sort of "Merry Wives of Windsor" of Shakespeare.

H:再后来您去了中国的北京大学。中国人又是怎么看莎士比亚的呢？他们有特别喜欢的剧吗？

F:Yeah, I think a great engagement with Shakespeare in tragedy. That sense of sacrifice and the questions of where you put the individual against society and how you define the one against the other, what has to go and what has to stay, how you hold it together. It's all being absorbing interests to Chinese Shakespeareans and Chinese students.

H:非常感谢您的分享！谢谢您！

F:You are welcome! It is my pleasure!

练习

假设孔子学院教学场景，不会说英语的中国老师在口译员的翻译下给母语为英语的学生讲解中国文化。自编讲解内容，进行中英口译，可参照15.3节的词汇。

15.3 词汇拓展

下面是中国文化交流常用英语[77]。

(1) 京剧 Beijing Opera

(2) 昆曲 Kunqu Opera

(3) 脸谱 facial paintings

(4) 唱念做打 singing, recitation, facial and body posturing and acting,

martial arts

(5) 生旦净丑 male role (sheng), female role (dan), male roles with facial paintings (jing), clown (chou)

(6) 民乐乐器 traditional Chinese musical instruments

(7) 弦乐 stringed instrument

(8) 打击乐 percussion instrument

(9) 汉字 Chinese character

(10) 文房四宝 four treasures of the study

(11) 笔画 stroke

(12) 书法家 calligrapher

(13) 象形文字 pictographic character

(14) 表意文字 ideographic character

(15) 表音文字 phonographic character

(16) 气脉 internal line of energy

(17) 行体 Xing style calligraphy

(18) 练字 practice one's calligraphy

(19) 年画 New Year painting

(20) 人物画 figure paintings

(21) 山水画 landscapes paintings

(22) 花鸟画 flower-and-bird paintings

(23) 横幅画 horizontal scroll

(24) 清明上河图 Riverside Scene at Qingming Festival

(25) 天人合一的道家原则 Taoist principles of balance and harmony, man and nature

(26) 临水亭榭 waterside pavilion

(27) 花窗 decorative window

(28) 幽径 footpath

(29) 卵石 pebble

(30) 官位的等级 ranks of officials

(31) 一品官 the first grade official

(32) 腊月 the last lunar month

(33) 月宫 Moon Palace

(34) 玉兔 Jade Rabbit

(35) 莲子馅 filling of lotus seeds

(36) 蛋黄馅 filling of salted duck eggs

(37) 年夜饭 Spring Festival meal

(38) 除夕夜 midnight of New Year's Eve

(39) 七夕节 Double Seventh Festival

(40) 银河 Milky Way

(41) 织女 Cowherd and Weaver Maid

(42) 天帝 God of Heaven

(43) 西天王母 Queen Mother of the Western Heavens

(44) 金簪 gold hairpins

(45) 喜鹊 magpie

(46) 抓周 grabbing test

(47) 剪纸 paper-cut

(48) 洞房 bridal chamber

(49) 科举考试 highest-level imperial examination

(50) 对联 couplet

(51) 岁寒三友 the three plant friends who thrive in cold weather

(52) 松、竹、梅 pine, bamboo and plum

(53) 杜莎夫人蜡像馆 Madame Tussaud's

(54) 蜡像 waxworks, wax model, wax figure

(55) 联票 a combined ticket

(56) 兵马俑 Terra Cotta Warriors and Horses

(57) 秦始皇陵墓 Emperor Qin Shi Huang's Mausoleum

(58) 下葬的财宝与祭奠物品 buried treasures and sacrificial objects

(59) 坑 pit

(60) 世界文化遗产 world cultural heritages

(61) 布达拉宫 Potala Palace

(62) 中国结 Chinese knot

(63) 折扇 folded fans

(64) 旗袍 cheongsam, qipao

(65) 旗人 banner people

(66) 养蚕 silkworm-raising

(67) 民间工艺 folk art

(68) 刺绣 embroidery

(69) 刺绣品 embroidered works

第16章 演讲发言

16.1 译前准备

背景介绍:李开复在 TED 发表"人工智能(AI)和人类将来会如何共处"的主题演讲[78]。

词汇准备如表 16.1 所示。

表 16.1 演讲发言的词汇准备

序号	词汇	翻译
1	take precedence over	高于
2	oxymoron	矛盾修辞法
3	gladiatorial flight	角斗士的战争
4	impregnable	不可战胜的;无法撼动的
5	computer vision	计算机视觉
6	drone	无人机
7	telesales	电话销售
8	hematologists	血液学工作者
9	radiologists	放射学工作者
10	lymphoma	淋巴瘤
11	PET scan	正子扫描
12	dementia	痴呆症
13	chemotherapy	化疗
14	in remission	在缓解期
15	PwC(Prince Waterhouse Coopers)	普华永道
16	serendipity	意外的运气

16.2 演讲全文

听下列演讲,进行英中口译(视频 16.2-1)。

I'm going to talk about how AI and mankind can coexist, but first, we have to rethink about our human values. So let me first make a confession about my errors in my values.

It was 11 o'clock, December 16, 1991. I was about to become a father for the first time. My wife, Shen-Ling, lay in the hospital bed going through a very difficult 12-hour labor; I sat by her bedside but looked anxiously at my watch, and I knew something that she didn't. I knew that if in one hour, our child didn't come, I was going to leave her there and go back to work and make a presentation about AI to my boss, Apple's CEO. Fortunately, my daughter was born at 11:30, sparing me from doing the unthinkable, and to this day, I am so sorry for letting my work ethic take precedence over love for my family.

视频 16.2-1

My AI talk, however, went off brilliantly.

Apple loved my work and decided to announce it at TED 1992, 26 years ago on this very stage. I thought I had made one of the biggest, most important discoveries in AI, and so did the "Wall Street Journal" on the following day.

But as far as discoveries went, it turned out, I didn't discover India, or America. Perhaps I discovered a little island off Portugal. But the AI era of discovery continued, and more scientists poured their souls into it. About 10 years ago, the grand AI discovery was made by three North American scientists, and it's known as deep learning.

Deep learning is a technology that can take a huge amount of data within one single domain and learn to predict or decide at superhuman accuracy. For example, if we show the deep learning network a massive number of food photos, it can recognize food such as hot dog or no hot dog.

Or if we show it many pictures and videos and sensor data from driving on the highway, it can actually drive a car as well as a human being on the highway. And what if we showed this deep learning network all the speeches made by President Trump? Then this artificially intelligent President Trump, actually the network.

You like double oxymorons, huh?

So this network, if given the request to make a speech about AI, he, or it, might say:

(Recording) Donald Trump: It's a great thing to build a better world with artificial intelligence.

Kai-Fu Lee: And maybe in another language?

DT: (Speaking Chinese)

Kai-Fu Lee: You didn't know he knew Chinese, did you?

So deep learning has become the core in the era of AI discovery, and that's led by the US. But we're now in the era of implementation, where what really matters is execution, product quality, speed and data.

And that's where China comes in. Chinese entrepreneurs, who I fund as a venture capitalist, are incredible workers, amazing work ethic. My example in the delivery room is nothing compared to how hard people work in China. As an example, one startup tried to claim work-life balance: "Come work for us because we are 996." And what does that mean? It means the work hours of 9 a.m. to 9 p.m., six days a week. That's contrasted with other startups that do 997.

And the Chinese product quality has consistently gone up in the past decade, and that's because of a fiercely competitive environment. In Silicon Valley, entrepreneurs compete in a very gentlemanly fashion, sort of like in old wars in which each side took turns to fire at each other.

But in the Chinese environment, it's truly a gladiatorial fight to the death. In such a brutal environment, entrepreneurs learn to grow very rapidly, they learn to make their products better at lightning speed, and they learn to hone their business models until they're impregnable. As a result, great Chinese products like WeChat and Weibo are arguably better than the equivalent American products from Facebook and Twitter. And the Chinese market embraces this change and accelerated change and paradigm shifts.

As an example, if any of you go to China, you will see it's almost cashless and credit card-less, because that thing that we all talk about, mobile payment, has become the reality in China. In the last year, 18.8 trillion US dollars were transacted on mobile internet, and that's because of very robust technologies built behind it. It's even bigger than the China GDP. And this technology, you can say, how can it be bigger than the GDP? Because it includes all transactions: wholesale, channels, retail, online, offline, going into a shopping mall or going into a farmer's market like this.

The technology is used by 700 million people to pay each other, not just merchants, so it's peer to peer, and it's almost transaction-fee-free. And it's instantaneous, and it's used everywhere.

And finally, the China market is enormous. This market is large, which helps give entrepreneurs more users, more revenue, more investment, but most importantly, it gives the entrepreneurs a chance to collect a huge amount of data which becomes rocket fuel for the AI engine. So as a result, the Chinese AI companies have leaped ahead so that today, the most valuable companies in computer vision, speech recognition, speech synthesis, machine translation and drones are all Chinese companies.

So with the US leading the era of discovery and China leading the era of implementation, we are now in an amazing age where the dual engine of the two superpowers are working together to drive the fastest revolution in technology that we have ever seen as humans.

And this will bring tremendous wealth, unprecedented wealth: 16 trillion dollars, according to PwC, in terms of added GDP to the worldwide GDP by 2030. It will also bring immense challenges in terms of potential job replacements. Whereas in the Industrial Age it created more jobs because craftsman jobs were being decomposed into jobs in the assembly line, so more jobs were created. But AI completely replaces the individual jobs in the assembly line with robots. And it's not just in factories, but truckers, drivers and even jobs like telesales, customer service and hematologists as well as radiologists over the next 15 years are going to be gradually replaced by artificial intelligence.

And only the creative jobs. I have to make myself safe, right? Really, the creative jobs are the ones that are protected, because AI can optimize but not create.

But what's more serious than the loss of jobs is the loss of meaning, because the work ethic in the Industrial Age has brainwashed us into thinking that work is the reason we exist, that work defined the meaning of our lives. And I was a prime and willing victim to that type of workaholic thinking. I worked incredibly hard. That's why I almost left my wife in the delivery room, that's why I worked 996 alongside my entrepreneurs. And that obsession that I had with work ended abruptly a few years ago when I was diagnosed with fourth stage lymphoma. The PET scan here shows over 20 malignant tumors jumping out like fireballs, melting away my ambition.

But more importantly, it helped me reexamine my life. Knowing that I may only have a few months to live caused me to see how foolish it was for me to base my entire self-worth on how hard I worked and the accomplishments from hard work. My priorities were completely out of order. I neglected my family. My father had passed away, and I never had a chance to tell him I loved him. My mother had dementia and no longer recognized me, and my children had grown up.

During my chemotherapy, I read a book by Bronnie Ware who talked about dying wishes and regrets of the people in the deathbed. She found that facing death, nobody regretted that they didn't work hard enough in this life. They only regretted that they didn't spend enough time with their loved ones and that they didn't spread their love.

So I am fortunately today in remission.

So I can be back at TED again to share with you that I have changed my ways. I now only work 965. Occasionally 996, but usually 965. I moved closer to my mother, my wife usually travels with me, and when my kids have vacation, if they don't come home, I go to them. So it's a new form of life that helped me recognize how important it is that love is for me, and facing death helped me change my life, but it also helped me see a new way of how AI should impact mankind and work and coexist with mankind, that really, AI is taking away a lot of routine jobs, but routine jobs are not what we're about.

Why we exist is love. When we hold our newborn baby, love at first sight, or when we help someone in need, humans are uniquely able to give and receive love, and that's what differentiates us from AI.

Despite what science fiction may portray, I can responsibly tell you that AI has no love. When AlphaGo defeated the world champion Ke Jie, while Ke Jie was crying and loving the game of go, AlphaGo felt no happiness from winning and certainly no desire to hug a loved one.

So how do we differentiate ourselves as humans in the age of AI?

We talked about the axis of creativity, and certainly that is one possibility, and now we introduce a new axis that we can call compassion, love, or empathy.

Those are things that AI can not do. So as AI takes away the routine jobs, I like to think we can, we should and we must create jobs of compassion. You might ask how many of those there are, but I would ask you:

Do you not think that we are going to need a lot of social workers to help us make this transition? Do you not think we need a lot of compassionate caregivers to give more medical care to more people? Do you not think we're going to need 10 times more teachers to help our children find their way to survive and thrive in this brave new world? And with all the new found wealth, should we not also make labors of love into careers and let elderly accompaniment or homeschooling become careers also?

This graph is surely not perfect, but it points at four ways that we can work with AI. AI will come and take away the routine jobs and in due time, we will be thankful.

AI will become great tools for the creatives so that scientists, artists, musicians and writers can be even more creative. AI will work with humans as analytical tools that humans can wrap their warmth around for the high-compassion jobs. And we can always differentiate ourselves with the uniquely capable jobs that are both compassionate and creative, using and leveraging our irreplaceable brains and hearts.

So there you have it: a blueprint of coexistence for humans and AI. AI is serendipity. It is here to liberate us from routine jobs, and it is here to remind us what it is that make us human. So let us choose to embrace AI and love one another. Thank you.

练习

假如你要为某美国中学学生做演讲，题为"人类未来如何与人工智能共处"，准备中文讲稿，并进行中英口译，可以参考16.2节的内容和16.3节的词汇。

16.3　词汇拓展

下面是即兴演讲常用语句[79]。

1. 应对问题

（1）请听众演讲结束时提问：

- I will be pleased to answer any questions you may have at the end of the presentation.
- Could you save your questions till the end?

（2）允许听众随时打断：

- Don't hesitate to interrupt if you have a question.
- Please feel free to interrupt me at any time.
- Please stop me if you have any questions.
- If you need clarification on any point, you're welcome to ask questions at any time.

（3）被打断后：

- Can I come back to that point later?
- I will be coming to that point in a minute.
- We will go into details later. But just to give you an idea of...
- I think I said that I would answer questions at the end of the presentation, perhaps you wouldn't mind waiting until then.

(4) 对问题的评论和拖延战术：

- That's a tricky question.
- I am afraid there's no easy answer to that one...
- Yes，that's a very good point.

(5) 同意听众提问：

- I think we have time for just one more question.

2. 欢迎听众

(1) 欢迎：

- I am pleased to be able to welcome you to our company.
- May I take this opportunity to thank you for coming.

(2) 茶歇后再次欢迎：

- Hello again everybody. Thank you for being on time.
- It's GREAT to be back here.

3. 受邀请在会议上致辞

- I am delighted/pleased/glad to have the opportunity to present/to make this presentation...
- I am grateful for the opportunity to present...

4. 引起听众的兴趣

(1) 重要性：

- I'm going to be speaking about something that is vitally important to all of us.
- My presentation will help solve a problem that has puzzled people for years.
- I am going to be talking about a product that could double your profit margins.

(2) 效果渲染：

- At the end of this presentation you will understand why this company has been so successful for so long...
- The next ten minutes will change your attitude to sales and marketing.

- Over the next ten minutes you are going to hear about something that will change the way your companies operate.
- By the end of this presentation you will know all there is to know about...

5. 结束语

（1）总之：
- Finally.../By way of conclusion...
- In conclusion, I'd like to... /Let me end by saying...
- That concludes our presentation...
- That, then was all I had to say on...
- Thank you for your attention.

（2）期望效果：
- I hope I have made myself understood.
- I hope you have found this useful.
- I hope this has given you some idea/clear idea/an outline of...
- I hope I've managed to give you a clearer picture of...

（3）允许提问：
- If there are any questions, I'd be delighted to...

（4）下一步安排：
- Let's break for a coffee at this point.

第3篇　参考答案和译文

第17章　第1篇中练习的参考答案

17.1　第2章口译基本技能(一)听辨的参考答案

1. 2.2 口译听辨的原则"得意忘形"的参考答案

练习

（1）<u>越不繁</u>,<u>越不凡</u>。

（2）他总是<u>入不敷出</u>。

（3）状况之好是<u>千言万语</u>都不能表达的。

（4）如果你是悲观的<u>人</u>,你还能乐观地看世界吗？

（5）《宣言》对全球石油工业产生了变革性影响。我们在过去20个月里看到的是<u>日新月异</u>的变化.

（6）能源是贯穿我们日常生活的一个核心需求；能源不可能招之即来,能源没有假日,能源也不能打电话请病假。能源必须提供24小时服务。

（7）我会爱你<u>一生一世</u>。

（8）他今天有<u>很多</u>事情要做。

（9）<u>十有八九</u>,我们将超额完成今年的生产计划。

（10）他<u>根据事实推断出</u>一个结论：机械能不等同于电能。

2. 2.3 口译听辨的训练方法的参考答案

练习1

（1）人与自然是生命共同体,人类必须尊重自然、顺应自然、保护自然。

（2）大学曾经是培养社会精英的殿堂,现在是集教学、科研、社会服务和引领文化于一身的机构。

（3）教育学导引课程旨在介绍教育的基本概念、原理、方法以及教育领域从业人员基本素质要求。

（4）在这辞旧迎新之际,我谨代表单位党委及我本人的名义,向各位领导的到来表示热烈的欢迎！向单位全体职工及其家属同志们致以节日的问候,并祝各位新年好!

(5) 中医药凝聚着深邃的哲学智慧和中华民族几千年的健康养生理念,是中国古代科学的瑰宝,也是打开中华文明宝库的钥匙。

(6) 随着工信部今年陆续为多家企业发放5G商用牌照,我国正式进入5G商用元年。从今年6月开始,国内手机厂商华为、小米、中兴等纷纷推出首批5G手机。

(7) 新疆事务纯属中国内政。在涉疆问题上,中国政府和中国人民最有发言权,不容许任何国家和外部势力干预。

(8) 不忘初心、牢记使命。我们的初心就是为人民谋幸福、为民族谋复兴,我们想的就是千方百计让老百姓都能过上好日子。

(9) 演讲是一种受过训练后的表演,只要进行刻意训练,每个人都可以完成一场80分的演讲。但是所有的技巧都代替不了内容和思想本身。

(10) 爱国主义是中华民族的民族心、民族魂。南开大学具有光荣的爱国主义传统,这是南开的魂。

(11) 全民健身运动的普及和参与国际体育合作的程度,也是一个国家现代化程度的重要标志。

(12) "慈母手中线,游子身上衣"。感恩母亲,就是在她操劳后习惯地为她送上一杯白开水,给她捶捶背。"春蚕到死丝方尽,蜡炬成灰泪始干"。感恩老师,就是在教师节上送上一句贴心的祝福。"有福同享,有难同当"。感恩朋友,就是在他伤心时与之同担痛苦。

(13) Many persons have a wrong idea of what constitutes true happiness. It is not attained through self-gratification but through fidelity to a worthy purpose.

(14) Perseverance is a great element of success. If you only knock long enough and loud enough at the gate, you are sure to wake up someone.

(15) Perhaps the most valuable result of all education is the ability to make yourself do the thing you have to do, when it ought to be done, whether you like it or not.

(16) Life is pleasant. Death is peaceful. It's the transition that's troublesome.

(17) The ideal engineer is a composite: he is not a scientist, he is not a mathematician, he is not a socialist or a writer; but he may use the knowledge and techniques of any or all of these disciplines to solve engineering problems.

(18) An education isn't how much you have committed to memory, or even how much you know. It's being able to differentiate between what you do know and what you don't.

(19) My Father taught me how to be a man. He taught me that a real man doesn't take, he gives; he doesn't use force, he uses logic; he doesn't play the role of trouble-maker, but rather, trouble-shooter.

(20) I am among those who think that science has great beauty. A scientist in his laboratory is not only a technician, he is also a child placed before natural phenomena which impress him like a fairy tale.

练习 2

(1) The Internet is like alcohol in some sense. It <u>accentuates</u> what you would do anyway. If you want to be a loner, you can be more alone. If you want to connect, it makes it easier to connect.

词义解释：加重，强调。To accentuate something means to emphasize it or make it more noticeable.

(2) It is the mark of an educated mind to be able to <u>entertain</u> a thought without accepting it.

词义解释：心存。If you entertain a thought, you allow yourself to consider it as possible or as worth thinking about seriously.

(3) Speak properly, and in as few words as you can, but always plainly; for the end of speech is not <u>ostentation</u>, but to be understood.

词义解释：卖弄，炫耀。If you decide someone's behavior as ostentation, you are criticizing them for doing or buying things in order to impress people.

(4) There are in fact two things, science and opinion; the former <u>begets</u> knowledge, the latter ignorance.

词义解释：产生。To beget something means to cause it to happen or be created.

(5) I spent five years and I don't want to tell you how much money on designing and constructing that little video camera. And now that we've lost it, well, it's <u>back to the drawing board</u>.

词义解释：俚语，重新开始。本句翻译：这个小摄像头是我们花了5年时间做成的，花在设计和制作上的钱更是不计其数，可现在我们把它弄丢了，没办法，只能一切从头开始。

练习 3

音频 2.3-3 Social networking

Today let's talk about social networking. First let's talk about networks. Networks get things done. Whether it's sending a letter or lighting your home. Networks make it happen. To get from Chicago to Santa Fe, we need to see the network of roads that will get us there. We see that Chicago is connected to St Louis, which is connected to Dallas which is connected to Santa Fe. Of course, people networks can help us with finding jobs, meeting new friends, and finding partners. You know how it works. Bob is your friend, he knows Sally, and Sally's friend Joe has a job for you. This is a network of people—a social network. The problem with social networks in the real world is that most of the connections between people are hidden. Your network may have huge potential, but it's only as valuable as the people and connections that you can see. This problem is being solved by a type of website called a social networking site. These websites help you see connections that are hidden in the real world. Here's how it works. You sign up for a free account and fill out your profile. Then, you look for people you know. When you find someone, you click a button that says, "Add as Friend". Once you do this, you and that person have a connection on the website that others can see. They are a member of your network, and you are a member of theirs. What's really cool is that you can see who your friends know, and who your friends' friends know. You're no longer a stranger, so you can contact them more easily. This solves a real world problem because your network has hidden opportunities. Social networking sites make these connections between people visible. Like a map for a highway, they can show you the people network that can help you get to your next destination, whether it's a job, a new partner, or a great place to live. Your network is suddenly more useful. You can get started at these sites, LinkedIn, Facebook, and MySpace.

3.2.4 各国口音特点的参考答案

练习1

音频2.4-1 英特尔手持设备业务部总监在中国移动娱乐产业发展论坛上的讲话

- 会议名称：CGBC中国移动娱乐产业发展论坛。
- 会议目的：探讨3G时代的移动娱乐价值观、移动娱乐良好沟通平台的搭建等话题，共同挖掘中国移动娱乐的市场潜力，分享成功经验。
- 听众：移动网络专家、游戏开发商、硬件生产商、移动娱乐爱好者。
- 发言人：英特尔中国手持设备业务部总监。
- 发言语速：约130词/分钟。
- 话语特点：信息密集程度为中等，冗余程度为中等，语言比较口语化，逻辑一般，英语表达稍有问题。

Good afternoon! Chinajoy is a great event and I love the event because when

I look around the show floor, the excitement, the energy, the enthusiasm is great, I think it's wonderful. At Intel we are also very excited because this is a tremendous opportunity in the gaming space and for the first time, we now have an opportunity to extend the PC gaming experience into small devices and make it available on the go for delivering great user experience of the gamers, and for the developers and service providers, create a new business opportunity. I think the future is very exciting. I think that it'll continue to grow, I think most of us know that, know this… That almost 10,000 new websites get added every day. And in China alone there is more than 13 million registered websites. And if you look at overall users, you can see that China is No. 1 country with more than 338 million Internet users. From a growth standpoint, the Internet is going extremely fast and very vibrant. The biggest trend that's happening is in the mobile Internet space. It is a global trend and I believe that in China this will be huge. And if you look at the number of people who are accessing the Internet from the mobile devices, I believe last year more than 150 million people is getting online from their mobile devices. But I think the biggest... The expectation for the users is that they expect the same experience and performance when they access the Internet from any device. But, the 3G I think it is helping. But I believe that from a user experience standpoint they have a lot of opportunity to improve. And that is one of the areas Intel is focused on. In PRC the gaming and the media are the biggest drivers of the growth. And when you look at these, what you have seen here is some of the most popular online PC games today. And what amazes me is that some of these games took a very short time to become so popular in the market. But the second, more important thing for me is that some of the games become popular for a very long time. You can see that the games like Mir2 has been introduced maybe 4 or 5 years ago but still have a very strong user base. So the full aspect of the online gaming is extremely vibrant and great. It's very interesting for me to watch. If you look at the online gaming itself in PRC, the China is No. 1 market today. I think in 2008 more than \$2.8 billion of revenue (were) generated from the online games. But more interesting thing to me about this online game is innovation in the business model. I think China led in creating new business models, things like the point-card systems or the micro-transactions where users pay for value-added services. Those are some of the great innovations that happened in the online market place. And today many of the other countries, most of them are emulating the success that China had in these innovation areas.

The third element that is happening, I think it is a very important aspect, is the 3G transitions. With 3G transitions, now it is possible to extend the PC gaming experience from anywhere. That means that users can get access to their same favorite games from anytime anywhere. I think that creates a tremendous opportunity from a developer's standpoint and from a growth perspective I think created a tremendous opportunity.

Intel Atom architecture is now one year old, so recently we celebrated the first-year birthday for Atom processors. It is same as the PC architecture, fully compatible with the PC architecture. And the reason we designed the Atom is for very special devices, very small devices, for like netbook or hand-held devices where we can extend the same experience. And for the first time we can now bring exactly the same PC architecture into much smaller devices. And that's creating new opportunities in the market place. And combining Atom with what is happening in the 3G space, I think it's creating a huge opportunity.

So Atom is designed for new classes of devices, especially for the mobile devices. So when we designed the Atom architecture, we make sure that it has enough headroom to deliver the need of the ever-growing mobile Internet market. So it has headroom to really support the emerging usages on the mobile devices. Secondly, it is also based on exactly the same architecture as the PC architecture so any applications that you have on PC will be fully binary compatible with Atom. That means the applications that is written for PC can be easily migrated to this new platform of devices. The second... The third element is its performance capability. We have rich features and capability together, great user experience such as 3D performance and the media performance and also support for some of the latest Internet technology. The most important aspect especially for mobile devices is the power. And with the low-power architecture we have been really able to bring in Atom in the very small devices, at the same time providing the performance and the rich user experience. And Intel is very focused on making sure that we deliver the rich user experience while the objective of Atom is exactly like we want. We want to deliver the rich, the great user experience while extending mobility without sacrificing the performance or... If you look at our roadmap, I believe we continue to invest in creating, bringing new-generation products, and you can see that there are 100% innovational products already under development.

Each one, we are making sure that they are 100% compatible so that the minute you made today can be fully leveraged even when we come up with new-generation products in the future. Currently we have a product and in 2010 we will be introducing a new product which will be almost double the performance but at the same time we will be reducing power by 50 times. And in 2011, we will come up with a new product again, which will once again deliver high performance at the same time reducing the power consumption.

So in summary, when you combine the 3G revolution that's going on in China and combine with the Intel Atom architecture, you can really hope to bring the entire online PC experience on portable devices. I think that's a tremendous opportunity.

No. 2 is the Atom will deliver very compelling user experience without sacrificing either compatibility or the performance. I think that's one of the unique advantages of interlocking architecture. And one thing, if you are developers, you did pay attention to is that given the architecture, given the fact that we are extending the exactly the same PC architecture from all the way to the desktop, to notebook to netbook, to hand-held devices, you should be thinking about optimizing your games from the beginning for multiple screen sizes. I think that creates a lot of opportunity for your ability to run these different multiple devices. We create a lot of opportunity for you in the future. And the last one is Atom will definitely establish Intel leadership in a variety of new generation platforms. And I think the opportunity is there and we are very excited about it. And my call to action will be if you are not thinking about these devices, it's the time to start thinking about them now because that's where the market is doing better, we are going, I think that's the opportunities.

17.2 第3章口译基本技能(二)记忆的参考答案

1. 3.3 信息组块法的参考答案

练习

音频 3.3-1 人工智能定义[80]

人工智能的定义可以分为两部分,即"人工"和"智能"。"人工"比较好理解,争议性也不大。有时我们会要考虑什么是人力所能及制造的,或者人自身的智能程度有没有高到可以创造人工智能的地步,等等。但总的来说,"人工系统"就是通常意义下的人工系统。关于什么是"智能",就问题多多了。这涉及到其他诸如意识、自我、思维等问题。人唯一了解的智能是人本身的智能,这是普遍认同的观点。但是我们对我们自身智能的理解都非常有限,对构成人的智能的必要元素也了解有限,所以就很难定义什么是"人工"制造的"智能"了。因此人工智能的研究往往涉及对人的智能本身的研究。其他关于动物或其他人造系统的智能也普遍被认为是人工智能相关的研究课题。

提示:首先将这一段的记忆组块为"人工"和"智能"两块,然后再进一步增加细节。

2.3.4 逻辑分层法的参考答案

练习1

音频3.4-1　张璐:如何给总理做翻译[81]

给领导人当翻译,首先要有较高的政治敏感。"翻译时要保持对原文的忠实,做到如实翻译。"她举例说:"在这次记者会上,温总理澄清所谓中国在哥本哈根大会上'傲慢'的传言时提到,'……我从一位欧洲领导人那里知道,那天晚上有一个少数国家参加的会议……'因为我跟着总理去过哥本哈根,知道他指的'那位领导人'是谁,也知道这个人的性别。但当时总理并未提及这位领导人的名字,所以我在翻译时也不能直接说出这个人的名字,甚至不能表示性别。英文里有男'他'和女'她'的区别,所以在翻译时,我选择用被动句式来表达。"

当一个好翻译还要了解领导人说话的意图,可以结合当时的语境去"巧译"。她说:"大家对我在翻译总理古诗词时的表现给予了肯定。其实,古诗词翻译并不是我的强项,哪怕能再多给我一秒钟时间,我都能翻译得更加准确。"张璐认为,自己这次的表现,主要归功于平时的积累。"我发现总理最喜欢引用刘禹锡、王安石和屈原的诗词。所以,给总理当翻译时,要结合他说话的语境,知道总理在这个时刻引用古诗词是想要传达怎样的一种精神。这一点很重要。"

提示:先记第一层的主干信息。

- 具有较高的政治敏感。
- 了解领导人说话的意图。

练习2

音频3.4-2　如何不负此生——沈祖尧[82]

我祈求你们离校后,都能过着"不负此生"的生活。你们或会问,怎样才算是"不负此生"的生活呢?

其一,我希望你们能俭朴地生活。过去的三至五年间,大家完成了大学各项课程,以真才实学和专业知识好好地装备了自己。我肯定大家都能学以致用,前程锦绣。但容我提醒各位一句:快乐与金钱和物质的丰盛并无必然关系。一个温馨的家、简单的衣着、健康的饮食,就是乐之所在。漫无止境地追求奢华,远不如俭朴生活那样能带给你幸福和快乐。

其二,我希望你们能过高尚的生活。我们的社会有很多阴暗面:不公、剥削、诈骗,等等。我呼吁大家,无比庄敬自强,公平待人,不可欺负弱势的人,也不可以做损及他人或自己的事。高尚的生活是对一己的良知无悔,维护公义,事事均以道德为依归。

其三,是我希望你们能过谦卑的生活。我们要有服务他人的谦卑心怀,时刻不忘为社会、国家以至全人类出力。一个谦卑的人并不固执己见,而是会虚怀若谷地聆听他人的言论。

假如你拥有高尚的情操、过着俭朴的生活并且存谦卑的心,那么你的生活必会非常充实。你会是个爱家庭、重朋友,而且是关心自己健康的人。你不会在意社会能给你什么,但会十分重视你能为社会出什么力。

提示:先记第一层的主干信息。
- 简朴。
- 高尚。
- 谦卑。

练习 3

音频 3.4-3　十大科技趋势[83]

(1) 人工智能从感知智能向认知智能演进。

人工智能已经在"听、说、看"等感知智能领域达到或超越了人类水准,但在认知智能领域还处于初级阶段。认知智能将从认知心理学、脑科学及人类社会历史中汲取灵感,实现从感知智能到认知智能的关键突破。

(2) 计算存储一体化。

类似于脑神经结构的存内计算架构将数据存储单元和计算单元融为一体,能显著减少数据搬运,极大提高计算速度和能效。

(3) 工业互联网的超融合。

工业互联网将实现超融合。制造企业将实现设备自动化、搬送自动化和排产自动化,进而实现柔性制造。同时工厂上下游制造产线能实时调整和协同。这将大幅提升工厂的生产效率及企业的盈利能力。

(4) 机器间大规模协作成为可能。

随着物联网协同感知技术、5G 通信技术的发展,将实现机器彼此合作、相互竞争,共同完成目标任务。例如,仓储机器人可协作完成货物分拣,无人驾驶车可以感知路况,群体无人机协同可以打通最后一公里配送。

(5) 模块化降低芯片设计门槛。

传统芯片设计模式无法高效应对芯片需求。开源芯片设计、模板化芯片设计方法推动了芯片设计与开源芯片的发展。

(6) 规模化生产级区块链应用将走入大众。

区块链服务将进一步降低企业应用区块链技术的门槛,专为区块链设计的各类固化核心算法的硬件芯片也将应运而生,实现物理世界资产与链上资产的锚定。

(7) 量子计算进入攻坚期。

"量子霸权"之争让量子计算再次成为世界科技焦点。超导量子计算芯片的成果增强了行业对超导路线和大规模量子计算的乐观预期。

(8) 新材料推动半导体器件革新。

当前,以硅为主体的经典晶体管很难维持半导体产业的持续发展。新材料将通过全新物理机制实现全新的逻辑、存储及互联概念和器件,推动半导体产业的革新。

(9) 保护数据隐私的 AI 技术将加速落地。

使用 AI 技术保护数据隐私正在成为新的技术热点,它能够保证数据安全和隐私,并实现数据的价值。

(10) 云成为 IT 技术创新的中心。

随着云技术的深入发展,云已经演变成所有 IT 技术创新的中心。云已经贯穿新型芯片、新型数据库、大数据、AI、物联网、区块链等,云正在重新定义 IT 的一切。

提示:第一层的主干信息如下。

1. AI 从感知智能向认知智能演进。
2. 计算存储一体化。
3. 工业互联网超融合。
4. 机器间大规模协作成为可能。
5. 模块化降低芯片设计门槛。
6. 规模化生产级区块链走入大众。
7. 量子计算进入攻坚期。
8. 新材料推动半导体器件革新。
9. 保护数据隐私的 AI 技术加速落地。
10. 云成为 IT 技术创新的中心。

3.3.5 顺时记忆法的参考答案

练习

音频 3.5-1　林金桐小传[84]

林金桐出生于江苏丹阳,一岁半时失去了父亲,自幼自立、自强和奋发向上。正是这种个性促使他成为上海市复兴中学的高才生,成为北大物理系同学中的佼佼者。后来,他来到河北一所农村中学当中学老师,而且一当就是 8 年,他没有因为条件艰苦而放弃责任,没有因为落后而失去信心。这 8 年里,他为穷乡僻壤培养了大学生,为乡村中学装上了日光灯,方圆百十里地,他奏响了第一架手风琴优美的旋律,组织了乡里第一支学生合唱队。后来他成为英国伦敦大学皇家学院的研究员,再后来成为北京邮电大学的系主任、副校长、校长。

提示:记忆要点是在记忆这段话的时候,应该按照以下时间节点帮助记忆。
- 出生:江苏丹阳。
- 一岁半:丧父。
- 中学:上海复兴中学。
- 大学:北大物理系。
- 后来8年:河北农村某中学教师。
- 后来:英国伦敦大学皇家学院研究员。
- 再后来:北京邮电大学校长。

音频3.5-2　扎克伯格小传[85]

扎克伯格出生于纽约的一个犹太人家庭。高中时,扎克伯格很喜欢程序设计,特别是沟通工具与游戏类。2004年,他在哈佛的大学宿舍创办了Facebook。短短数年,这一网站迅速风靡全世界,如今,它已成为世界上最重要的社交网站之一。20岁的扎克伯格虽然考入知名的哈佛大学,但却是该学校计算机系和心理学系的辍学生。有媒体曾对他俭朴的生活方式进行了报道,据悉,扎克伯格成为全球最年轻的亿万富翁之后,依然住着租来的一套一室一厅的小公寓,地板上放着的一个床垫、两个椅子、一张桌子,这就是全部家具。他的早餐通常都是一碗麦片。每天,他都走路或骑自行车上班。

提示:在记忆这段话的时候,应该按照以下时间节点帮助记忆。
- 出生:纽约,犹太人。
- 高中:程序设计。
- 2004年:哈佛、Facebook。
- 数年后:风靡世界。
- 如今:世界最重要的社交网络之一。
- 20岁:计算机、心理系辍学。
- 亿万富翁后:简朴生活方式。

音频3.5-3　李彦宏演讲[86]

如果让我回想的话,还是应该从我北大的这四年生活说起。说实话,这四年对我的影响是非常大的。在我的印象当中,1988年,也就是我入学的第二年,赶上了北大九十周年的校庆,一百周年的校庆没有赶上,非常遗憾。但是九十周年的校庆对我来说已经是非常深刻了。那时北大出版了一本书,叫《精神的魅力》。当中的一些话和一些概念,在往后的十几年当中,一直在指导我做出人生的选择,指导我的思考,让我去选择最适合我做的事情,以及去选择真正能够对人们的生活发生改变、产生影响的一条人生道路。

如同很多北大毕业的同学一样,1991年我从北大毕业以后,就到美国读书去了。在那里,导师要求我跟踪世界上最先进的信息检索技术。到1994年的时候,我放弃了在美国大学里读博士的机会,进入工业界,因为那时候我看到很多的机会在工业界产生。我先到了华尔街,做了有关金融信息的检索系统,也帮助设计了华尔街日报的网络版。1997年夏天,我到了硅谷,加入互联网早期的一个搜索引擎公司,在硅谷,我知道了什么是创新。一直到今天,当人们提起硅谷的时候,可能第一概念想到的还是创新,硅谷就是依靠它这种不竭的创新动力和坚持不懈的创业精神,吸引着一代又一代的技术人员,在那里实现自己的梦想,实现自己的技术理想,所以跟很多在硅谷的工程师一样,我也有一个理想、一个梦想,那就是用技术来改变世界。

提示:在记忆这段话的时候,应该按照以下时间节点帮助记忆。
- 90年校庆。
- 1991年。
- 1994年。
- 1997年夏天。
- 直到现在。

音频3.5-4 Frank Hawkins[87]

Yesterday afternoon Frank Hawkins was telling me about his experiences as a young man. Before he retired, Frank was the head of a very large business company, but as a boy he used to work in a small shop. It was his job to repair bicycles and at that time he used to work fourteen hours a day. He saved money for years and in 1958 he bought a small workshop of his own. In his twenties Frank used to make spare parts for aeroplanes. At that time he had two helpers. In a few years the small workshop had become a large factory which employed seven hundred and twenty-eight people. Frank smiled when he remembered his hard early years and the long road to success. He was still smiling when the door opened and his wife came in. She wanted him to repair their grandson's bicycle!

提示:在记忆这段话的时候,应该按照时间节点进行整理加工,帮助记忆。
- 小时候:在一家小铺里做工。
- 1958年:买下小铺子。
- 20多岁:生产飞机零配件、两个帮手。
- 几年之后:小铺子→大工厂(728人)。
- 退休前:商业公司经理。
- 昨天下午:回忆过往,妻子,修孙子自行车。

音频 3.5-5　Wilma Subra

Wilma Subra had no intention of becoming a public speaker. After graduating from college with degrees in chemistry and microbiology, she went to work at Gulf South Research Institute in Louisiana. As part of her job, she conducted field research on toxic substances in the environment, often in minority communities located near large industrial polluters. She found many families were being exposed high, sometimes deadly levels of chemicals and other toxic substances. But she was not allowed to make her information public. Frustrated by these restrictions, Subra left her job in 1981, created her own company and has devoted the past two decades to helping people fight back against giant industrial polluters. She works with families and community groups to conduct environmental tests, interpret test results, and organize for change. Because of her efforts, dozens of toxic sites across the country have been cleaned up. And one chemical industry spokesperson calls her "a top gun" for the environmental movement. How has Subra achieved all this? Partly through her scientific training, partly through her commitment to environmental justice. But just as important is her ability to communicate with people through public speaking. "Public speaking," she says, "is the primary vehicle I use for reaching people." If you had asked Subra before 1981, "Do you see yourself as a major public speaker?" She would have laughed at the idea. Yet today she gives more than 100 presentations a year. Along the way, she's lectured at Harvard, testified before Congress, and addressed audiences in 40 states, as well as in Mexico, Canada, and Japan.

提示：在记忆这段话的时候，应该按照时间节点进行整理加工，帮助记忆。
- 毕业前。
- 工作后。
- 1981年辞职后。
- 现状。

4．3.6 形象记忆法的参考答案

练习1

提示：均是利用形象化的方法。

第一组略。

第二组可以想象火灾情景，联想"9·11"事件，会更容易记忆。

第三组可以利用形象化＋归类的方法，如图17.1所示。

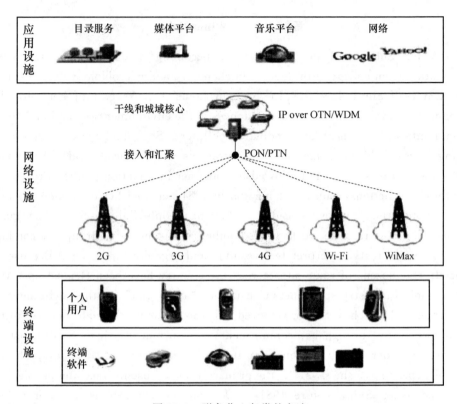

图 17.1　形象化＋归类的方法

练习 2

音频 3.6-1　I love trees

　　I love trees because they have many different shades of green, so many that it is almost impossible to count. When I paint a picture of a tree I use many shades of green and many more shades of brown. My favorite thing about trees is that they always seem to have a glow around them. I love trees because they always smell so fresh and clean. I like to go to the nursery because I love the smell of the trees, it's so refreshing. It's a glass of cool water on a hot day, or a damp cloth on a hot forehead.

　　One of my favorite things about trees is that they are fun to climb. I started climbing trees when I was very little. I especially like to climb my grandpa's apple tree. I love to wind through the branches, and climb up to a board that has been placed there. Once up, I like to think and relax or bring a book up there with me. It's fun to let my imagination run away with me while eating apples.

　　I love trees in the autumn when they display their beautiful colors. In the autumn time, splashes of red, yellow, orange, and green decorate the mountainsides. The maples go red, the oak and aspen go yellow while the evergreens maintain their beautiful shade of green.

Trees make life possible because they use the carbon dioxide and release oxygen which makes it so that we can breathe. If we exterminate trees, the effects could be fatal. There may be global warming, lack of oxygen, and we would definitely not have any lumber or paper.

17.3 第4章口译基本技能(三)笔记的参考答案

1. 4.3 口译笔记符号举例的参考答案

练习

音频4.3-1和音频4.3-2 中印希望加强经济纽带

The Chinese and Indian foreign ministers have discussed ways to ease tensions and increase economic ties.

中国和印度外长探讨了化解紧张和加强经济纽带的措施,

It was the first high-level meeting between the Asian powers since a new government took power in India.

这是自印度新政府掌权以来这两个亚洲大国之间的首次高端会议。

Chinese Foreign Minister Wang Yi and his Indian counterpart, Sushma Swaraj, met for three hours in the Indian capital New Delhi.

中国外长王毅和印度外长瓦拉吉在印度首都新德里进行了三小时的会谈。

Afterwards, Indian official said both countries agreed much could be done to improve their economic relationship.

随后,印度官方称两国都认为需要做更多努力来改善两国经济关系。

Gautam Bambawale of India's foreign ministry says China will consider the possibility of expanding economic cooperation between the two countries.

印度外交部的班浩然称中国将考虑扩展两国经济合作的可能性。

"Foreign Minister Wang Yi also said that the economic development of India is something that is supported by the Chinese government."

班浩然说,"外交部部长王毅也说印度的经济发展得到了中国的支持。"

Indian Officials say more Chinese investment could reduce India's trade deficit with China.

印度官员称，增加中国投资将减少印度对中国的贸易逆差。

That deficit has increased to more than ＄30 billion. India says it wants more Chinese investment in roads, ports and other systems.

这一逆差目前已增加到300多亿美元。印度称希望中国更多投资于道路、港口和其他系统。

India also would like increased investment in manufacturing-areas in which India is behind China.

印度还希望能增加在制造业的投资，在这个领域印度落后于中国。

Some foreign policy observers in India expect new Prime Minister Narendra Modi to increase economic ties with China as he tries to meet his campaign promise to develop India's economy.

印度一些外交政策观察家期待新总理莫迪能加强与中国的经济纽带，从而兑现他发展印度经济的竞选承诺。

【笔记参考】

此处笔记参考如图17.2所示。

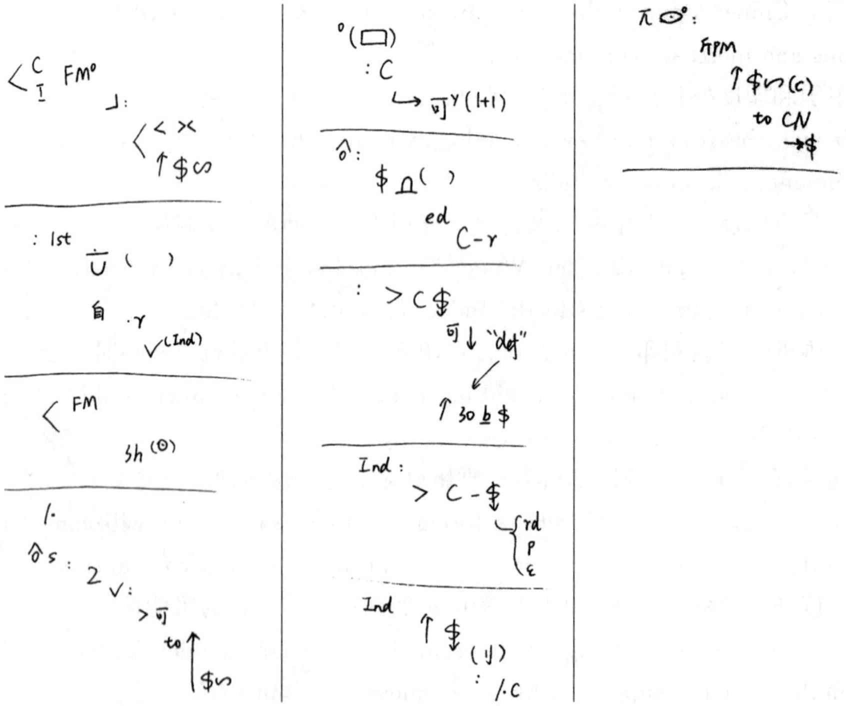

图17.2　此处的笔记参考

第 17 章　第 1 篇中练习的参考答案

【笔记解释】

对应的笔记解释如图 17.3 所示。

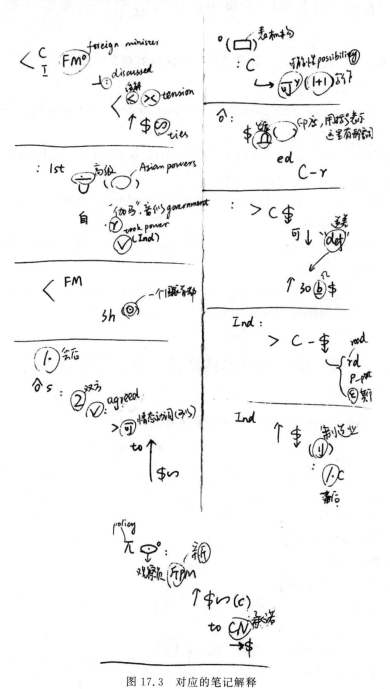

图 17.3　对应的笔记解释

17.4 第5章口译基本技能(四)表达的参考答案

1. 5.5 英语正式语体与非正式语体的区别的参考答案

练习1

(1) Consumer interest in electronic billing and payment is <u>getting bigger and bigger</u>. (increasing)

(2) The competition faced by U.S. growers from imports of fresh vegetables has <u>gotten more intense</u>. (intensified)

(3) Many urban areas <u>do not have enough</u> land to build new public schools. (have insufficient/lack)

(4) Allergic reactions to local dental anesthesia <u>do not happen very often</u>. (rarely occur)

(5) The doors on these ferries were <u>made bigger to make it easier to load and unload</u> vehicles. (enlarged to facilitate loading and unloading)

17.5 第6章口译基本技能(五)数字口译的参考答案

1. 6.2 数字增减及倍数的译法的参考答案

练习1

(1) 38 5176 0000

(2) 46 5494 6000

(3) 90 4578 1038

(4) 135 7500 0000

(5) 781 1203 0331

(6) 4782 4300 0000

(7) 6976 7820 1000

练习2

(1) 泰国:514 000;61 797 751;Bangkok。

(2) 英国:244 820;59 647 790;London。

(3) 法国:547 030;59 551 227;Paris。

（4）意大利：301 230；57 679 825；Rome。

（5）刚果：2 345 410；53 624 718；Kinshasa 金莎萨。

（6）乌克兰：603 700；48 760 474；Kiev 基辅。

（7）韩国：98 480；47 904 370；Seoul。

（8）南非：1 219 912；43 586 097；Pretoria 比勒陀利亚。

第18章 第2篇中各章的译文

18.1 第7章接待外宾的译文

对话全文(中方为 C;外方为 F;口译员为 I)

C:请问您是来自美国的普里斯先生吗?

I:Are you Mr. Price from America?

F:Yep. That's me. Please do call me Larry.

I:是的,是我,叫我徕瑞吧。

C:好的,很荣幸见到您,Larry! 我是杨思嘉,英文名是 Scarlet。

I:OK,it's a great honor to meet you, Larry! I am Yang Sijia,my English name is Scarlet.

F:Nice to meet you,Scarlet.

I:很高兴见到你,Scarlet。

C:我们的车就在外面,这边不让停车,咱们边走边谈好吗?

I:Our car is just over there. Parking is not allowed here. Shall we go and talk on the way to the hotel?

F:Sure. Let's go.

I:好的,我们走吧!

C:您是第一次来中国吗?

I:Is this your first trip to China?

F:Actually not. My wife June is a Chinese. We had been pen pals before we first met face to face in Beijing in 2000. We married three months later.

I:不是的。我太太 June 是中国人。我们曾经是笔友,然后 2000 年我们第一次在北京见面。三个月后我们结婚了。

C:听起来很浪漫呢! 真是"有缘千里来相会"呢。

I：Sounds romantic! As the saying goes, though born a thousand li apart, souls which are one shall meet.

F：Well said! I like Chinese sayings. They are full of wisdom and puns. Chinese culture is so broad and profound.

I：说得好。我喜欢中国的谚语,又有智慧又俏皮。中国文化真是博大精深。

C：看来您真是喜欢中国。

I：I see you do like China.

F：Indeed. Actually, I plan to settle down here when this business is done. June needs to take care of her grandparents, they are in their 90s.

I：是的。实际上,我打算这次生意做完,就在中国定居,June 也需要照顾她的爷爷奶奶,他们已经九十多岁了。

C：爷爷奶奶?

I：Grandparents?

F：Yes. June was raised by her grandparents. Now that they are old, June will come back to look after them.

I：是的,June 是爷爷奶奶带大的。现在他们老了,June 回来照顾他们。

C：真孝顺! 就像俗语说的,羔羊跪哺,乌鸦反哺。

I：What a filial granddaughter! Just as saying goes, the lamb kneels down to suckle, the crown feeds its parents.

F：What do you mean?

I：什么意思呢?

C：是表示对父母的感恩:羔羊跪下表达感激和敬意,乌鸦长大后喂养年迈的父母。

I：Those were signs of their gratitude to their parents. The lamb kneels down to show its gratitude and respect to its mother. The crown feeds its old parents once it grows up.

F：How touching! Filial piety is truly a merit of the Chinese people. Thanks for the teaching. In return, I'd like to teach you a few Chinese characters.

I：真让人感动! 孝顺是中华民族的一个优秀品质。受教了。作为回报,我教你几个中国汉字吧。

C：您教我汉字?! 我没听错吧? 有意思,我洗耳恭听。

I：You teach me Chinese characters? ! Seriously? Interesting! I am all ears.

F：Yep. Now let's begin by the character "wo".

I：没错,我们先从汉字"我"开始吧。

18.2 第8章宴请饮食的译文

对话全文(中方为 C;外方为 F;口译员为 I)

C:杰克逊先生,我们到了。今晚我们吃中国菜。

I: Mr. Jackson, here we are. We'll have Chinese food tonight.

F: Wow, what a magnificent restaurant! It is decorated in red and gold, typical Chinese colors. I think the Chinese food here must be very delicious.

I:哇,这家饭店真气派,用红色和金色装饰,典型的中国颜色。我想这家的中国菜一定很好吃吧。

C:这的确是一家有名的餐厅。杰克逊先生,这是菜单。今天您是客人,请随便点。

I: This is indeed a famous restaurant. Mr. Jackson, here is the menu. Please be my guest and order whatever you want.

F: Thanks. But I don't know anything about Chinese food. What would you recommend?

I:谢谢,不过我对中国菜不了解,您有什么推荐的吗?

C:请问您喜欢吃辣吗?

I: Would you like to eat spicy food?

F:I'm afraid I can't. I love fried mutton slices and baked fish with butter in my country, does China have something similar?

I:我吃不了辣。在我们国家我喜欢吃炸羊肉片和奶油烤鱼,中国也有类似的菜吗?

C:中国也有很多关于羊肉的菜,如烤羊排和清蒸羊肉。鱼的话在中国不同的菜系中做法会各不相同,最常见的是松鼠鳜鱼和水煮鱼。

I: China also has a lot of dishes made of mutton, such as roast lamb chops and steamed lamb. As for fish, there is a variety of dishes cooked in different manners. The most common are Squirrel-shaped mandarin fish and Boiled fish.

F:The Squirrel-shaped mandarin fish soundsyummy, what do you think?

I:松鼠鳜鱼听起来很好吃。您觉得呢?

C:很好的选择!中国菜十分注重"色""香""味"三方面。我想这道菜应该和您以前吃的鱼味道不一样。

I: Good choice! Chinese dishes attaches great importance to three aspects, namely, color, aroma and taste. I think this dish might taste quite different from what you have had before.

F: That'll be great. Well, I can't find coffee on the menu, you guys don't drink coffee?

I:不错。我没在你们的菜单里看见咖啡,你们不喝吗?

C:我们一般不在吃饭的时候喝咖啡。来点啤酒怎么样,北京当地产的燕京啤酒在全国都非常有名。

I: We usually don't have coffee in dinner time. How about beer? The local beer-Yanjing beer is a well-known brand in China.

F:OK. Could you tell me about the custom of drinking in China?

I:好的。中国人喝酒有什么特殊的规矩吗?

C:我们会以"干杯"的方式向对方敬酒,需要一口喝干杯中的酒,表示敬酒人的心诚和相聚的欢乐。

I: We usually say "Gan Bei" when toasting each other. And you need to dry up the glasses to show your sincerity and joy of gathering.

F:Sounds very interesting. But for me, it might be a challenge, since I get drunk quickly. And are there any taboos about using chopsticks?

I:听起来十分有趣,对我来说或许是个挑战,因为我酒量不行。请问,使用筷子有什么禁忌吗?

C:筷子作为用餐工具,是不能用来指向别人的,这在中国是不礼貌的行为。还有就是不能把筷子竖直插在米饭碗里,因为这象征着祭祀。实际上,在中国请人吃饭更多是一种社交,在饭桌上人们可以增进了解,成为朋友。

I: Chopsticks as a tableware can't be used to point to others, which is considered bad manners in China. Also don't stick your chopsticks upright in a bowl of rice, which mimics a funeral rite. In fact, taking someone to dinner is more of a social activity. People get to know each other better and even become friends over dinner.

F:I am sure we will become good friends.

I:我相信我们会成为好朋友的。

C:我同意。杰克逊先生,来,为我们的友谊和合作干杯。

I: I agree. Mr. Jackson, may I propose a toast, to our friendship and cooperation, Cheers!

F:Gan Bei!

I:干杯!

18.3 第 9 章礼仪致辞的译文

音频 9.2-1 第一段

下面是 9.2 节中演讲的原文和译文。

原文[66]20-21 如下。

各位嘉宾,女士们、先生们:

初秋时节的北京,万木葱茏,金风送爽。今天,第二十二届万国邮政联盟大会将在这里隆重开幕。这是万国邮政联盟成立 125 年和中国加入万国邮政联盟 85 年来,首次在中国举行这样的大会。我代表中国政府和中国人民,并以我个人的名义,向大会致以衷心的祝贺!向与会的各国代表和来宾表示诚挚的欢迎!

人类即将迈入新的世纪。在这样的时刻,大家共同探讨面向二十一世纪邮政发展的战略和行动纲领,其意义十分重要。我相信,这次大会将在国际邮政史上留下光荣的一页。……

最后,预祝大会取得圆满成功。祝各位在北京度过愉快的时光。

现在,我宣布:第二十二届万国邮政联盟大会开幕!谢谢!

译文[66]213-214 如下。

Distinguished Guests, Ladies and Gentlemen,

Today we are gathering here for the grand opening ceremony of the 22nd Universal Postal Congress (UPC) at a time when golden autumn is embracing Beijing, bringing refreshing and pleasant breeze to the capital city. This Congress is the first of its kind ever convened in China in the 125-year history of the Universal Postal Union (UPU) and in the past 85 years since China's accession to the organization. On behalf of the Chinese Government and people, and in my own name, I wish to extend our sincere congratulations on the convocation of the Congress and our hearty welcome to all the deputies and guests.

Mankind now stands at the threshold of the 21st century. At this important moment, it is of great significance that we meet here and discuss the postal service development strategies and programs of action for the new century. I am confident that this Congress will be remembered as a splendid chapter in the annals of the international postal services…

Finally, I wish the 22nd UPC a complete success and wish all of you a pleasant stay in Beijing.

Now, I have the pleasure to declare the 22nd Universal Postal Congress open. Thank you!

视频 9.2-2[67] 第二段

演讲全文及译文[67]如下。

Bridging the Standardization Gap
缩小标准化差距
ITU Secretary-General Houlin Zhao's Message
on World Telecommunication and Information Society Day
国际电联秘书长赵厚麟世界电信和信息社会日致辞

On 17 May, we will be celebrating the 50th World Telecommunication and Information Society Day.

我们将于5月17日庆祝第50个世界电信和信息社会日。

This year, we will focus on "bridging the standardization gap."

今年,我们将重点关注"缩小标准化差距"。

Setting standards is a fundamental pillar of ITU's mission as the specialized agency of the United Nations for information and communication technologies.

作为联合国负责信息通信技术的专门机构,国际电联使命的一个基本支柱就是制定标准。

You want to connect to the internet, enjoy a sports event on TV, listen to radio in your car or watch a video on your smartphone? ITU standards make it possible.

您想上网,在电视上观看体育赛事,在汽车里收听广播,或者在智能手机上看视频吗?国际电联制定的标准使之成为可能。

The upcoming 5G standards, especially if coupled with artificial intelligence, will support a new range of applications which we will soon take for granted: from self-driving cars to safer and smart cities.

即将到来的5G标准,特别是在与人工智能结合之后,将支持一系列我们将很快视为理所当然的新应用:从自动驾驶汽车到更为安全的智慧城市。

ITU standards ensure interoperability, open up global markets and spur innovation and growth. They are good for developed and developing countries.

国际电联的标准能够确保互操作性,有利于开拓全球市场并刺激创新和增长。发达国家和发展中国家均可因此受益。

They help accelerate ICTs for all Sustainable Development Goals.

这将有助于加速利用信息通信技术实现所有可持续发展目标。

I call upon ITU Member States, industry members, SMEs and academia, together with UN sister agencies, our partners and all stakeholders, to support ITU's "Bridging the Standardization gap" programme and prosperity and well-being for all. Thank you.

我向国际电联成员国、行业成员、大小公司和学术界,以及联合国姐妹机构、我们的合作伙伴及所有利益攸关方发出呼吁,请大家支持国际电联开展的"缩小标准化差距"项目,为实现所有人的繁荣、福祉而添砖加瓦。谢谢各位。

练习1

演讲全文及译文[68]如下。

音频9.3-1　Secretary-General Message on World Telecommunication and Information Society Day
联合国秘书长2010世界电信和信息社会日致辞

In today's world, telecommunications are more than just a basic service-they are a means to promote development, improve society and save lives. This will be all the more true in the world of tomorrow.

当今世界,电信不仅仅是一项基本服务,它是促进发展、改进社会和拯救生命的一种手段。未来的世界更将如此。

The importance of telecommunications was on display in the wake of the earthquake which devastated Haiti earlier this year. Communications technologies were used to coordinate aid, optimize resources and provide desperately sought information about the victims. The International Telecommunications Union (ITU) and its commercial partners contributed scores of satellite terminals and helped to provide wireless communications to help disaster relief and clean-up efforts.

在今年初发生了摧毁海地的地震之后,电信的重要性体现了出来。通信技术被用来协调援助、优化资源和提供迫切需要的伤亡人员信息。国际电信联盟及其商业伙伴捐赠了数十部卫星终端,并帮助提供无线通信服务,以协助救灾和清理工作。

I welcome those efforts and, more broadly, the work of ITU and others to promote broadband access in rural and remote areas around the world.

对于这些努力,更广泛地讲,对于国际电联和其他各方促进世界各地农村和偏远地区宽带接入的工作,我表示欢迎。

Greater access can mean faster progress toward the Millennium Development Goals (MDGs). The Internet drives trade, commerce and even education. Telemedicine is improving health care. Earth monitoring satellites are being used to address climate change. And green technologies are promoting cleaner cities.

更广泛的宽带接入可能意味着在实现千年发展目标方面取得更快的进展。因特网推动了贸易、商业、甚至教育的发展。远程医疗正在改善保健服务。地球监测卫星正被用于应对气候变化。绿色技术正在使城市变得更加清洁。

As these innovations grow in importance, so, too, does the need to bridge the digital divide.

随着这些创新的重要性日益加强,也越来越有必要弥补数字鸿沟。

The theme of this year's observance, "Better Cities, Better Life with ICTs," is a reminder that communications technologies must be employed – and disposed of – in a manner that raises living standards while protecting the environment.

今年的纪念活动以"利用信通技术优化城市和生活"为主题,它提醒我们,必须以提高生活水平并同时保护环境的方式采用和处理通信技术。

The United Nations is committed to ensuring that people everywhere have equitable access to information and communication technologies. On this International Day, let us resolve to fully harness the great potential of the digital revolution in the service of life-saving relief operations, sustainable development and lasting peace.

联合国致力于确保任何地方的人都可以公平地利用信息和通信技术。值此国际日之际,让我们下定决心,在拯救生命的救济活动、可持续发展和持久和平中充分发挥数字革命的巨大潜力。

【笔记参考】

此处的笔记参考如图 18.1 所示。

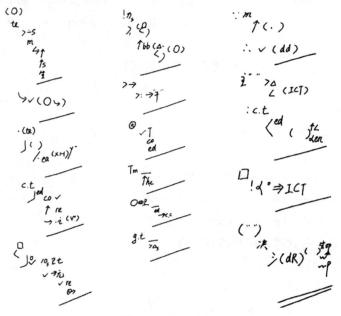

图 18.1　笔记参考

18.4　第10章参展参会的译文

对话全文(中方为 C;外方为 F;口译员为 I)

Dialogue 1

Scenario: initial business talk.

C:您好!我是销售代表王雷,有什么可以帮您?

I:Hi! I'm Wang Lei, sales representative. How can I help you?

F:Hi! I'm interested in your range of sweaters. Could I look at your samples?

I:您好!我对您公司的针织衫很感兴趣。可以看看样品吗?

C:当然可以,我陪您到处看看,边走边讲解我们的产品。这些产品在国内外很受欢迎。

I:Sure. I'll show you around and explain our products as we go along. They've been very popular home and abroad.

F:That'll be great.

I:那太好了。

C:右边是我们的最新产品,您是否愿意先看看货?

I:The products on the right are the latest. Would you like to have a look?

F:Quite interesting, this is the style I am looking for. How about the prices?

I:有意思,这正是我想找的款式。价格如何?

C:这是价格表。

I:Here is the price list.

F:Thank you. What about delivery time?

I:谢谢,何时能发货?

C:我们收到订单后几天之内即可发货。

I:We can deliver the goods within the days upon receipt of your order.

F:Can I have the catalog for all styles?

I:能给我所有款式针织衫的目录吗?

C:好的。给您。

I:Of course. Here you are.

F:I'll come again tomorrow.

I：明天我再来。

C：好的,明天见。

I： All right. See you tomorrow.

Dialogue 2

Scenario：bargaining in negotiations.

C：我们开始吧?

I：Shall we begin?

F：Sure. I have read through the materials of your company and found the price you quote is too high.

I：好的。我看了贵公司的材料,你们的报价太高了。

C：俗话说一分钱一分货,如果您考虑一下质量,就会觉得我们的价格是非常合理的。我们用的原材料是最好的,而且现在全国物价都在上涨,原材料成本也上涨了。

I：As the saying goes, every extra penny deserves its value. You'll find our price very reasonable considering the quality of our products. We use the best raw materials whose cost has gone up since prices are soaring all over the country.

F：Why not try meeting each other half way?

I：为什么不试试各让一步呢?

C：如果你们订单下得大一些,我们价格也可以更优惠。

I：If your order is bulk, we may offer a better price.

F：We would like to order 50 000 sweaters. As far as a trial order is concerned, the quantity is by no means small. And generally speaking, people profit from a trial order. I hope you understand.

I：我们买5万件毛衣,作为试购,这个数量绝不算少了。一般来说,试购总应得到些利润,希望您能理解。

C：好吧,因为这是我们的第一次交易,我们同意给您9折优惠价。

I：Well, since this is the first deal between us, we agree to offer you a 10% discount.

F：Good, I can accept that. And, I'd like to know your usual way of packing.

I：好的,这个价格我能接受。我想了解一下你们的常规包装方法。

C：我们用纸箱,内衬防潮纸,外打铁箍两道。

I： We use cantons lined with waterproof paper and bound with two iron straps outside.

F: Sounds all right.

I: 听上去还可以。

C: 贵方希望怎样发货,铁路还是海运？

I: How do you like the goods dispatched, by railway or by sea?

F: By sea, please. And we can assume freight.

I: 请海运发货。如果海运,我们可以承担运费。

C: 太好了。

I: That is great.

F: When can you effect shipping?

I: 你们什么时候能交货？

C: 我们最晚在今年12月或明年年初就交货。

I: We can effect shipment in December or early next year at the latest.

F: That's good.

I: 好。

Dialogue 3

Scenario: signing the contract.

C: 这是草拟的合同,请您过目。

I: Here is the draft of the contract. Please check it.

F: OK.

I: 好的。

(F 看合同。)

C: 看完了吗？

I: Have you finished?

F: Yes, I have got one question about Clause 7. Are these the terms we agreed on?

I: 看完了。关于第7款我有个问题,这是我们议定的条款吗？

C: 是的,我们来看看。

I: Yes. Let's have a look at it.

F: 20 percent down and the balance at the time of shipment?

I: 百分之二十付现款,余额在装运时付清？

C: 是的。

I: Yes.

F: I'll need a few minutes to check over my notes again.

I: 请给我点时间,让我查一下我的记录。

（F 查阅谈判记录。）

C：如果您有什么意见的话，请提出来。

I：If you have any questions on the details, feel free to ask.

F：OK, that's all right. I have no questions.

I：好的，没问题了。

C：我们现在可以签合同了吗？

I：Shall we sign the contract now?

F：Sure. Where shall I put my signature?

I：好的，我在哪里签字？

C：最后一页上。我们签署两份文本，一份中文，一份英文，两份具有同等效力。

I：On the last page. We will sign the two originals, one in Chinese and the other in English. Both are equally effective.

F：OK. I hope this will lead to further cooperation between us. All we have to do now is shake hands.

I：好的。我希望以后我们继续合作。现在我们该握手了。

C：好的，谢谢您！

I：OK, thank you!

18.5　第 11 章送客道别的译文

对话全文（中方为 C；外方为 F；口译员为 I）

Dialogue 1

Scenario：at the closing ceremony of World Internet Conference.

C：时间过得真快！互联网大会这么快就结束了，今晚准备为您饯行，不知道您有时间吗？

I：How time files! World Internet Conference ended so soon. I'm planning a farewell dinner for you tonight and wondering if you will be available.

F：I think so. Thank you very much.

I：应该可以。非常感谢！

Dialogue 2

Scenario：at farewell dinner.

C：这次互联网大会举办得真不错，不但互通有无，我也结交了新朋友。史密斯先生,和您有一种相见恨晚的感觉呢!

I:This WIC is really a good one—it doesn't only help sharing of needed information, but also build up friendship. Mr. Smith, I just regret not have known you before!

F:Me too. It's been great pleasure knowing you. I'm deeply impressed by your vision and insights into "Internet plus". And I found myself nodding quite often during your speech.

I:我也这样觉得。认识您真高兴。您对"互联网+"的真知灼见给我留下了深刻印象。您做演讲的时候我常常点头赞同。

C:哪里哪里。不过,也许是"英雄所见略同"。我提议,为我们的友谊,为我们第一次以及今后的合作,喝一杯吧,干杯!

I:Well, thank you! Maybe it is just "great minds think alike". May I propose a toast? To our friendship, to our first and much more cooperation! Cheers!

F:Cheers!

I:干杯!

Dialogue 3

Scenario:on the way to the airport.

F:Thank you, Mr. Wang, for coming over to pick me up.

I:王先生,感谢您过来接我!

C:我很荣幸呢。这几天会议日程比较满,也没多少机会和您交流。

I:It's my honor. There haven't been many opportunities to talk with you during the fully packed days of the conference.

F:Same here. We did have a very tight schedule during the conference.

I:我也一样。我们这次会议的确日程很紧呢。

C:您有时间逛逛乌镇景区吗?

I:Did you spare some time visiting the tourist area of Wuzhen?

F:Actually yes, I stayed in Waterside Resort, which is located within the West Scenic Zone. So I took a walk in the evening. It was so beautiful! By the way, the buildings on both sides of the street look great too, they have similar roofs and windows like those in the houses in the scenic zone, but they are modern.

I:实际上有的。我住在枕水度假酒店,位于西栅景区。晚上我就出来走走。很美!顺便说一下,这条路两旁的建筑也很美,它们的屋顶和窗户有着景区内房子的样子,但又是现代建筑。

C:对的,这些都是仿古建筑,不过您知道吗,几年前,这些房子就是白送老百姓都不愿意住呢。

I:Yep, these are reproductions of ancient buildings. But you know what? A few years ago, no one would have lived in these houses even for free.

F:Really? Why?

I:是吗,为什么?

C:几年前,乌镇还没有成为互联网大会的永久会址,这里不发达,人们一般都去大城市打工去了,留下的都是老人和小孩儿。

I:A few years ago, before Wuzhen became a permanent venue for WIC, this area wasn't quite developed. Local people would go to big cities for a job, leaving only senior people and children behind.

F:Oh, I see. Wuzhen is truly becoming more developed now.

I:哦,是这样。乌镇现在真是越来越发达了。

Dialogue 4

Scenario:at the airport.

C:我们到了,这就是虹桥机场了。

I:Here we are. This is Shanghai Hongqiao International Airport.

F:Thank you for the ride. It's been a pleasure knowing you.

I:谢谢您送我过来。认识您高兴。

C:我也很荣幸。俗话说"送君千里,终有一别",我们就此道别吧。另外,请收下这份小礼物作为中国之行的纪念吧。

I:My honor too. As the old saying goes, "no matter how far away you escort a guest, there will be the time to say goodbye". Now it is time. Please take this little present as a souvenir from China.

F:What a nice pair of chopsticks! Thank you a lot!

I:好漂亮的筷子! 非常感谢!

C:祝您一路平安!

I:I wish you a safe journey!

F:Thanks! Let's keep in touch!

I:谢谢! 我们保持联系!

C:好的,常联系,再见!

I:Sure we will. Goodbye!

F:Bye!

18.6　第12章商贸洽谈的译文

对话全文（中方为 C；外方为 F；口译员为 I）

Dialogue 1

Scenario：initial talk.

C：欢迎来到海尔！我是海尔公司的 CEO 严昊涵。

I：Welcome to Haier! I'm Haohan Yan, CEO of Haier Corporation.

F：Thanks! I'm Larry, the general manager of Carrier Corporation.

I：谢谢！我是徕瑞，开利公司总经理。

C：您现在来北京正是时候，十月的北京，气候适宜。不知您是否适应这边的饮食？

I：You came to Beijing at the right time. The weather here in October is most agreeable. Are you comfortable with the food here?

F：Indeed, we are also impressed with the fascinating scenery and exquisite dishes.

I：的确，另外这边风景宜人，食物也很精美，给我们留下深刻印象。

C：今晚，我们为您安排了本地最具代表性的晚宴——满汉全席，期待您能赴宴。

I：Tonight, we've arranged in your honor the Man-Han banquet, the most typical local cuisine combining Manchurian and Chinese delicacies. We are looking forward to your coming.

F：Thank you very much! I'm pleased to receive your invitation. Your company has received a favorable reputation. We hope we can settle the deal through this negotiation.

I：非常感谢！很高兴接受您的邀请。贵公司声名远扬，我们期待此次商谈能够达成合作。

Dialogue 2

Scenario：bargaining.

C：好的，那我们开始吧？

I：OK, shall we begin?

F：Sure.

I：同意。

C：看来贵公司提供的新型空调很符合我方的采购要求，请问贵方报价如何？

I: It seems your company's new product is in line with our purchase requirements, how much are you offering?

F: 600 U.S. dollars per set.

I: 报价 600 美元一台。

C: 贵方的报价实在是太高了,这远远超出我们的财政预算。

I: I'm afraid the price is way too high and exceeds our financial budget.

F: Mr. Yan, you'll find our price very reasonable if you consider the high-tech quality of our product.

I: 严总,考虑到我们产品的科技含量,您会觉得这个报价是合理的。

C: 非常合理? 贵方的报价如此离谱,我实在怀疑贵方的诚意。我们所能接受的价格为 400 美元一台。

I: Reasonable? Your offer is so outrageous, I really doubt the sincerity of your company. We can only accept 400 dollars per set.

F: We really cannot take your offer. We've invested huge amounts of labor, resources and funds in R&D in this product. However, to show our sincerity, we could lower our price to 500.

I: 这个价格我们实在无法接受,我们对这个产品的研发投了大量的人力、物力、财力。不过为了表示我们的诚意,我们将价格降到 500 美元一台。

C: 我们已经感受到了您的诚意。我们有意订购 2 000 台,不知贵方可否将价格降到 450 美元?

I: We appreciate your good faith. If we order 2 000 sets, could you lower the price to 450 dollars?

F: Considering the costs we've paid, 480 is really our bottom line.

I: 算上成本,我们能接受的最低价格是 480 美元。

C: 虽然贵方已经做出一定的让步,但是此价格我方仍然难以接受。如果我们把订单提高到 3 000 台,您看 460 美元能接受吗? 六在中国也是个吉祥数字。

I: Though you have made concession, the price is still unacceptable to us. Would You take 460 if we increase our order to purchase 3 000 set? By the way, six is an auspicious number in China.

F: Alright. We can take that. Hopefully this deal will bring us good fortune. Well, we've settled the price. Let's talk about the terms of payment?

I: 好吧,我们可以接受。希望这次交易可以给我们带来好运。既然价格已经谈妥,现在来谈谈付款方式,怎么样?

C: 好的!

I: Sure.

F: We only accept payment by irrevocable letter of credit payable against shipping documents.

I：我们只接受不可撤销的、凭装运单据付款的信用证。

C：我明白了。您能不能破例接受承兑交单或付款交单？

I: I see. Could you make an exception and accept documents against acceptance or payment?

F: I'm afraid not. We always require a letter of credit for our exports.

I：恐怕不行，我们出口一向要求以信用证付款。

C：老实说，信用证会增加我方进口货的成本。要在银行开立信用证，我得付一笔押金。这样会占压我的资金，因而会增加成本。

I: To tell you the truth, a letter of credit would increase the cost of my import. When I open a letter of credit with a bank, I have to pay a deposit. That will tie up my money and increase my cost.

F: You could consult your bank and see if they will reduce the required deposit to a minimum.

I：您可以和开证行商量一下，看他们能否把押金减少到最低限度。

C：我们都各让一步，货价的百分之五十用信用证，其余的采用付款交单，您看怎么样？

I: To meet you half way, what do you say if 50% by letter of credit and balance by documents against payment?

F: Alright, we can do that.

I：好，也可以。

C：这很合理。我们已谈妥大部分的合同条款，贵方是否有疑问？

I: That's fair. We've covered most of the contract terms, do you have any doubt?

F: We've reached agreement and expect further cooperation.

I：我们已达成一致，期待进一步的合作。

18.7　第13章参观访问的译文

对话全文（中方为C；记者为F；口译员为I）

F: Hi, I'm Sam from China Matters. I'm very honored to visit the new research center of Huawei.

I：您好，我是外文局融媒体 China Matters 的 Sam，非常荣幸能来参观华为的新研发中心。

C：您好，我是华为新研发中心的工程师邹博士。接下来将由我带领您参观中心。

I：Hello, I'm Dr. Zou, an engineer from Huawei research center. I will show you around the center.

F：Huawei is now 12 months ahead of its rivals like Nokia and Ericsson because of its superior technology especially in 5G. I'm very curious about the 5G technique and what is powering Huawei.

I：华为凭借以 5G 为代表的高端技术，已经将竞争对手诺基亚和爱立信远远地甩在了身后。我对华为的 5G 技术和推动华为发展的动力非常好奇。

C：好的，希望今天的参观过程将会满足你的好奇心。请这边走。

I：Great. Hopefully this visit will satisfy your curiosity. This way please.

C：这里是 5G 无线基站，那是 4G 无线基站。在 4G 时代，无线基站的平均功率约为 300 瓦。在 5G 时代，平均功率高达 1 000 瓦。这意味着功率是原来的三倍多。

I：This is a 5G wireless base station. That is a 4G wireless base station. In 4G time, the average power of a wireless base station is around 300 watts, while in 5G time, it goes up to 1000 watts. So, the power more than tripled.

F：Awesome! I have just heard that Huawei has been developing telecoms gear to handle higher 5G performance. But how does this 5G wireless base station work?

I：厉害！我早就听说华为不断优化 5G 通信设备的性能。但是这个 5G 通信基站是如何发挥作用的呢？

C：5G 基站是必不可少的通信设备，它以超高的速度向我们的移动设备传输信号。

I：5G base stations are an essential telecoms gear because they make sure we get 5G signals on our mobile devices at higher speed.

C：由于 5G 基站的数据传输速度更快，其消耗的能量更多，温度也会越来越高，因此需要研发新的冷却技术。你可以看到里面有一种特殊液体，不是水，这个液体很特别，它的沸点是 18 ℃。华为有很多像我一样的工程师，正在研究如何通过巧妙的设计和材料的使用来改变部件内热气流的流速和方向，从而达到散热的目的。

I：With this speed, 5G base stations consume more power. This means they get increasingly hot. And this is why new cooling techniques need to be developed. In the inner part, you could see some liquid. It is not water, but a special liquid with boiling point at 18 degrees Celsius. Engineers like me are studying how different designs and materials can change the speed and direction that heated air flows away from the components.

F: I think these designs by your team have been funded by Huawei's massive investment in research. I have heard that the investment spent on research is more than the total of its rivals combined.

I：我认为这些创造性的设计背后,是华为对科研的大规模投入。我之前听说华为的研发经费比它对手加起来的研发经费总和还要多。

C：是的。截止到2017年,华为的研发经费已经高达130亿美元,到2019年为止,华为几乎包揽了5G中最重要的专利科技,高达2 570个,全球占比20%。这些专利技术成为推动5G在国内外发展的最坚实的保障。

I: Yes. Until 2017, Huawei had spent a whopping 13 billion US dollars on research. By 2019, Huawei has owned most of the essential 5G patents, as many as 2 570, 20% of the global total. These patents are considered the fundamental blocks for rolling out 5G at home and abroad.

F: Excellent! But please allow me to interrupt, what you said before is too technical. Could you please introduce me to some applications about 5G techniques in our daily life?

I：太棒了！但是请允许我打断一下,您之前说得有点太专业了。您可以向我介绍一下5G在我们日常生活中的应用吗？

C：当然。请跟我来这边。大量的研发投入使得一项项新的技术应运而生,室内数字系统就是其中之一。有了它,就算你用的不是5G手机,也可以在室内接收5G信号。

I: Of course, this way please. The research funding has also enabled new technologies. One of them is DIS-Digital Indoor System, which allows 5G signal to be received inside buildings.

F: So does that mean we can enjoy 5G at home even without a 5G mobile phone?

I：所以这意味着即使我们没有5G手机,也可以在家里享受5G的网速吗？

C：是的。

I: Yes.

F: With the 4G network, I especially struggle to make video calls. That's probably because the speed is slow, and somehow the screen freezes from time to time, which I find to be annoying. This DIS is such an amazing product!

I：用4G的时候,我最怕视频聊天了,可能因为网速很慢,聊着聊着就卡了,让人非常恼火。这个室内的数字系统真是一个超好的发明!

C:是的,当然你也可以用4G的手机卡,或者在4G和5G卡之间自由切换,都没有问题。华为的手机基站可以同时支持这两种选择。

I: Yeah. You can also use your 4G (phone) sim, and you can switch between the two. And that's because Huawei's base stations, they offer you two options.

F: At a time when many of the world's 5G players have been held back by the high cost of setting up more 5G base stations. Huawei is offering a solution. I do admire your company.

I:当建设基站的高昂成本令世界上许多5G供应商望而却步时,华为却能给出解决方案。我太敬佩你们公司了。

C:谢谢您的赞美,接下来请让我带您参观推动基站实现"极简"模式的研发核心——"天罡"芯片。请这边走。

I: Thanks for your compliment. Now let me show you the core Tiangang chipsets powering the base stations, which plays a vital role in making the base stations "simpler". This way please.

18.8　第14章教育合作的译文

对话全文(陈月为C;记者为J;口译员为I)

J:Hi Ms. Chen! could you introduce yourself to our online audience?

I:您好!陈女士,您可以向我们的在线观众介绍一下自己吗?

C:好的,我是陈月,2003年开始在玛丽女王学院工作。现在是伦敦玛丽女王学院-北京邮电大学合作项目主任。

I: Sure, I'm Yue Chen. I started working for Queen Mary in 2003. I'm the Queen Mary director of the joint program with BUPT.

J:Could you tell me a bit about the BUPT Program?

I:您可以介绍一下与北京邮电大学的合作项目吗?

C:好的。这个合作项目是由伦敦玛丽女王学院和北京邮电大学联合举办的双学位本科项目,始于2004年。北京邮电大学是中国一流大学之一,在信息和通信工程领域排名第一。合作项目的理念是将两国教育体系的优势结合起来。

I: Yes. The Queen Mary and BUPT Joint Program is a set of dual-award undergraduate programs run jointly by Queen Mary University of London and Beijing University of Posts and Telecommunications. This partnership started back in 2004. BUPT is one of the leading universities in China. The university ranked number One in Information and Communication Engineering. The idea of the Joint Program is to combine the strengths of both education systems.

J: How is the teaching program organized?

I: 你们是如何组织教学的呢?

C: 目前我们有三个学位课程,三个专业是:电信工程及管理、电子商务与法律和物联网工程。在教学方面,整个课程由两所大学共同设计,大约一半课程由北京邮电大学教授,另一半由玛丽女王学院教授。

I: Currently we have three degree programs, the subject areas are: Telecommunications Engineering with Management, E-Commerce Engineering with Law, and Internet of Things Engineering. In terms of the teaching, the whole curriculum was designed jointly by the two universities. Roughly half of the modules are delivered by BUPT and the other half by Queen Mary staff.

J: Who are the students on the program?

I: 你们是如何招生的呢?

C: 我们通过高考选拔招生,今年招生 680 人,他们来自中国各地,遍布 30 多个省份。

I: We recruited the students via the standard Chinese college entry admission systems. This year intake is 680. The students come from 30 provinces all over China.

J: What have been some challenges of managing the Joint Program?

I: 您管理这个合作办学项目时遇到的挑战是什么?

C: 合作项目是一种特殊的跨国项目,作为东道主大学玛丽女王学院,我们为中国学生提供学位。因此,我们面临着和其他跨国教育项目面临的一样的挑战:一方面保证项目质量符合英国标准;另一方面要调整教学风格,使之适应中国背景下的学生。这是我们在执行这个项目时面临的挑战之一。

I: The Joint Program is a particular type of transnational program where as the host university, Queen Mary offers a degree to the students in China. So we face the same range of challenges as all the other transnational education programs do, which is to meet the quality standard of the program accredited by the UK while catering the pedagogical styles to the Chinese students in their context. That's one of the challenges we have in running this program.

J: What have been some of the benefits?

I: 这个合作项目的优势在哪呢?

C: 优势嘛,从学生的角度来说,这些有天分的学生可以得到更多的学习机会。

如果没有这个合作项目,就没有这样的机会。此外,学生可以不用出国就能接触中英两国的教育系统。从学校的角度看,这个合作项目通过提升教育合作,提升了玛丽女王学院和北京邮电大学的国际知名度。

I: As for the benefits, from the students' perspective, these talented students could have more learning opportunities, which were inaccessible to them without this Joint Program. Besides, they could have experience of both UK and Chinese education systems without leaving their home country. From the perspectives of universities, this program has raised both Queen Mary and BUPT's international profile through enhanced teaching partnership.

J: Why is the program important for Queen Mary? What do you think its wider impact will be?

I: 这个项目对玛丽女王学院的意义是什么呢?您认为这个项目的更广阔的影响在于什么呢?

C: 正如西蒙指出,国际化是一个现代化大学发展的战略计划。玛丽女王学院坐落于伦敦,教职员工和学生都来自世界各地,已经具备很高的国际化程度。这个国际合作项目提升了我校跨国教育的可信度。我们学生的毕业去向显示,迄今为止,已经有三千余名毕业生,其中,大约80%选择在中国或海外继续修读研究生学位,其余20%选择直接进入职场。我们为毕业生的成就深感自豪。大学追求的目标之一,就是培养学生,让他们有更好的未来,这对学生和学校而言都是非常有益的事情。

I: As Simon pointed out, internationalization is one of the strategic plans for the modern university. Queen Mary, being located in London, is already very international with faculties and students from all over the world. This transnational program gives us more credibility in terms of transnational education. The data of our students' career development show, so far, there are over 3000 graduates, about 80% of them continued their postgraduate study either inside or outside China, the remaining 20% went straight into employment. So we are very proud of the students' achievement. One of the things a university strives for is to prepare students for a better future, which is beneficial for the students as well as the university.

J: What do the students get out of the program, aside from the qualification?

I: 除了拿到学位,学生还能从这个项目中获得哪些收获呢?

C: 我认为学生还可以获得丰富的学习经验,接触不同国家的教师和课程。举个例子,我们引入个人发展计划,这是一个特别设计的模块,旨在培养学生的通用技能、工程伦理意识、研究评估能力等。与传统学位课程的学生相比,这个模块丰富了他们的学习体验。我们还努力为中英两国的学生组织交流活动。由于时空的差距,组织这样的活动不太容易。不过我很高兴地看到,从这个学年开始,我们举办了"设计与建造"夏令营。其实本周就在进行,有10个中国学生去了伦敦,他们和玛丽女王学院电子工程与计算机专业的学生一起,做设计和建造项目,准备最后的比赛。这是个好活动,希望在未来持续下去。

I: I think students could have rich learning experience and the access to staff in a different country and the mixed curriculum. For example, we have introduced personal development plan, which is a module specially designed to bring out transferable skills, awareness of engineering ethics, research assessment, etc. This module has enriched the students' study experience compared to the students who are on a traditional degree program. We also endeavor to organize exchange activities for the students in China and the UK. It is not easy, due to the geographic distance and time difference. But I'm very pleased to know from this academic year on, we have managed to host a summer camp called "Design and Build". It is actually happening this week, ten Chinese students have gone to London to be mingled and mixed with the EECS students in Queen Mary. They are doing "Design and Build" projects in order to attend the final contest. That's really a good activity and we would like to continue it in the future.

J: Finally, do you have any advice for colleagues who might be embarking on similar transnational educational projects?

I: 最后,给可能从事类似跨国教育项目的同行,您有什么建议吗?

C: 在我看来,良好的质量是任何跨国项目可持续运作的关键,对不同教育体系的深入了解至关重要。要建立双学位项目,必须确保课程满足双方的要求,学生应具备成为未来工程师所需的技能,以满足市场的需要。除了质量把控和良好计划外,积极进取、高效工作的团队也是必不可少的。我们的工作人员对这个项目非常投入,工作一直非常努力。虽然这项工作是一个挑战,但很有益处。

I: I think good quality is key for any sustainable operation of transnational programs, and deep understanding of different education systems are quite essential. To establish a dual award program, one has to make sure the curriculum satisfies the requirement from both sides, and the students would be equipped with the skills necessary as future engineers to meet the market's needs. Apart from the quality control and good planning, a well motivated and well-functioning team is also pivotal. We have staff really committed to the program. They have been working very hard. It's a challenge, but also very rewarding.

18.9　第15章文化交流的译文

对话全文(主持人为 H;外方为 F;口译员为 I)

H:今天我们很荣幸请到了伯明翰大学莎士比亚研究所所长 Michael Dobson 教授。让我们一起对 Dobson 教授的到来表示最热烈的欢迎。我想先从您的专业领域——莎士比亚开始。想请问您,您对于莎士比亚的兴趣和热情来自哪里呢?

I:We are very honored to have Professor Michael Dobson with us today. He is Director of the Shakespeare Institute of Stratford, University of Birmingham. Let's extend our warmest welcome to Professor Dobson. We'd like to start from your specialist subject, Shakespeare. So where does this passion or interest come from?

F:Well, it comes from Shakespeare's works themselves and the influence of my family. Almost everyone has to study Shakespeare in schools around the world and many of them fall in love with his works. To be honest, I am one of the group. But what really excited me about Shakespeare was seeing it performed. I have some sort of formative memories of this. One is to see students from a local school performing "Midsummer Night's Dream" when I was quite young, which I thought was absolutely weird and incredibly funny. All of the girls dressed up as fairies and acting this play out which was extremely powerful and interesting. It was just a brilliant production and was beautifully designed. So that was a revelation. But actually, there'd been an enthusiasm for Shakespeare in a previous generation of my family. My grandfather was passionately keen on Shakespeare and even founded an amateur theatre group when he was in college. So you can see that Shakespeare is a popular writer in Britain and around the world among not only the professionals but also the amateurs. And I started to know that this was something absolutely extraordinary for me long before I left school.

I:我对于莎士比亚作品的热情主要来自作品本身和我家人的影响。几乎每个人在上学的时候都要学习莎士比亚的作品,许多人就喜欢上了。老实说,我也是其中的一员。不过真正让我感到兴奋的还是看到莎士比亚的戏剧搬上舞台。我对此有一些特别深刻的记忆。其中一个记忆是去观看一个当地学校的学生表演莎士比亚的《仲夏夜之梦》,那时候我还很小。我认为表演既怪异又无比有趣。所有的女孩子们都打扮成仙女的样子来表演这部戏,非常震撼和有趣。那一场表演让我产生了顿悟。不过实际上，我们家的老一辈也非常喜欢莎士比亚的作品。我祖父就非常热衷莎士比亚，甚至在上大学的时候成立了一个业余的莎剧剧组。所以说莎士比亚不仅仅在英国，在全世界范围内都是备受欢迎的。不仅专业人士喜欢他的作品，业余爱好者也喜欢。因此，我在毕业之前很早就意识到了莎士比亚作品对我的非凡意义。

H：您提到英国的专业人士和业余爱好者都喜欢莎士比亚，在全球也是这样。那么您认为莎士比亚为什么能享誉全球呢？

I：You've mentioned that not only the professionals and amateurs in the UK but also the world love Shakespeare. So how does he have such a global appeal?

F：To some extent it's historical luck. Some British people who liked Shakespeare spread out across the world, so the English language carries Shakespeare with it simultaneously. He has such an influence on the development of the English language and English culture. But also, he's the medium through which lots of stories get into wide circulation. He tells stories about families. There is a tremendous sort of core appeal of Shakespeare in that he keeps dramatizing what happens between fathers and children, what happens between lovers, what happens between siblings, as well as how does history change, how do people arguing together produce a new society. And because his works have different styles and registers between the intellectual and the popular, there will be something in the Shakespeare canon that resonates with their particular interests and their particular styles. He does some rational political plays about how people pragmatically get on with things in a secular world. But he also writes plays about ghosts, magic and the supernatural. His works are so broad that each can take what he needs from them.

I：从某种角度上来讲，这是时势造英雄。因为一些喜爱莎士比亚的英国人去往世界各地，英语便将莎士比亚的作品同时带到了全世界。莎士比亚对英语语言和文化的发展有着巨大的影响。与此同时，他也是许多故事得以广泛流传的媒介。他讲述有关家庭的故事。莎士比亚有着巨大的吸引力，因为他用戏剧化的笔触描绘了父子之间、爱人之间、兄弟姐妹之间的故事，并讲述了历史是如何变迁的，相互争论的人们是如何建立一个新社会的。又因为他的作品混合了不同人物的风格和语言，有知识分子，也有市井百姓，因此他的经典作品中总有某种东西能与不同人的兴趣和风格产生共鸣。莎士比亚创作了一些理性的政治类型剧本，描述人们如何在世俗的世界为人处世。但同时他也创作有关幽灵、魔法和超自然的作品。他的作品包罗万象，每个人都能从中找到自己所需的东西。

H：其他国家的观众要欣赏戏剧的话，翻译就十分重要，尤其是对于莎士比亚的作品。您认为翻译会让他作品的精髓丢失吗？或者翻译反而能丰富他的作品？

I:The translation plays a huge part for audiences in other country to enjoy a play, especially for Shakespeare's plays. Does it get lost in translation or can translation add to Shakespeare?

F:Well, one thing that gets found in translation is Shakespeare's newness. Performing Shakespeare, especially translating Shakespeare keeps these texts and plays new. And you will discover things about your own language through working out how you're going to render Shakespeare's effects and how you're going to recreate them in your own context. The problem of translating Shakespeare's blank verse, the kind of rhythm in which he habitually writes in English, into Mandarin, is a great example. Because there are so many different rhythm and verse patterns in Mandarin and you get to choose which one, for particular bits of blank verse. Therefore Shakespeare's blank verse metamorphoses into different versification patterns in Mandarin, which is fascinating.

I:在翻译中的发现之一是莎剧的新意。表演莎士比亚的剧目,尤其是翻译这些剧目,能够防止文本和剧目过时。当研究用本国的语言来渲染喜剧效果时,以及在本国的语境中重塑莎剧时,也会对自己的语言有一个全新的认识。将莎士比亚的无韵诗,就是那些他习惯用英语而写就的韵律,翻译成中文,就是一个很好的例子。因为在中文里,韵的种类和诗歌体裁非常多,翻译某小段无韵诗时,需要选择合适的韵律和诗体。所以莎士比亚的无韵诗可以翻译成不同的中文诗体,很有意思。

H:近年来,更多的莎士比亚剧目在中国的各大剧场上演。您对于这些文化交流是怎么看的？文化交流有什么重要意义？

I:In recent years, increasing amount of Shakespeare's plays has been performed in China. So what do you think of these cultural exchanges? How important are they?

F:They are terribly important, because they renew both parties involved. Shakespeare is all about dialogue and his plays foment dialogue. It enables culture to understand one another or for both as audiences or both as practitioners, that's tremendously enlightening. For instance, when a performer goes on a global tour, he or she may be very curious about what Chinese audience are going to make of it, where the laughs are going to be, where the attentions are going to be, which bits of the play are going to really excite a Chinese audience, compared to a British audience or a New York audience. Shakespeare's plays themselves are interested in relations between countries, they are a great means of producing discussion about that in the afterlives they have. I've seen some great Chinese Shakespeare with subtitles. And I thought that Beijing People's Art Theatre's "Coriolanus" that came to Edinburgh a couple of years ago was a terrific show.

I: 文化交流真的极其重要,因为文化交流能使交流双方都有新的收获。莎士比亚的戏剧妙就妙在对白,而他的戏剧也能促进交流。莎剧能让不同文化之间相互了解、互为观众和被关注的对象,有极大的启发作用。例如,某个演员正要进行莎剧的全球巡演时,他可能很想知道中国的观众会有什么反应,如观众的笑点在哪里;这部戏剧在哪个方面会让中国观众振奋;与英国观众和纽约观众相比,中国观众与他们有何区别。而莎剧很关注国家间的关系,莎剧本身也能够在表演之后引起广泛的讨论。我看过中国一些优秀的带字幕的莎剧演出。我觉得北京人民艺术剧团几年前在爱丁堡演出的《科里奥兰纳斯》简直精彩绝伦。

H: 对,我也知道那场演出。那么既然您已经欣赏了许多表演和作品,您也在世界各地讲授莎士比亚的课程,请问您是否发现在与不同国家的学生和人们聊天时,由于成长在不同的文化氛围中,他们对莎剧会有不同的看法?

I: Yes, I know that one. You've seen plays and productions as well as taught Shakespeare around the world. When you talked to students and people with different nationalities, have you found that they have different opinions on the same thing based on how they've grown up in their culture?

F: Absolutely, and it's really fascinating. Quite different priorities and different responses to the stories, different things that they want to explore and want to go with. The question of political legitimacy in history plays has been very important for different countries at different times and lots of students have wanted to argue about that. In different places I've taught, for example in America, where there are some aspects of Shakespeare in comedy that don't really work for Americans. And some of them work extremely well. I remember being quite taken aback when I was first teaching at Harvard where I was teaching a class on "Henry IV" Part I, Shakespeare's great play about a prince who is waiting to inherit the crown. While he's waiting to inherit the crown, he's hanging about down at the pub with this complete fat dropout reprobate called Sir John Falstaff. And These Harvard students, they can see the point of this prince waiting to inherit the crown, but they just couldn't see the point of Falstaff at all. You know, why doesn't he just get on with inheriting the corporation? Why are they wasting our time with this fat guy. You know the sort of pub element of "Henry Ⅳ", and it just didn't translate for them at all, which I thought was very intriguing. Whereas when I met students in Central Europe, they wanted Shakespeare to be very noble and elevated, and they've been slightly embarrassed by the jokes sometimes. They prefer that kind of Julius Caesar-ish side of Shakespeare rather than the sort of "Merry Wives of Windsor" of Shakespeare.

I:肯定有,这也十分有趣。他们对故事的侧重点和反应差别很大,想去探究和追随的东西也不一样。历史性剧目中的政治合法性问题在不同时期、不同国家都非常重要,许多学生都想讨论这些问题。在我教过的许多地方,例如,在美国,莎剧喜剧中的一些方面并不讨美国人喜欢,有一些方面却反响特别好。我记得第一次在哈佛大学讲课的时候,学生的反应让我很惊讶,当时正在讲解《亨利四世》的第一部分,那是一部很好的莎剧,讲了一位等待继承王位的王子,在等候继承王位时,在酒吧与胖子无赖约翰·福斯塔夫一起玩乐。这些哈佛学生可以理解王子在等待继承王位,却一点也不能理解福斯塔夫存在的意义。他们不明白王子为什么不好好等着继承王位,却要把时间浪费在这个胖子身上。对于《亨利四世》中的酒吧这个元素,他们没办法理解,这一点让我觉得很有趣。然而当我遇到中欧的学生时,他们希望莎士比亚的作品是高贵典雅的,所以有时他们会对某些玩笑感到有点儿尴尬。他们青睐有恺撒气质的莎剧,而不是《温莎的风流娘们儿》那种类型的作品。

H:后来您去了北京大学。中国人又是怎么看莎士比亚的呢?他们有特别喜欢的剧吗?

I:And then you spent some time in Peking University. What do you find about the Chinese angle on Shakespeare? Do they have particular favorites?

F:Yeah, I think a great engagement with Shakespeare in tragedy. That sense of sacrifice and the questions of where you put the individual against society and how you define the one against the other, what has to go and what has to stay, how you hold it together. It's all being absorbing interests to Chinese Shakespeareans and Chinese students.

I:有的,他们很喜欢莎士比亚的悲剧。崇尚那种牺牲的精神,个人利益与集体利益谁先谁后,如何区别个人利益和社会利益,什么该舍弃,什么该保留,怎样将二者结合,这些问题是中国莎剧迷和学生一直都很感兴趣的问题。

H:非常感谢您的分享! 谢谢您!

I:Thank you for sharing your opinions with us! Thank you very much!

F:You are welcome! It is my pleasure!

I:不客气! 我很乐意。

18.10　第16章演讲发言的译文

李开复演讲英文及译文

I'm going to talk about how AI and mankind can coexist, but first, we have to rethink about our human values. So let me first make a confession about my errors in my values.

我将会谈谈人工智能和人类如何能够共存,但首先,我们需要重新思考人类的价值观。首先,让我承认自己价值观的错误。

It was 11 o'clock, December 16, 1991. I was about to become a father for the first time. My wife, Shen-Ling, lay in the hospital bed going through a very difficult 12-hour labor; I sat by her bedside but looked anxiously at my watch, and I knew something that she didn't. I knew that if in one hour, our child didn't come, I was going to leave her there and go back to work and make a presentation about AI to my boss, Apple's CEO. Fortunately, my daughter was born at 11: 30, sparing me from doing the unthinkable, and to this day, I am so sorry for letting my work ethic take precedence over love for my family.

那是1991年12月16日的11点,我即将第一次成为父亲。我的妻子先铃,躺在病床上,经历着一段艰辛的12个小时的分娩过程。我坐在床边,焦虑地望着手表,知道一件妻子不知道的事。我知道,如果在一小时后孩子还不出生,我将要将妻子留在产房,自己去上班,向我的老板——苹果的首席执行官——做有关人工智能的汇报。幸运的是,我女儿11点半出生了,免得我去做难以想象的事,而直到今天,我为爱工作高于爱家人而感到抱歉。

My AI talk, however, went off brilliantly.

我有关人工智能的汇报,倒是进行得十分精彩。

Apple loved my work and decided to announce it at TED 1992, 26 years ago on this very stage. I thought I had made one of the biggest, most important discoveries in AI, and so did the "Wall Street Journal" on the following day.

苹果十分认可我的工作,决定在1992年的TED上将其发布,26年前就在这个台上。我以为自己做出了人工智能领域最重大的发现之一,第二天的"华尔街日报"也持这样的观点。

But as far as discoveries went, it turned out, I didn't discover India, or America. Perhaps I discovered a little island off Portugal. But the AI era of discovery continued, and more scientists poured their souls into it. About 10 years ago, the grand AI discovery was made by three North American scientists, and it's known as deep learning.

但随着越来越多新发现的出现，结果是，我并没有发现新大陆。或许我发现的是葡萄牙附近的一个小岛。不过人工智能的发现时代持续了下去，越来越多的科学家倾心投入其中。大约在 10 年前，三名北美科学家做出了重大的人工智能发现，那就是人们所知的深度学习。

Deep learning is a technology that can take a huge amount of data within one single domain and learn to predict or decide at superhuman accuracy. For example, if we show the deep learning network a massive number of food photos, it can recognize food such as hot dog or no hot dog.

深度学习是一种技术，它能在单一领域中利用海量数据进行学习，并以超人的精确度做出预测或决定。例如，如果向深度学习网络展示海量的食物照片，那它就可以辨认出食物，如是不是热狗。

Or if we show it many pictures and videos and sensor data from driving on the highway, it can actually drive a car as well as a human being on the highway. And what if we showed this deep learning network all the speeches made by President Trump? Then this artificially intelligent President Trump, actually the network.

或者，如果向它展示许多在高速公路上汽车拍摄的图片、视频或者传感器数据，那它其实可以在高速公路上开车，与人相媲美。如果向它展示特朗普总统发表过的所有演说呢？那这就是人工智能（英文也可译为"假聪明"）的特朗普总统，其实是这个网络。

You like double oxymorons, huh?

你们喜欢矛盾修辞法，对吧？

So this network, if given the request to make a speech about AI, he, or it, might say：

所以这个网络，如果让它发表一场关于人工智能的演说，他，或它，或许会说：

(Recording) Donald Trump：It's a great thing to build a better world with artificial intelligence.

（录音）特朗普：运用人工智能来建立一个更完美的世界是件美事。

Kai-Fu Lee：And maybe in another language?

李开复：或许用另一种语言来说？

(Recording)：(Speaking Chinese)

（录音）：人工智能正在改变世界。

Kai-Fu Lee：You didn't know he knew Chinese, did you?

李开复：你们以前不知道他会说中文吧？

So deep learning has become the core in the era of AI discovery, and that's led by the US. But we're now in the era of implementation, where what really matters is execution, product quality, speed and data.

所以深度学习成了人工智能发现时代的核心，并由美国领导着。不过我们现在所处的是实践时代，关键的是执行力、产品质量、速度和数据。

And that's where China comes in. Chinese entrepreneurs, who I fund as a venture capitalist, are incredible workers, amazing work ethic. My example in the delivery room is nothing compared to how hard people work in China. As an example, one startup tried to claim work-life balance: "Come work for us because we are 996." And what does that mean? It means the work hours of 9 a.m. to 9 p.m., six days a week. That's contrasted with other startups that do 997.

这就是中国上场的时候了。对于中国企业家，我作为风险投资人为他们投资资本，他们是非凡的实干者，工作拼命。我在产房的例子和中国企业家工作卖力程度相比根本不算什么。例如，有个创业公司声称注重工作与生活的平衡："加入我们吧，因为我们是 996。"这是什么意思呢？早 9 点到晚 9 点，每周工作 6 天。这与其他实施 997 的创业公司形成了对比。

And the Chinese product quality has consistently gone up in the past decade, and that's because of a fiercely competitive environment. In Silicon Valley, entrepreneurs compete in a very gentlemanly fashion, sort of like in old wars in which each side took turns to fire at each other.

在过去的十年中，中国制造的产品质量在持续地提升，这归功于竞争极其激烈的环境。在硅谷，企业家用非常绅士的方式竞争，有点像是旧时双方轮流向对方开火的战争。

But in the Chinese environment, it's truly a gladiatorial fight to the death. In such a brutal environment, entrepreneurs learn to grow very rapidly, they learn to make their products better at lightning speed, and they learn to hone their business models until they're impregnable. As a result, great Chinese products like WeChat and Weibo are arguably better than the equivalent American products from Facebook and Twitter. And the Chinese market embraces this change and accelerated change and paradigm shifts.

但在中国环境内，就像是角斗士的殊死搏斗。在这种极其残酷的环境内，企业家学习如何迅速成长，学习如何光速地将产品变得更好，直到将企业模式打磨得坚不可摧。结果是，像微信和微博这样杰出的中国产品，虽然有争议，但是可以说比同类的美国产品脸书和推特更好。而且中国的市场欣然接受这种变化，加速了变化和范式转变。

As an example, if any of you go to China, you will see it's almost cashless and credit card-less, because that thing that we all talk about, mobile payment, has become the reality in China. In the last year, 18.8 trillion US dollars were transacted on mobile internet, and that's because of very robust technologies built behind it. It's even bigger than the China GDP. And this technology, you can say, how can it be bigger than the GDP? Because it includes all transactions: wholesale, channels, retail, online, offline, going into a shopping mall or going into a farmer's market like this.

例如，如果你到中国，将会看到人们几乎不用现金和信用卡，因为我们常常讨论的移动支付在中国已成了现实。在过去一年，归功于背后强劲的科技，通过移动网络交易的金额高达18.8万亿美金，这比中国的国内生产总值还高。你可能会问：它怎么能比国内生产总值还高呢？因为它包括了所有的交易：批发、渠道、零售、线上、线下、购物商场或者农贸市场等。

The technology is used by 700 million people to pay each other, not just merchants, so it's peer to peer, and it's almost transaction-fee-free. And it's instantaneous, and it's used everywhere.

这项技术被7亿人用来互相支付，不仅仅局限于商家，因为它是点对点的，而且几乎是零手续费的，并且是即时的，在每个地点都能使用。

And finally, the China market is enormous. This market is large, which helps give entrepreneurs more users, more revenue, more investment, but most importantly, it gives the entrepreneurs a chance to collect a huge amount of data which becomes rocket fuel for the AI engine. So as a result, the Chinese AI companies have leaped ahead so that today, the most valuable companies in computer vision, speech recognition, speech synthesis, machine translation and drones are all Chinese companies.

最后，中国市场十分巨大。巨大的中国市场给企业家提供了更多的用户、更高的收入、更大的投资，但最重要的是给企业家一个收集海量数据的机会，海量数据又成了人工智能引擎的燃料。结果，中国人工智能公司已往前飞跃，所以如今，在计算机视觉、语言识别、语言合成、机器翻译和无人机领域中最有价值的公司都是中国公司。

So with the US leading the era of discovery and China leading the era of implementation, we are now in an amazing age where the dual engine of the two superpowers are working together to drive the fastest revolution in technology that we have ever seen as humans.

所以，美国引领发现时代，中国引领实践时代，两个超级大国作为双联引擎正合作并进，驱动着我们从未见过的最迅猛的科技革命。

And this will bring tremendous wealth, unprecedented wealth: 16 trillion dollars, according to PwC, in terms of added GDP to the worldwide GDP by 2030. It will also bring immense challenges in terms of potential job replacements. Whereas in the Industrial Age it created more jobs because craftsman jobs were being decomposed into jobs in the assembly line, so more jobs were created. But AI completely replaces the individual jobs in the assembly line with robots. And it's not just in factories, but truckers, drivers and even jobs like telesales, customer service and hematologists as well as radiologists over the next 15 years are going to be gradually replaced by artificial intelligence.

这将带来极大的财富，前所未有的财富。普华永道称：2030年，人工智能将带来16万亿全球GDP的增长。人工智能也将带来巨大的挑战，可能造成失业和再就业。在工业时代，因为工匠的工作被分解成生产线中的各式工作，所以创造了更多工作。但是人工智能用机器人替代了生产线中的独立工作。这不只是发生在工厂内，货车司机、驾驶员，甚至电话销售、客服、血液科和放射科医生的工作，在未来的15年内都将会慢慢被人工智能所取代。

And only the creative jobs. I have to make myself safe, right? Really, the creative jobs are the ones that are protected, because AI can optimize but not create.

而只有创造性的工作才能不被取代。我必须保护我自己，对吧？真的，创造性的工作是有保障的，因为人工智能可以优化但不能创造。

But what's more serious than the loss of jobs is the loss of meaning, because the work ethic in the Industrial Age has brainwashed us into thinking that work is the reason we exist, that work defined the meaning of our lives. And I was a prime and willing victim to that type of workaholic thinking. I worked incredibly hard. That's why I almost left my wife in the delivery room, that's why I worked 996 alongside my entrepreneurs. And that obsession that I had with work ended abruptly a few years ago when I was diagnosed with fourth stage lymphoma. The PET scan here shows over 20 malignant tumors jumping out like fireballs, melting away my ambition.

然而，比失去工作更严重的是失去意义，因为工业时代的工作伦理已经给我们洗脑，让我们以为工作就是我们存在的原因，工作定义了我们生活的意义。而我就是个典型的并自愿接受工作狂思想的受害者。我工作异常卖力。所以我几近将妻子独自留在产房，所以我996地与企业家们工作。我对工作的痴迷在几年前戛然而止，因为被确诊患上了第四期淋巴瘤。这个正子断层扫描显示有超过20个的恶性肿瘤向火球那样跳了出来，令我的壮志雄心付之一炬。

　　But more importantly, it helped me reexamine my life. Knowing that I may only have a few months to live caused me to see how foolish it was for me to base my entire self-worth on how hard I worked and the accomplishments from hard work. My priorities were completely out of order. I neglected my family. My father had passed away, and I never had a chance to tell him I loved him. My mother had dementia and no longer recognized me, and my children had grown up.

　　但更重要的是，癌症让我重新审视人生。知道可能只剩下几个月的生命时，令我看清将自我价值完全建立在工作强度和工作成就上是多么的愚蠢。我人生的优先级完全本末倒置了。我忽视了我的家人。我父亲过世了，而我从来没有机会告诉他我爱他。我母亲患上了痴呆症并从此认不出我了，而我的孩子们也已经长大了。

　　During my chemotherapy, I read a book by Bronnie Ware who talked about dying wishes and regrets of the people in the deathbed. She found that facing death, nobody regretted that they didn't work hard enough in this life. They only regretted that they didn't spend enough time with their loved ones and that they didn't spread their love.

　　在化疗的过程中，我读了布朗妮·维尔的一本书，写的是人临终前的心愿和遗憾。她发现面对死亡时，没人遗憾工作得不够努力，只后悔自己没有花足够的时间与所爱的人相处，后悔没有传递自己的爱。

　　So I am fortunately today in remission.

　　幸运的是，现在我的病情有所缓解。

　　So I can be back at TED again to share with you that I have changed my ways. I now only work 965. Occasionally 996, but usually 965. I moved closer to my mother, my wife usually travels with me, and when my kids have vacation, if they don't come home, I go to them. So it's a new form of life that helped me recognize how important it is that love is for me, and facing death helped me change my life, but it also helped me see a new way of how AI should impact mankind and work and coexist with mankind. , AI is taking away a lot of routine jobs, but routine jobs are not what we're about.

　　所以我可以重返TED舞台，和你们分享我生活方式的改变。现在我965地工作，偶尔996，但通常965。我搬到母亲附近住，常和妻子一起旅行，孩子们放假时，如果他们不回家，我就到他们那儿去。这种新的生活方式帮我认清爱对我来说是多么的重要,而面对死亡帮助我改变自己的生活,也帮助我用新的方式来看待人工智能该如何影响人类、影响工作、与人共存,确实,人工智能带走了很多重复性的工作,但我们存在的意义并不在于这些重复性的工作。

Why we exist is love. When we hold our newborn baby, love at first sight, or when we help someone in need, humans are uniquely able to give and receive love, and that's what differentiates us from AI.

我们存在的意义是爱。当我们抱着自己刚出生的宝宝时,当我们一见钟情时,或当我们帮助有需要的人时,唯有人类才能爱与被爱,是爱将我们与人工智能区分开来。

Despite what science fiction may portray, I can responsibly tell you that AI has no love. When AlphaGo defeated the world champion Ke Jie, while Ke Jie was crying and loving the game of go, AlphaGo felt no happiness from winning and certainly no desire to hug a loved one.

不管科幻作品怎么描写,我可以很负责任地告诉你,人工智能没有爱的能力。当阿尔法围棋打败了世界冠军柯洁时,柯洁哭了并深爱着围棋,但阿尔法围棋没有从胜利中感受到开心的滋味,也不会渴望拥抱一个心爱的人。

So how do we differentiate ourselves as humans in the age of AI?

那我们该如何在人工智能时代中,将自己与人工智能区分出来?

We talked about the axis of creativity, and certainly that is one possibility, and now we introduce a new axis that we can call compassion, love, or empathy.

我们说到了创造性的维度,那当然是一个可能性,现在我们介绍一个新维度,称之为同情心、爱或同理心。

Those are things that AI can not do. So as AI takes away the routine jobs, I like to think we can, we should and we must create jobs of compassion. You might ask how many of those there are, but I would ask you:

这些都是人工智能做不到的事情。所以当人工智能带走重复性工作的同时,我想我们可以、应该也必须创造关爱型的工作。你或许会问这样工作到底有多少?但我想问你:

Do you not think that we are going to need a lot of social workers to help us make this transition? Do you not think we need a lot of compassionate caregivers to give more medical care to more people? Do you not think we're going to need 10 times more teachers to help our children find their way to survive and thrive in this brave new world? And with all the new found wealth, should we not also make labors of love into careers and let elderly accompaniment or homeschooling become careers also?

你不认为我们将需要许多社工,来帮助我们平稳过渡吗?你不认为我们需要许多富有同情心的看护,来为更多人提供更多的医疗看护吗?你不认为我们将需要多10倍的老师,来帮助我们的孩子勇敢探索在新世界中的生存和发展之道吗?拥有了这些新获得的财富,我们不应该将爱心活动变为一种工作吗?不应该把陪护老人或在家教育孩子变成一种工作吗?

This graph is surely not perfect, but it points at four ways that we can work with AI. AI will come and take away the routine jobs and in due time, we will be thankful.

这个图表不甚完美,但它指出了四种我们与人工智能共事的方式。人工智能未来将带走重复性的工作,到时候,我们会感到欣慰。

AI will become great tools for the creatives so that scientists, artists, musicians and writers can be even more creative.

人工智能将成为创造者的好工具,所以科学家、艺术家、音乐家和作家能变得更有创造力。

AI will work with humans as analytical tools that humans can wrap their warmth around for the high-compassion jobs.

人工智能将成为分析工具,与人共事,所以人们可以将温暖倾注于高同情心的工作。

And we can always differentiate ourselves with the uniquely capable jobs that are both compassionate and creative, using and leveraging our irreplaceable brains and hearts.

而且,只要充分利用我们无法替代的大脑和心灵,我们总是可以通过独有擅长的工作来区分自己,这些工作既富有同情心,又富有创造性。

So there you have it: a blueprint of coexistence for humans and AI. AI is serendipity. It is here to liberate us from routine jobs, and it is here to remind us what it isthat make us human. So let us choose to embrace AI and love one another. Thank you.

所以你可以看到:人类与人工智能共存的蓝图。人工智能是机缘巧合。它来,是将我们从重复性工作中解放出来;它来,也是提醒我们人因何为人。所以让我们选择欣然接受人工智能并彼此相爱。谢谢。

参考文献

[1] LI P, LU Z. Learners' needs analysis of a new optional college English course—interpreting for non-English majors[J]. Theory and Practice in Language Studies, 2011, 1(9):1091-1102.

[2] LI P. A Learning-centered Course Design of Interpreting for Non-English Majors—An Empirical Study[J]. Theory and Practice in Language Studies, 2015, 5(12):2469-2479.

[3] NIDA E A, TABER C R. The Theory and Practice of Translation[M]. Leiden: United Bible Societies, 1969: 178-179.

[4] 李田心. 奈达翻译定义的错误译文曲解了奈达翻译理论[J]. 衡阳师范学院学报, 2011, 32(1): 126-130.

[5] 李长栓. 非文学翻译理论与实践[M]. 北京: 中国对外翻译出版公司, 2004:5.

[6] 郭力嘉, 张丽, 李砚颖. 口译职业化趋势下的西部口译人才培养探究:一项基于川、渝两地口译职业调查的研究报告[J]. 外语电化教学, 2011(5):54-59.

[7] 黄忠廉. 科学翻译的分类及其作用[J]. 四川外语学院学报, 2004(4):106-110+131.

[8] 刘向红, 罗晓语. 科技英语文体的名词化结构及其翻译策略[J]. 湖南工程学院学报(社会科学版), 2015, 25(3):43-46.

[9] 毛荣贵. 翻译美学[M]. 上海: 上海交通大学出版社, 2005:464-469.

[10] 罗琳. 浅谈科技翻译口译的几个基本点[C]//中国翻译协会广东省翻译协会. 第十四届全国科技翻译研讨会论文集. [S.l.:s.n.], 2011:345-347.

[11] 崔艳秋, 郭炎华. 科技英语翻译:培养简洁的文风及文体意识[J]. 疯狂英语(教师版), 2010(3):220-221.

[12] 韦孟芬. 英语科技术语的词汇特征及翻译[J]. 中国科技翻译, 2014, 27(1):5-7+23.

[13] 吕世生. 科技口译策略选择与操作问题[J]. 中国科技翻译, 2004(2):24-26.

[14] GILE D. 口笔译训练的基本概念和模型(修订版)[M]. 上海: 上海外语教育出版社, 2011:163-164.

[15] 李越然.论口译的社会功能——口译理论基础初探[J].中国翻译.1999，20(3):8-12.

[16] 仲伟合、王斌华.基础口译[M].北京:外语教学与研究出版社,2009:4.

[17] MOSER-MERCER P. Expectations of users of conference interpretation [EB/OL]. (1995-01) [2020-04-10]. https://aiic.net/page/attachment/1044.

[18] BUHLER H. Linguistic (semantic) and extra-linguistic (pragmatic) criteria for the evalution of conference interpretation and interpreters [J]. Multilingua，1986，5(1):692-708.

[19] 刘和平.科技口译与质量评估[J].上海科技翻译.2002(1):33-37.

[20] 张威.科技口译质量评估:口译使用者视角[J].上海翻译.2010(3):43-47.

[21] 王斌华.从口译标准到口译规范:口译评估模式建构的探索[J].上海翻译.2012(3):49-54.

[22] GILE D. Basic Concepts and Models for Interpreter and Translator Training [M]. Amsterdam/ Philadelphia: John Benjamins Publishing Company，1995:77-79.

[23] 柴明颎.口译职业化带来的口译专业化[J].广东外语外贸大学学报.2007(3):12-14.

[24] 雷天放,陈菁.口译教程[M].上海:上海外语教育出版社,2006:230.

[25] 蔡小红.以跨学科的视野拓展口译研究[J].中国翻译.2001,22(2):26-29.

[26] 鲍刚.口译理论概述[M].北京:中国对外翻译出版公司,2005:93.

[27] 卢信朝.英汉口译①听辨:认知心理模式、技能及教学[J].山东外语教学.2009(5):53-59.

[28] ADANK P，EVANS B G，Stuart-Smith J and Scott S K. Comprehension of familiar and unfamiliar native accents under adverse listening conditions. [J]. Journal of Experimental Psychology: Human Perception and Performance. 2009,35(2):520-529.

[29] Pöchhacker F. Introducing Interpreting Shudies [M]. 2nd ed. London and New York: Routledge, 2016:129.

[30] 狄建茹.掌握英语口音,从容做口译[J].校园英语.2018(7):239.

[31] 邱少波.加拿大英语的特点[J].英语知识.1998(7):6-10.

[32] 朱巧莲,汤倩.英语各类口音听译突破[M]北京:人民教育出版社,2011:4-13.

[33] ThoughtCo. How to Fake a French Accent. [EB/OL]. (2019-03-11) [2020-11-22]. https://www.thoughtco.com/how-to-fake-a-french-accent-1368758.

[34] NEVDULL. How to Type and Talk With a German Accent. [EB/OL]. [2020-11-22]. https://www.instructables.com/How-To-Type-and-Talk-With-a-German-Accent/.

[35] DETERDING D and KIRKPATRICK A. Emerging South-East Asian Englishes and intelligibility[J]. World Englishes, 2006, 25(3/4): 391-409.

[36] YOUNG C. "You dig tree tree to NUS": understanding Singapore English from the perspectives of international students[A]. In L G Ling, L Ho, L Meyer, C Varaprasad & C Young (eds.). Teaching English to Students from China[C]. Singapore: University of Singapore Press, 2003: 94-106.

[37] NOSRATINIA M, ZAKER A. An analysis of Iranian EFL learners' pronunciation errors[J]. International Journal of Language Learning and Applied Linguistics World, 2014, 5(3): 97-108.

[38] KHORASGANI A T, KHORASGANI A T & ARAY N K. A survey on several potentially problematic areas of pronunciation for Iranian EFL learners[J]. Indonesian EFL Journal, 2015, 1(2): 189-198.

[39] KHAN M. The myth of reference varieties in English pronunciation across the subcontinent, Egypt and Kingdom of Saudi Arabia[J]. International Journal of English Linguistics, 2015, 5(3):19-36.

[40] 张玉芳. 非洲英语：中非贸易道路上的语言关[J]. 考试周刊, 2014, (11): 86-87.

[41] 卢信朝. 英汉口译技能教程——听辨[M]. 北京: 北京语言大学出版社, 2012: 56-58.

[42] 佚名. 改变世界的锂离子电池摘得诺贝尔化学奖[EB/OL]. (2019-10-10) [2020-05-04]. https://new.qq.com/omn/20191010/20191010A03X1V00.html.

[43] CASTELVECCHI D, STOYE E. Chemistry Nobel honours world-changing batteries [EB/OL]. (2019-10-09) [2020-05-04]. https://www.nature.com/articles/d41586-019-02965-y.

[44] 鲍刚. 口译理论概述[M]. 北京: 旅游教育出版社, 1998: 159.

[45] JONES R. Conference Interpreting Explained[M]. 2nd ed. Manchester: St. Jerome Publishing, 2002: 14-21.

[46] CHASE W G, SIMON H A. Perception in chess[J]. Cognitive Psychology, 1973(4): 55-81.

[47] C114中国通信网安迪. 李开复: 猛烈的AI三部曲才正揭开序幕[EB/OL]. (2017-04-28) [2020-05-04]. http://www.c114.com.cn/topic/5128/a1005597.html.

[48] 吴钟明.英语口译笔记法实战指导[M].武汉:武汉大学出版社,2008:1.

[49] SKELESKOVITCH D. Language and memory: a study of note-taking in consecutive interpreting[M]// Pochhacker F,Shelesinger M,et al. The Interpreting Studies Reader. London and New York: Routledge, 2002: 121-129.

[50] 王文宇,周丹丹,王凌.口译笔记特征与口译产出质量实证研究[J].外语界,2010(4):9-18.

[51] 孙海琴,杨瑛.口译基础[M].上海:上海交通大学出版社,2011:141.

[52] 韩刚.口译实战训练法[M].北京:北京大学音像出版社,2010.

[53] 佚名.外交部口译的笔记符号[EB/OL].(2010-06-23)[2020-05-04]. https://wenku.baidu.com/view/1a076fe79b89680203d8259b.html.

[54] 杨永芳.英语书面语语体特征及中国学生英语语体意识的培养[J].西南农业大学学报(社会科学版),2010,8(3):206-207.

[55] 赵军峰,刘洪泉.论口译中的语体识别与对等转换[J].中国科技翻译,1997,10(3):35-38.

[56] 文军,高晓鹰.归化异化,各具一格——从功能翻译理论角度评价《飘》的两种译本[J].中国翻译,2003,24(5):40-43.

[57] 耿小辉.9小时快学国际音标[M].北京:中国科学文化音像出版社,2008:32-246.

[58] 秦秀白.英语语体和文体要略[M].上海:上海外语教育出版社,2001:126.

[59] JOOS M. The Five Clocks[M]. New York and London: Harcourt Brace Jovanovich,1961:24-39.

[60] 丁闯.英语语体特征差异分析[J].长春理工大学学报(社会科学版),2013,26(4):155-156+172.

[61] SWALES J M,FEAK C B. Academic Writing for Graduate Students: Essential Tasks and Skills[M]. University of Michigan Press,2012:21.

[62] MCCARTHY M,O'DELL F. Academic Vocabulary in Use with Answers[M]. Cambridge: Cambridge University Press,2008:116-119.

[63] 泛瑞翻译.数字增减及倍数的译法[EB/OL].(2015-02-02)[2020-05-04]. https://wenku.baidu.com/view/d424d272eff9aef8941e0682.html.

[64] 佚名.陪同口译资料一(迎来送往,宾馆入住)[EB/OL].(2011-01-16)[2020-11-22]. https://wenku.baidu.com/view/2a6de8c34028915f804dc25c.html.

[65] 佚名.陪同口译资料四(餐馆用餐)[EB/OL].(2011-01-16)[2020-11-22]. https://wenku.baidu.com/view/f65bd51ba8114431b90dd85c.html.

[66] 梅德明.英语口译资格考试分类词汇精编[M].北京:人民教育出版社,

2003:20-21,213-214.

[67] 佚名.双语:国际电联秘书长赵厚麟2019年世界电信和信息社会日致辞[EB/OL].(2019-05-17)[2020-05-04]. https://www.en84.com/7072.html.

[68] 佚名.联合国秘书长2010世界电信和信息社会日致辞[EB/OL].(2011-04-26)[2020-05-06]. https://www.hjenglish.com/movieworld/p160163/.

[69] 青岛国展工程.展会常用英语词汇[EB/OL].(2016-12-17)[2020-05-02]. https://www.meipian.cn/aeoiwk9?from=weibo.

[70] 胡鹏.商务洽谈(谈判)步骤与技巧[EB/OL].(2019-08-26)[2020-05-02]. https://wenku.baidu.com/view/4957859b2f3f5727a5e9856a561252d381eb2068.html.

[71] 佚名.(整理)商务英语谈判对话900句[EB/OL].(2019-11-08)[2020-05-02]. https://wenku.baidu.com/view/22f81d660342a8956bec0975f46527d3250ca624.html?fr=search.

[72] LETSVIDEO.【REAL5G】歪果仁参观华为研发中心:科研经费超过竞争对手之和,活该你第一(EB/OL).(2019-08-06)[2020-05-08]. https://b23.tv/BV1V4411Z7bV.

[73] KENNEDY E. Transnational teaching: the BUPT programme.[EB/OL].(2016-04-19)[2020-05-03]. https://adept.qmul.ac.uk/resource/transnational-teaching-qmul-bupt/.

[74] MA L. Cross-course collaboration between software and hardware modules to improve student learning experience[R]. Queen Mary University of London: QMUL Teaching and Learning Conference, 2018.

[75] 佚名.陪同口译资料六(参观访问)[EB/OL].(2011-01-16)[2020-11-22] https://wenku.baidu.com/view/a2dfeb878762caaedd33d45c.html.

[76] 智慧课堂.专访英国莎士比亚研究所所长[EB/OL].(2016-02-24)[2020-05-06]. https://v.qq.com/x/page/h0185ntl7sf.html.

[77] 姜怡,姜欣主编.文化交流英语[M].北京:高等教育出版社,2007.

[78] LEE K. How AI can save our humanity[EB/OL].(2018-04)[2020-05-06]. https://www.ted.com/talks/kai_fu_lee_how_ai_can_save_our_humanity.

[79] 佚名.即兴英语演讲万能句子[EB/OL].(2017-06-08)[2020-05-04]. http://www.xuexila.com/koucai/yanjiang/jixing/910556.html.

[80] 佚名.人工智能[EB/OL].[2020-05-04]. https://baike.so.com/doc/2952526-3114987.html.

[81] 佚名.走近张璐:如何给总理做翻译[EB/OL].(2012-05-24)[2020-05-04].

http://www.translators.com.cn/archives/2012/05/4912.

[82] 尹世昌.香港中文大学校长沈祖尧:不流俗不盲从,不负此生(新语)[N].人民网-人民日报,2014-07-15(8).

[83] 佚名.重磅!阿里达摩院发布《2020十大科技趋势》[EB/OL].(2020-01-05)[2020-05-06]. http://sike.news.cn/statics/sike/posts/2020/01/219552709.html.

[84] 于晋图,华资料.林金桐:真情润物激情挥洒——《华夏英才》采访稿[EB/OL].[2020-05-04]. http://nuoha.com/book/70988/00028.html.

[85] 人民网.IT大佬奋斗史:马云蹬三轮送书 刘强东创业遭女友嫌弃[EB/OL].(2015-06-05)[2020-05-04]. http://tech.cnr.cn/techit/20150605/t20150605_518762540_2.shtml.

[86] 佚名.央视《经济半小时》创新论坛:李彦宏[EB/OL].(2006-01-13)[2020-05-07]. http://news.sina.com.cn/c/2006-01-13/14078858633.shtml.

[87] ALEXANDER L G,何其莘.新概念英语[M].北京:外语教学与研究出版社,1997:146.

附录 以学习为中心的《初级英语口译》课程设计

A Learning-Centered Course Design of Interpreting for Non-English Majors
——An Empirical Study[2]

Ping Li

School of Humanities, Beijing University of Posts and Telecommunications, Beijing, China

Email: byliping@bupt.edu.cn

Abstract—Curriculum design is crucial for any courses, however, there seems to be sparse published literature that relates curriculum theory to interpreter education. Even scarcer is the study on the curriculum design of interpreting courses for non-English majors. To address such a scarcity of study, the author designed an optional course named Interpreting for Non-English Majors (IFNEM), drawing upon a learning-centered approach to course design in the ESP theories. After being implemented for one semester, the course design was evaluated by relating to the learning outcomes to the objectives, using instruments including a questionnaire on the course design and the students' learning journals and semester summaries. Results showed the course was well designed: the students had improved their interpreting scores with a statistical difference ($p < 0.01$), enhanced their English proficiencies and learning autonomy; the students' feedback on the course and the teacher was very positive. This study may bring insights into the curriculum design of similar courses.

Index Terms—Course Design, Learning-Centered, Interpreting

I. Introduction

Curriculum design is one of the aspects that directly affect the quality of an educational program. However, there has been sparse published research that relates curriculum theory to interpreter education (Li, 2012; Sawyer, 2011). Even scarcer is the study on the course design of an interpreting class for non-English majors (IFNEM), a new existence in China's colleges, which requires emergent research attention.

Interpreting courses used to be set only for English majors, who were considered more competent linguistically for an interpreting task. However, non-English majors have improved greatly their English proficiencies. Many of them are capable candidates for interpreting training. Besides, results of both social and students' needs analysis have indicated the necessity to establish IFNEM as an optional College English course (Deng, 2007; Li, 2011; Luo, Huang, & Xu, 2008). As China's college English policy advocates curricular diversity and individuality (Ministry of Education, 2007, p. 19), the time is ripe for optional courses like IFNEM to open. Then follows a practical problem of how to design it.

As the language teaching paradigm shifts from teaching to learning and from the instructor to the learner, the learning-centered curriculum design is gaining wider recognition. To design IFNEM, a new course for a certain group of students with special needs, a learning-centered approach of English for Special Purposes (ESP) seems to fit just well, for ESP is "an approach to language teaching which aims to meet the needs of particular learners" (Hutchinson and Waters, 1987, p. 21). Therefore the course design of IFNEM adopts this approach.

II. Rationale

A. Learning-Centered Approach to Course Design

There are three basic curriculum designs: subject-centered designs, learned-centered designs and program-centered designs (Ornstein & Hunkins, 2009, p.

191). Among them, the learner-centered design in line with constructivism learning theory has gained popularity since the early 1900s, when the learner became in the limelight of educational programs.

Building upon the learner-centeredness, Hutchinson and Waters (1987) proposed a learning-centered approach based on their understanding of learning. They held that learning is not just an internal process of the learner, but also a process of negotiation between the society that sets the target and the individual who tries to attain it. In other words, the learner is not the only factor to consider in learning. The learning-centered approach, as they suggested, involves both what competence that enables someone to perform and how that competence is acquired (pp. 72-73). This indicates that the learner should be considered at every stage of course design. Fig. 1 illustrates this approach (p. 74) with the author's modifications.

Figure 1. A learning-centered approach to course design with modifications

B. Factors Affecting ESP Course Design

To design a ESP course one should start by asking questions concerning language descriptions, learning theories and needs analysis (Hutchinson & Waters, 1987, p. 22). Considering the difference between a language course and an interpreting course, the author altered the framework by replacing "language descriptions" with "descriptions of oral translation competence". The modified framework is demonstrated in Fig. 2.

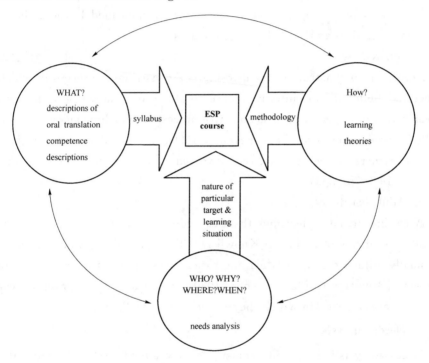

Figure 2. Factors affecting ESP course design

1. Descriptions of oral translation competence

To define components of oral translation competence one can refer to those of translation competence, since oral translation is one mode of translation. Gile (2011) summarized the components of translation competence as good passive knowledge of passive working language(s); good command of active working language(s); adequate world knowledge; and good command of the principles and techniques of translation (p. 18). Studies on oral translation competence (Lin, 1994; Zhong, 2003) shared similar views. A consensus has been reached that there are three key elements that comprise interpreter education, namely, interpreting skills, encyclopedia knowledge and proficiencies of languages (Wang, 2009, p. 209). A training program for professional interpreters should address all of the three aspects in its goals and objectives.

2. Learning theories

The starting point for all language teaching should be an understanding of how people learn. To avoid danger of basing too narrowly on one learning theory, Hutchinson and Waters suggested an eclectic approach and proposed a model for learning (1987, pp. 49-51). In addition to this learning model, the author drew upon constructivism and adult learning theories.

a. Constructivism

According to constructivists, learning is a constructive process in which the learner is building an internal representation of knowledge, a personal interpretation of experience. It is an active process in which meaning is developed on the basis of experience (Bednar et al., 1999, p. 22). This nature of learning requires learners to become actively involved and participate in a community (Lauzon, 1999, p. 263).

b. Adult learning

According to adult learning theories, education is defined as a process of mutual, self-directed inquiry (Knowles, 1972, p. 36). Adult learners are profoundly influenced by past learning experiences, present concerns and future prospects (Brundage & MacKeracher, 1980, pp. 21-31). This group of learners prefer a process design in which they participate as well.

3. Needs analysis

Needs analysis is a vital prerequisite for developing a course. Before IFNEM was established, the designer carried out a needs analysis through a questionnaire to 156 freshmen and junior students at her university, some of whom would be potential learners of the IFNEM that she later set up. The questionnaire was based on an adapted checklist of analyzing learning needs by Hutchinson and Waters (1987, p. 62).

Results showed that it is highly necessary to provide an IFNEM as an optional course. The students hoped to have free access to it in the second semester of the freshman year or the sophomore year, either in the evening or in the morning. They also expected a small-sized class of 20 to 40 students. The teaching environments were expected to include multi-media appliances, computers and movable tables and chairs. Students' motivation to take this course was mainly instrumental, many expecting to improve their English skills. They expected the teaching goals to be improvement of both interpreting skills and language abilities, especially English listening and speaking abilities. (Li, 2011, pp. 1100-1101).

III. Course Designing and Implementation

The process of course design involves initial planning, implementation, and evaluation (Nunan, 1988a, p. 8). Traditionally this process is finished by curriculum designers before any encounters of the teacher and the students. This leads to difficulties to consider the learner at every stage of course design, as required in a learning-centered approach. Ideally the key participants of pre-course planning should be both the teachers who are to direct a course and the learners who are to take part in it (Nunan, 1988b, p. 45), and "the most valuable learner data can be obtained, especially after relationships have been established between the teacher and learners" (p. 5).

Fortunately, the IFNEM design lived up to the ideal: the designer of the IFNEM is also the teacher (and the author) who had been teaching English to the potential learners of IFNEM in their freshmen year. The teacher had known the class so well that she could remember all of the students' names and general English proficiencies. During that period, the teacher proposed the new course of IFNEM to the students and received many "reservation requests" from interested candidates. Much discussion was led afterwards to elicit the learners' opinions about the course design, especially on the content and assessment. For instance, as part of the formative assessment, the number and frequency of quizzes and learning journals was decided after rounds of negotiation between the ambitious teacher and realistic students. The decision proved to be a wise one as the course turned out. Without consulting with the learners, the assessment could have been too intensive and scared away many candidates.

The teacher was also able to collect comprehensive data about the learners before the class, encompassing their current proficiency level, age, previous learning experiences, preferred learning arrangement, learning-style preferences, personal learning objectives and motivation, etc., through tests, questionnaires, and most importantly, causal chats via WeChat, a communication tool of instant messaging. In fact, this effective channel of communication continued to the period during the implementation of IFNEM class, enabling ongoing supervision, modification and evaluation of the course.

The final design of IFNEM is as follows.

A. Aims and Objectives

This course aims to introduce the fundamental knowledge of interpreting to students, and equip them with basic interpreting skills, higher English listening and speaking skills and independent learning strategies. A subdivision of fundamentals of interpreting knowledge and skills is elaborated in Table 1:

Table 1.
Objectives on fundamentals of interpreting and basic interpreting skills

1. On fundamental knowledge of interpreting		
	The course is to help students to understand:	
	-	competence required for an interpreter;
	-	principles of de-verbalization;
	-	Effort Model;
	-	principles and techniques of listening for interpreting tasks;
	-	principles and techniques of note-taking for interpreting tasks;
	-	principles and techniques of short-term memory for interpreting tasks;
2. On interpreting skills		
	The course is to help students to learn and practice:	
	-	listening for meaning;
	-	short-term memory techniques;
	-	note-taking techniques;
	-	public speaking skills;
	-	critical thinking skills (e.g., to summarize, to identify main ideas and to reconstruct);
	-	interpreting figures;
	-	coping tactics
3. On professionalism		
	The course is to help students learn about:	
	-	short-term preparation for interpreting tasks;
	-	cross-cultural communication;
	-	professional standards.

The list is not exhaustive. For instance, more advanced objectives like analysis of different registers and artistic delivery of interpreting are not included. For "it is essential to select the number of objectives that can actually be attained in significant degree in the time available, and that these be really important ones" (Tyler, 1949, p. 31).

B. Syllabus

In view of the introductory nature of this course and learners' varied proficiency levels, the teaching content is decided upon liaison interpreting in common settings (tourism, business and culture, etc), which are less challenging and more practical. The materials for this course are from multiple sources, including textbooks, online recourses and training materials that the teacher accumulated from her own education and interpreting experiences. The textbooks selected are *Liaison Interpreting* (Wang & Wu, 2010), *Basic Interpreting Skills* (Su & Deng, 2009), and *Asia Link-Interpreting Asia Interpreting Europe* (Xiao & Yang, 2006). Additional multi-media resources are uploaded online to the "iclass" teaching platform, a MOODLE-like course management system, which the students have access to via computers or a smart phone application named "Blackboard Mobile Learn".

The teaching content attempts to address the three components of translation competence as mentioned before, with interpreting skills ranking the first in importance. This is in line with the interpreter educationalist Zhong's viewpoint (2001, p. 31). He maintains that training of interpreting skills should be the top priority of interpreting education, which can be arranged according to different themes of situations that interpreting takes place. Accordingly, the IFNEM is arranged by themes, except for an introduction to fundamentals of interpreting at the beginning.

The theme-based syllabus is presented below:

1. fundamental knowledge of interpreting,
2. short-term memory techniques,
3. listening techniques in interpreting,
4. note-taking techniques,
5. receiving guests,
6. tourism and shopping,
7. food and catering,
8. seeing guests off,

9. exhibition and fairs,
10. business negotiation,
11. business etiquettes,
12. cooperation talks,
13. cultural communication,
14. preparation for an interpreting task,
15. interpreting practicum.

This theme-based syllabus, however, fails to demonstrate the actual focus on training interpreting skills which happen in almost every class, regardless of the theme. To present an overview of what and how those interpreting skills are trained and assessed, a skills-based syllabus is elaborated in Table 2, drawing upon Zhong's summary of basic interpreting skills and training methods (2001, p. 31).

Table 2.
The Skills-Based Syllabus of IFNEM

Content	Objectives	Materials	Activity	Assessment
interpreting competence	to understand competence required for an interpreter and learn what long-term preparation is needed as a self-directed learner of interpreting	Gile's comprehension equation, etc.	lecture; impromptu interpreting practice	quiz on fundamentals of interpreting
Effort Model	to enhance awareness of better distribution of efforts during interpreting and the importance of proficiency of languages, especially listening and speaking skills	Gile's Effort Model, related practice	repeating practice, retelling the gist	pretest, learning journal
de-verbalization	to be more cautious about common mistakes of literal translation by beginners	de-verbalization model	mini-lecture, related interpreting practice	learning journal
listening in interpreting	to understand and practice "listening for meaning"	Chinese and English listening materials	listening and retelling in source and target language	retelling quiz, learning journal
short-term memory	to learn and practice short-term memory techniques; to learn to summarize, identify main ideas and reconstruct	a celebrity's speech, etc.	listening and retelling in source and target language	retelling quiz, learning journal

continued

Content	Objectives	Materials	Activity	Assessment
note-taking	to learn and practice note-taking techniques	logical passages	lecture and note-taking at the sentence, passage level	quiz on basic principles of note-taking
interpreting figures	to master at least one of the ways to interpret large numbers	speeches containing figures	related interpreting practice	figure interpreting quiz
short-term preparation	to learn what short-term preparation to make for an interpreting task	a lecture in source language	listening and memorizing related vocabularies	simulation of the interpreting task
coping tactics	to learn possible solution to frequent difficulties in interpreting	practicum	a real-life interpreting practicum	practicum, video-recording, learning journal
professionalism	to learn about professional standards	textbook DVD	lecture and DVD watching	learning journal

C. Method and Organization

1. Course arrangement

The arrangement of the course is, for the most part, a fulfillment of the students' wishes and expectations, as expressed in the Needs analysis mentioned before. The IFNEM is established as an optional course in Tuesday evenings for Non-English majors of the second year and above. It is a 16 week program for two credits. The course is conducted in a language lab equipped with a multi-media console for the teacher, computers for each student and movable chairs-basically everything necessary for interpreting training, which entails presenting and sharing multi-media resources, carrying out simulation activities, and collecting the students' data. However, there is only one discrepancy from the original plan. The enrollment of the class is limited to 46 instead of the ideal 20, a balance between the teacher's hope to give due attention to each student in a small class and the administrative staff's concern with students' large demand for such a course.

2. Class organization

The course is organized in ways to maximize the learners' participation in interpreting practice. More than half of the class time was devoted to the interpreting practice. This emphasis on students' participation is grounded in constructivism and adult learning theories which stress the importance of the students' personal experience. It also echoes the golden rule in interpreter education that "practice makes perfect", which is also phrased as "the practice-based principle" of interpreting training (Zhong, 2007, p. 52).

There are different activities in the practice, ranging from individual interpreting, role-play, three-corner simulation and whole-class interpreting. Every learner is required to participate either in a three-corner simulation or a role-play task, which provides source materials for the rest to interpret. In order for the students to practice public speaking skills, a stimulus plan is added that bonus points could be gained by delivering a speech on the theme of that class, which serves also as a source text of interpreting for the class.

As advocated in translation programs (Li, 2012, p. 159), the principle of authenticity is applied in IFNEM for the practice to have relevance to the learners. Authentic training signifies authentic training materials and training methods (p. 160). The teacher adopts authentic training methods especially, having foreigners come to her class physically and via Skype to be interpreted by the learners, in which the students learn interpreting by doing it for real instead of for exams.

D. Assessment

In accordance with the focus on the process of learning, the assessment of IFNEM is largely formative (70%). Summative assessment accounts for only 30%. The assessment breakdown is shown in Table 3.

Table 3.

Assessment Breakdown of IFNEM

formative assessment 70%					summative assessment 30%
attendance & class Participation	three-corner simulation/ role play	5 quizzes	5 learning journals & 1 portfolio	bonus items	final interpreting project
20%	10%	25%	15%	2-10%	30%

The learning journal is used to help develop students' independent learning abilities. It follows a structure of "SEEDS" and "GPS". "SEEDS" is an acronym the designer coined from "Summary", "Evaluation of oneself", "Evaluation of others", "Difficulties" and "Solution"-five parts of the learner's reflection after a particular class. "GPS" is a record of the students' autonomous learning efforts during the week, organized by the titles of "Gains", "Problems" and "Solution". The students are to submit this homework every other week, though they are encouraged to do so every week for bonus points. This assignment is designed for the students to increase meta-cognition awareness as they reflect regularly on their learning. It also helps the teacher to adjust content and methods during the course.

The bonus items in Table 4 needs explanation. As mentioned before, one of them is the extra learning journal, which is 2 points each; other bonus-winning items include deliverance of speeches (5 points each), and contribution of model three-corner simulation video (5 points each). Obviously the stimulus plan intends to encourage students' regular reflection and active participation in learning.

Ⅳ. Evaluation

No curriculum design would be complete without being evaluated. Evaluation addresses the value and effectiveness of curricular matters and activities (Ornstein & Hunkins, 2009, p. 304). Essentially, it consists of gathering data and relating them to goals (p. 279). In this empirical study, the designer examined the effectiveness of the course against its aims through both quantitative and qualitative methods, including tests, a questionnaire on course evaluation, students' learning journals and semester summaries.

A. Results Relating to the Aims

1. Fundamental knowledge of interpreting

As an introductory course to interpreting, the preliminary goal is to inform the students of the basic knowledge on the subject. This objective has been attained: the students' scores of the quiz on fundamentals of interpreting averaged at 3.52 (full mark: 5), indicating a fairly good mastery. In addition, all of them reported in their learning journals and semester summaries that they had gained a general understanding of interpreting. Many "demystified the allegedly 'fancy and classy' interpreting competence", and discarded prejudices like "interpreting is no big deal but a matter of vocabulary".

2. Improved interpreting skills

At the end of the course, the students' interpreting skills saw a marked progress with a statistical significance ($p<0.01$), manifested by the results of a paired samples test of their pre- and post-test scores as shown in Table 4. Both examinations used authentic tests from China Accreditation Test for Translators and Interpreters (CATTI), a national qualification exam of high validity and reliability.

Table 4.
Paired Samples Test of The Students' Pre- and Post-Tests

	Paired Differences					t	df	Sig. (2-tailed)
	Mean	Std. Deviation	Std. Error Mean	99% Confidence Interval of the Difference				
				Lower	Upper			
Pair 1 pretest-posttest	−6.58974	4.27180	.68404	−8.44455	−4.73494	−9.634	38	.000

This progress is also confirmed by their learning journals and semester summaries. Many expressed joy and pride at their achievement of being able to interpret long dialogues in the final exam, in comparison with their "bleak" starting points when they had difficulties in interpreting short sentences. Two of them described their first experiences of interpreting in real life after class and gave credit to IFNEM, saying they would had shied away from the challenges without the knowledge and skills equipped in this class.

In fact, all of the students ascribed their growth in interpreting skills to the course. In their responses to the questionnaire on the course evaluation, all of them acknowledged the helpfulness of this class to their English interpreting skills, half of them (51.52%) considered this course "greatly helpful" (Table 5).

Table 5.
The helpfulness of IFNEM in improving English interpreting skills

Items	Percentage
A. greatly helpful	51.52%
B. somewhat helpful	39.39%

continued

Items	Percentage
C. helpful	9.09%
D. Not very helpful	0%
E. No help at all	0%

3. Language enhancement

As a byproduct of interpreting training, the students' English improved as well. In their semester summaries most of them mentioned that they had increased their vocabulary on the themes covered in the course, and saw "surprisingly" a growth of their English listening and speaking abilities, especially in comparison with their peers who failed to enroll in this class. Another evidence lies in their increased scores of interpreting tests, which alone could indicate an increase of language proficiency, as prerequisites of interpreting involve a certain amount of vocabularies and good English listening and speaking skills. Again, all of them agreed that the class had helped with their English listening and speaking skills (Table 6).

Table 6.
The helpfulness of IFNEM in improving English listening and speaking skills

Items	Percentage
A. greatly helpful	27.27%
B. somewhat helpful	57.58%
C. helpful	15.15%
D. Not very helpful	0%
E. No help at all	0%

In fact, the role interpreting practices play in language enhancement is confirmed in other studies. Research found that the students who took an IFNEM scored far higher than those who did not. The enrollers' English listening, speaking and translation abilities advanced in particular (Xiong & Luo, 2006). They improved in both translation and writing, embodied by a raised language sense and better choice of word collocation (Deng, 2007).

4. Independent learning strategies and abilities

One of the teaching objectives is to assist the students to further their interpreting skills through independent learning, which requires both the knowledge of interpreting training strategies and abilities of autonomous learning. The former has been mastered, judging from the students' scores and writings as evaluated before. Their autonomous learning abilities have also been strengthened, as they mentioned the learning journals had helped them to summarize and reflect, and form a habit of learning English. Most of them (81.82%, a combined percentage of Item A and B, in Table 7) claimed that they did take further action upon finishing the journals. Admittedly, even with the students' claims, it is hard to prove or quantify the development of independent learning abilities. However, it is safe to assert that a regular reflection on one's learning could be a good beginning to increase one's meta-cognition awareness, an integral part of independent learning ability. After all, action starts from a thought. In this sense, the designer believes that the students' autonomous learning abilities should have been promoted.

Table 7.
Whether the students took further action upon finishing the learning journal

Items	Percentage
A. I will take action accordingly	21.21%
B. It helped me to reflect, though with little further action.	60.61%
C. It helped me to reflect, though without further action.	12.12%
D. I forgot everything after finishing it. There is no further action.	6.06%
E. Others. Please specify:	0%

B. The Students' Feedback on the Course

The course has met the students' expectations in general. According to the results of the questionnaire, the majority of the students acknowledged that the teaching model had been greatly (27.27%) and largely (60.61%) in accordance with their expectations, as Table 8 shows.

Table 8.
The degree to which the teaching model is in line with the students' expectations

Items	Percentage
A. greatly	27.27%
B. largely	60.61%
C. somewhat	9.09%
D. not quite the same	3.03%
E. complete different	0%

Specifically, the participants rated the course elements on a 5-point scale in terms of the teaching content (4.24), methods (4.15), assessment (4.13) and effects (4), as Table 9 illustrates. More than half of them were "very satisfactory" with all the course elements. Though there were five votes for "very unsatisfactory" options, no supporting evidence was found in any of their writings, including the answers to questions eliciting feedback on the course in the same questionnaire.

Table 9.
The Students' Ratings of the Course Elements

Items	Very Unsatisfactory	Unsatisfactory	Fairly satisfactory	Satisfactory	Very satisfactory	No comment	Average
Content	5(15.15%)	0(0%)	0(0%)	5(15.15%)	23(69.7%)	0(0%)	4.24
Method	5(15.15%)	0(0%)	0(0%)	8(24.24%)	20(60.61%)	0(0%)	4.15
Assessment	5(15.15%)	0(0%)	0(0%)	8(24.24%)	19(57.58%)	1(3.03%)	4.13
Effects	5(15.15%)	0(0%)	2(6.06%)	9(27.27%)	17(51.52%)	0(0%)	4

The teaching content is described as "appropriate" (51.52%) and "a bit difficult" (42.42%), indicating a challenge and potential for growth that the course has brought (Table 10). The students further explained that their difficulty lied mainly in a relatively low English proficiencies, especially English listening and speaking skills.

Table 10.
The difficulty level of the teaching content

Items	Percentage
A. Very difficult, because:	6.06%
B. A bit difficult, because:	42.42%
C. Appropriate	51.52%
D. A bit too easy, because:	0%
E. Too easy, because:	0%

As for the implementation of practice-based methodology, 60.61% (a combined percentage of Item A and B in Table11) affirmed that half and more of class time was invested in interpreting practice. One explanation is needed here that this opinion was based on the whole semester, including the beginning lecture-based orientations to interpreting fundamentals. The proportion of interpreting practice in the skills-based classes was actually even lager. The multiple patterns of interpreting activities have met students' expectations, as the patterns were "always" (21.21%) and "largely" (66.67%) the same as their preference (Table 12).

Table 11.
The proportion of the time spent on students' interpreting practice in class

Items	Percentage
A. over 75%	9.09%
B. 50-75%	51.52%
C. 25-50%	30.30%
D. 10-25%	9.09%
E. under 10%	0%

Table 12.
The frequency of the patterns of interpreting activities preferred by the students

Items	Percentage
A. always	21.21%
B. largely	66.67%
C. sometimes	9.09%
D. seldom	0%
E. Never	0%
Blank	3.03%

The students also approved of the predominance of formative assessment in the course evaluation, deeming it was more comprehensive and helped them to focus on the learning process instead of cramming for tests. All of the students agreed the quizzes held on a regular basis had been helpful to their study (Table 13), because "Otherwise I would probably slack off", as some students confessed. The majority of them (90.91%) believed multiple learning journals had also helped with their interpreting learning, as Table 14 shows.

Table 13.
Helpfulness of having a quiz every other week to the students' interpreting learning

Items	Percentage
A. greatly helpful	30.30%
B. somewhat helpful	48.48%

continued

Items	Percentage
C. helpful	21.21%
D. Not very helpful	0%
E. No help at all	0%

Table 14.
Helpfulness of regular learning journals to the students' interpreting learning

Items	Percentage
A. greatly helpful	24.24%
B. somewhat helpful	30.30%
C. helpful	36.36%
D. Not very helpful	9.09%
E. No help at all	0%

On the whole, the students regarded their IFNEM learning experience as intensive, interesting and meaningful. Quoting from them in semester summaries, "It had never occurred to me that an optional course could be so informative and intensive, even better than compulsory English courses"; "I have never learnt so much in a course before"; "I wish there would be another IFNEM next semester".

C. The Students' Comments on the Teacher

The success of a course can be exemplified by the students' recognition of the teacher. The teacher of this IFNEM is highly thought of and appreciated. In fact, one of the reasons some students selected this course is that they believed in the teacher, as revealed in the semester summaries. From their encounters with the teacher during a one-year English program before IFNEM, the students found her "highly responsible and committed" and her class "interactive and relaxing". Many mentioned that they were so touched by the devotion of the teacher that they increased their efforts during the course.

D. Room for improvement

There have been few complaints about the course. One or two students advised to reduce the class size and increase real-life interpreting practice, which might be hard to realize due to practical constraints. A very feasible suggestion from the students is to replace some learning journals with video recordings of their interpreting practice after class, which is a more interesting way to improve their interpreting skills. In the teacher's opinion, a lack of updated and authentic materials that caters to the learners' needs is the most pressing problem, which calls for academic attention and contribution of practitioners.

V. Conclusion

As an attempt to address the scarcity of curriculum study in interpreting education, the author designed an IFNEM class based on Hutchinson & Waters' learning approach to course design, and a three-pronged framework of oral translation competence, learning theories and needs analysis results.

During the course design process, the designer was able to consider learners at every stage of course planning, thanks to the ideal condition that the teacher had been personally acquainted with and consulted directly the students who were to be enrolled in this new course.

The final product of the course design is presented in terms of aims and objectives, syllabus, method and organization and assessment, the four key elements of curriculum. The IFNEM is designed with the aims to introduce the fundamental knowledge of interpreting to students, and equip them with basic interpreting skills, higher English listening and speaking skills and independent learning strategies. It is arranged mainly by theme-based interpreting situations, with an introduction to interpreting fundamentals at the beginning. Meanwhile, there is a hidden skills-based syllabus, specifying the subdivision of interpreting skills and how those are trained and evaluated in class (in Table 2). The practice- and authenticity-based methodology of IFNEM is grounded in constructivism and adult learning theories, emphasizing the students' maximum and active participation. Finally, the assessment of the course is mostly formative (70%), focusing on the students' learning process.

At the end of the IFNEM, the course was evaluated through tests, a questionnaire on course evaluation, students' learning journals and semester summaries. It is found that this course design had been effective, judging from the results relating to the objectives, the students' feedback on the course and the teacher.

There were only a few suggestions for improving the course. One constructive suggestion is to include in the students' homework video recordings of their interpreting practice after class. From the perspective of the instructor, a pressing problem is a lack of authentic materials specifically for non-English major students, which calls for further academic endeavors.

Acknowledgment

This paper is supported by "Beijing Higher Education Young Elite Teacher Project"(Grant No. YETP0465).

References

[1] Bednar, A. K., D. Cunningham, T. M. Duffy & J. D. Perry (1992). Theory into practice: How do we link? In T. M. Duffy & D. H. Jonassen (Eds.), *Constructivism and the technology of instruction*, New Jersey: Lawrence Erlbaum & Associates Hillsdale, 18-34.

[2] Brundage, D. H. & D. MacKeracher (1980). Adult learning principles and their application to program planning. Ontario: Ontario Institute for Studies in Education.

[3] Deng, Z. J. (2007). Investigation of non-English majors' oral translation abilities. Journal of Xichang College (Social Science Edition) 19. 1, 131-134, 142.

[4] Department of Higher Education. (2007). College English curriculum requirements. Beijing: Foreign Language Teaching and Research Press.

[5] Gile, D. 2011. Basic Concepts and Models for Interpreter and Translator Training. (revised edn). Shanghai Foreign Language Education Press.

[6] Hutchinson, T. & Waters, A. (1987). English forspecific purposes: a learning-centered approach. Cambridge: Cambridge University Press.

[7] Knowles, M. S. (1972). Innovations in teaching styles and approaches based upon adult learning. *Journal of Education for Social Work* 8. 2, 32-39.

[8] Lauzon, A. C. (1999). Situating cognition and crossing borders: resisting the hegemony of mediated education. *British Journal of Educational*

Technology 30, 261-276.

[9] Li, D. F. (2012). Curriculum Design, Needsassessment and translation pedagogy. Beijing: Foreign Language Teaching and Research Press.

[10] Li, P., & Lu, Z. H. (2011). Learners' needs analysis of a new optional College English course—interpreting for non-English majors. *Theory and Practice in Language Studies* 1.9, 1091-1102.

[11] Luo X. M., Q. Huang & L. N. Xu. (2008). Investigation and thought on College English interpreting teaching. *Foreign Language World* 5, 75-83.

[12] Nunan, D. (1988a). Syllabus design. Oxford: Oxford University Press.

[13] Nunan, D. (1988b). The learner-centered curriculum: a study in second language teaching. Cambridge: Cambridge University Press.

[14] Ornstein A. C., & P. H. Hunkins (2009). Curriculum: foundations, principles, and issues (5th edn). Beijing: China Renmin University Press Co. LTD.

[15] Sawyer, D. B. (2011). Fundamental Aspects of Interpreter Education: Curriculum and Assessment. Shanghai: Shanghai Foreign Language Education Press.

[16] Su, W. & Y. Deng (2009). Basics of interpreting skills. Shanghai: Shanghai Foreign Language Education Press.

[17] Tyler, R. W. (1949). Basic Principles of Curriculum and Instruction. Chicago: The University of Chicago Press.

[18] Wang, B. H. (2009). Curriculum design and methodology of Interpreting majors. Journal of Hunan University of Science and Engineering 30.3, 208-213.

[19] Wang, B. H. & Z. W. Wu. (2010). Liaison interpreting. Wuhan: Wuhan University Press.

[20] Xiao, X. Y. & L. Y. Yang (2006). Asia Link-interpreting Asia Interpreting Europe. Shanghai: Shanghai Foreign Language Education Press.

[21] Xiong, L. J. & C. X. Luo (2006). Study on non-English majors' College English teaching. *Computer-Assisted Foreign Language Education* 2, 44-48.

[22] Zhan, C. (2010). Interpreting education in China in three decades: development and status quo. *Journal of Guangdong University of Foreign Studies* 21.6, 30-33.

[23] Zhong, W. H. (2001). Interpreting training: model, content, and methodology. *Chinese Translators Journal* 2, 30-33.

[24] Zhong, W. H. (2003). Interpreters' knowledge structure and interpreting curriculum design. *Chinese Translators Journal* 4, 63-65.

[25] Zhong, W. H. (2007). Curriculum design and teaching principles of interpreting programs. *Chinese Translators Journal* 1, 52-53.

Li Ping was born in Weifang, Shandong Province in 1982. She received her M. A. degree of Foreign Linguistics and Applied Linguistics at Nankai University, Tianjin, China in 2007.

She is currently a Lecturer in School of Humanities, Beijing University of Posts and Telecommunications, Beijing, China. Her research interests include English language teaching and translation & interpretation.